ELEANOR H. PORTER'S *POLLYANNA*

ELEANOR H. PORTER'S

Pollyanna

A Children's Classic at 100

Edited by Roxanne Harde and Lydia Kokkola

University Press of Mississippi / Jackson

Children's Literature Association Series

www.upress.state.ms.us

The cover image is used with the permission
of the Town of Littleton, New Hampshire.

The University Press of Mississippi is a member
of the Association of American University Presses.

First printing 2014
∞
Library of Congress Cataloging-in-Publication Data

Eleanor H. Porter's Pollyanna : a children's classic at 100 /
edited by Roxanne Harde and Lydia Kokkola.
pages cm. — (Children's Literature Association series)
Includes bibliographical references and index.
ISBN 978-1-62846-132-9 (cloth : alk. paper) — ISBN 978-1-62846-133-6
(ebook) 1. Porter, Eleanor H. (Eleanor Hodgman), 1868–1920. Pollyanna. 2. Orphans in literature. 3. Aunts in literature. 4. Conduct of life
in literature. 5. Cheerfulness in literature. I. Harde, Roxanne, editor of
compilation. II. Kokkola, Lydia, 1967– editor of compilation.
PS3531.O7342P634 2014
813'.52—dc23   2014013905

British Library Cataloging-in-Publication Data available

To Arwyn, who has made being her grandma
one of the gladdest parts of my middle age.
—*Roxanne*

To Kirsti, who taught me gladness wasn't just a game.
—*Lydia*

CONTENTS

Part I: Pollyanna's World

Part II: Ideological *Pollyanna*

Part III: Adapted *Pollyanna*

ACKNOWLEDGMENTS

While writing is often a solitary endeavor, assembling a collection is not. We each put in our share of hours writing and editing, but we had many people—our partners and other family members, friends, colleagues, and editors—literally and figuratively at our side. Without them, this book would never have been completed.

Together we want to extend our gratitude to

Teya Rosenberg and the Children's Literature Association's editorial board

Katie Keene, our astute editor at the University Press of Mississippi

the people of Littleton

and our contributors, for their hard work over the past two years, and for their devotion to our subject and this book.

Lydia is glad to have the opportunity to publicly thank

Roxanne Harde, for all our collaborations to date. Roxanne saw potential in me that I had not seen myself. She has helped me grow professionally more than she knows. I admire her greatly for her diligence, creativity and dedication, but I appreciate her most for her kindness.

Luleå University of Technology, for inviting me to take up the chair in English and Education, and the staff and students for making me feel so welcome.

Roxanne is grateful to

Lydia Kokkola, for her good humor, and for achieving a level of productivity and organization to which I can only aspire. She brings energy, wit, and joy to our work and, indeed, to even the most mundane conversations, and I look forward to our next collaboration.

Kim Misfeldt, Chair of Humanities, and Allen Berger, Dean, Augustana Faculty, University of Alberta, for their wisdom and leadership, and, more, for their friendship.

Samantha Christensen, Tia Lalani, and Taylor Kraayenbrink for being the best of research assistants. Each of them brought an inimitable work ethic to their duties and then developed genuine interest in and enthusiasm for my research. I expect every success in their future endeavors.

Nancy Goebel and the stellar staff at Augustana Library, for their efficiency and interest in this and all my projects.

ELEANOR H. PORTER'S *POLLYANNA*

This statue of Pollyanna, with her arms spread wide in gladness and welcome, sits in a park near the library in Littleton, New Hampshire, Porter's hometown. Littleton's promotional material notes that visitors and passers-by make it a point to return Pollyanna's "welcome wave" and rub her bronze hightop shoe for luck and gladness.

Glad to be 100: The Making of a Children's Classic

LYDIA KOKKOLA AND ROXANNE HARDE

You breathe all the time you're asleep, but you aren't living. I mean living—
doing the things you want to do: playing outdoors, reading (to myself of
course), climbing hills, talking to Mr Tom[1] in the garden, and Nancy, and
finding out all about the houses and the people and everything everywhere
all through the perfectly lovely streets I came through yesterday. That's what
I call living, Aunt Polly. (Porter, *Pollyanna* 51)

Eleanor H. Porter's *Pollyanna* was first published as a serial in a weekly
journal, the *Christian Herald*, from 27 November 1912 until 19 February
1913.[2] Later in 1913, *Pollyanna* was published in book form. This story of
an impoverished orphan girl, who travels from America's western frontier
to live with her wealthy maternal aunt, Polly Harrington, in the fictional
East Coast town of Beldingsville, went through forty-seven printings in
seven years and remains in print in its original version, as well as in various translations and adaptations today. The story's lasting appeal lies in
Pollyanna's enduringly sunny personality and in her "glad game." Her missionary father, who had requested a doll for his young daughter in a missionary barrel and instead received a pair of crutches, taught the glad game
to Pollyanna by asking her to come up with something to be glad about;
in this case, Pollyanna was taught to be glad she did not need crutches. As
Pollyanna settles into life in Beldingsville, she teaches the game to everyone except Aunt Polly, who has forbidden her to speak about her father; in
so doing, she changes many of the town's citizens. Subplots involve Pollyanna's favorite companion, another orphan (Jimmy Bean), and old love
affairs (Mr. Pendleton's love of Pollyanna's mother as well as Aunt Polly
and Dr. Chiltern's mutual love). The crisis of the novel happens offstage:
Pollyanna is hurt in an automobile accident and at first it seems she will
never walk again. The whole town joins in the effort to cheer her up, and

3

so Aunt Polly finally learns of the game. The result is not only a return to health for Pollyanna, but also the resumption of a romance between Aunt Polly and Dr. Chiltern.

After *Pollyanna*'s incredible success and an impassioned public demand for a sequel, Porter published *Pollyanna Grows Up* in 1915. The sequel is in two sections. In the first, young Pollyanna is sent to Boston to visit an embittered woman (Mrs. Carew) whose character resembles Aunt Polly before her transformation, but who—unlike Aunt Polly—is anxious to find her dead sister's child (who eventually turns out to be none other than Pollyanna's friend, Jimmy Bean). Pollyanna befriends a disabled boy (Jamie) whose positive outlook on life surprises even Pollyanna. In the second half of the sequel, a grown-up Pollyanna needs to support her recently widowed and impoverished Aunt Polly. Pollyanna invites her Boston friends to visit Beldingsville as paying guests. The novel concludes with three couples (Mr. Pendleton and Mrs. Carew, Jamie and Sadie, Pollyanna and Jimmy Bean Pendleton) all marrying for love, albeit all remaining within or returning to their original social class.

The author of these and other novels for young people was born Eleanor Hodgman on December 19, 1868, in Littleton, New Hampshire, upon which *Pollyanna*'s Beldingsville was modeled. Porter was a talented singer who studied music at the New England Conservatory of Music in Boston before becoming a teacher and then a successful author (Overton 262). After her marriage to John Lyman Porter in 1892, she began to publish short stories in periodicals, and then her first novel, *Cross Currents*, in 1907. She eventually published fifteen novels and over two hundred short stories. Porter's first major success came with *Miss Billy* (1911), a romantic comedy featuring an eighteen-year-old protagonist. It was popular enough that Porter followed it with *Miss Billy's Decision* (1912) and *Miss Billy Married* (1914). Porter's success with this exuberant young woman seems to have motivated her to create an even more irrepressible and robust young girl.

Porter was often compared with her most popular fictional character, as is evident from the epitaph on her tombstone: WHO BY HER WRITINGS BROUGHT SUNSHINE INTO THE LIVES OF MILLIONS. Porter's hometown, Littleton, continues to celebrate her achievement with an Official Pollyanna Glad Day every June and a birthday party for Porter every December. Even more fittingly, the town features a bronze statue of Pollyanna in its central park (see page 2). She spreads her arms wide and welcomes all, to the town, to her story, and to gladness.

As the chapters in this volume will attest, much of Pollyanna's tenacity is closely tied to her positive outlook on life, concretized most obviously in the glad game, which transforms the lives of everyone who comes into contact with her. However, Pollyanna's gladness is evident even when she is not playing the game. Porter created a character who can take pleasure in watching flies, playing with kittens and "just . . . living" (Porter, *Pollyanna* 51). Porter explained the gladness of her most popular protagonist this way: "I have been placed often in a false light. People have thought that Pollyanna chirped that she was 'glad' at everything. . . . I have never believed that we ought to deny discomfort and pain and evil; I have merely thought that it is far better to 'greet the unknown with a cheer'" (qtd. in Overton 262).[3] Pollyanna's glad game may have caught and held the public's lasting attention, but Porter intended to bring a combination of cheerfulness and resilience to her young audience, a worldview deeper than an optimistic party trick.

In the epigraph to this introduction, Pollyanna explains at some length what she regards as "living." While Porter clearly engages with the growing trend of her era to see playtime as necessary for all children, Pollyanna's mandates for living include her rather breathtaking list of activities that insist on a child's thoroughgoing engagement with her community and the natural world. Pollyanna's cheerful immersion in the life around her, her gladness, and the fervent immediacy of her presence are Porter's real contributions to children's literature and popular culture. These are also the features that have enabled her story to travel so well, as they can easily be adapted to fit cultural contexts other than the early-twentieth-century New England home in which she was born.

The Pollyanna Story: From Porter to Parcheesi

During the course of the century since she first stepped off the train in Beldingsville, Pollyanna Whittier has taken on a life that is not bound by the text from which she originated. She has taught more than four generations how to play the glad game through film adaptation, fan sequels, television programs, and club activities. This very American girl has been well received around the world. The first translation of *Pollyanna* into Norwegian in 1914 was soon followed by translations into French, Turkish, Hebrew, and Japanese. Available in at least twelve languages, *Pollyanna* has proven particularly popular in Japan and Turkey, countries where more than one translation is available.

Pollyanna's adventures have not been confined to replications of Porter's novel or its sequel, *Pollyanna Grows Up* (1915). After Porter's early death in 1920, other authors, most notably Harriet Lummis Smith and Elizabeth Borton, responded to the public's desire for more stories about Pollyanna and contributed to the "The Glad Series," which follows Pollyanna through her marriage to Jimmy, motherhood, into the Great Depression, and onward. To date, the series contains fourteen additional titles; the latest, *Pollyanna Plays the Game* by the established Christian author Colleen Reece, was added in 1995. Like the original serialized version of Porter's novel, *Pollyanna Plays the Game* was released through a Christian publishing house, thereby retaining the connection between Pollyanna and Christian education.

The introduction to the Puffin Classics edition of *Pollyanna* summarily dismisses those books that were not produced by Porter: "any success these books enjoyed was due only to their reflection of the two classic originals, *Pollyanna* and *Pollyanna Grows Up*" (n.p.). Readers' responses, judged from the successful sales figures, online reviews, and blogging activity, are more positive. Responses to the blogger Melody at "Redeeming Qualities," for instance, reveal that many readers regarded the series as a complete set despite the changes of author, and they retain fond memories of their childhood reading well into adulthood. For young readers, these sequels are very much part of the story of Pollyanna (Melody 5 and 6 June 2007). The earliest of the posthumous Glad Books, *Pollyanna of the Orange Blossoms* by Harriet Lummis Smith (1927), was produced before the notion of syndicate authorship had become established, and before fanzines became ubiquitous. These books reveal a readership ready for the Stratemeyer Syndicate that produced characters such as the Rover Boys, the Bobbsey Twins, Nancy Drew, and the Hardy Boys. If young readers are happy to accept the characters produced by Smith, Borton, Chalmers, Moffitt, and Reece as part of the continuance of the Pollyanna story, then at the very least we, as critics, must acknowledge them as part of the positive reader response to Porter's novels. The Pollyanna and Jimmy who appear in the later Glad Books may be derivative, but they attest to Porter's ability to inspire and engage her readers.

The popularity of Porter's novel has resulted in a veritable Pollyanna industry, comprised of far more than novels. One of the earliest adaptations was a stage play written by the composer Catherine Chisholm Cushing (1874–1952). *Pollyanna: A Comedy in Four Acts* opened in New York on 18 September 1916.[4] The play is primarily an adaptation of the first novel, but ends like the sequel with the blossoming of a romance between Pollyanna and Jimmy, which required two different actors to play the part of Jimmy Bean in order to be credible. Starring Helen Hayes for its two-year run, the play was a considerable financial success ("Pollyanna" *Master-piece Theatre*).

There have also been a number of film adaptations. The first English-language version, a silent film with subtitles filmed in black and white starring Mary Pickford, was released in 1920, the year Porter died. One of the key differences between this version and Porter's creation was that Pickford was an adult, but an actress whose success depended upon her retention of childlike qualities. The highly popular 1960 Disney version, starring Hayley Mills, presented Pollyanna as a child again. The Disney version proved so popular that one of the key changes to the plot—the town's fund-raising fete to raise money for a new orphanage—was to become so well integrated into the Pollyanna story that it was repeated in later adaptations, such as the film *Polly* directed by Debbie Allen.

Polly (1989) reframes Pollyanna's story as a commentary on racial politics. Polly is cast as an African American girl who moves from Detroit to Alabama in the mid-1950s. This north-to-south move for African American Polly picks up on many of the same themes as Porter's white protagonist's move from the West to the East Coast. In both cases, the girl character brings positive ideas from a region that offers more freedom to a region so steeped in tradition it is stagnating. *Polly* was a made-for-TV musical film starring Keisha Knight Pulliam and Phylicia Rashād.⁵ *Polly* is set in segregated Alabama in 1956, and so when the orphan, Polly, unites her community by playing the glad game, she engages in a form of political activism. With a cast that includes few white actors, the film does not add scenes directly related to the civil rights movement, although allusions are abundant. For instance, when the white doctor who diagnoses Polly's paralysis describes her as "a fine brave pickaninny," he is severely chastised by Aunt Polly. The doctor accepts that he has done wrong and that "times have changed," and the assembled townspeople promise, with considerable irony, to "help" the doctor change accordingly. For the most part, however, Polly's political activism is expressed through a celebration of African American culture. Aunt Polly's dress style and manners suggest that she is trying to emulate the white community, whereas Polly's sense of gladness is expressed in a distinctively African American way. This is most obvious in how musical styles are played against one another. Aunt Polly prefers the staid hymns that are also sung in white churches, but Polly brings her love of the new music of the northern city of Detroit with her when she travels south, and happily joins Jimmy as he tap dances and sings outside the church. *Polly* garnered a number of Emmy nominations and was followed with its own sequel, *Polly: Comin' Home!* (1990).

Pollyanna has fared well in other Anglophone contexts. In Britain, the BBC aired a six-part television series starring Elizabeth Archard as Pollyanna and Elaine Stritch as Aunt Polly in 1973, as part of series of adaptations of classic children's novels considered suitable for "teatime viewing." This was the era in which color televisions had become affordable for the majority of the population. Instead of sitting down to eat together around a table in the kitchen, families gathered together to watch the television. The BBC series tapped into this trend and provided family entertainment that encouraged the culture of families eating meals in front of the television together. Other adapted children's classics in this series included Burnett's *The Secret Garden* and Nesbit's *The Railway Children*. Although produced for a newly technologized society in an era when the sexual revolution and "women's liberation," as it was then known, were starting to affect family life, all the books chosen for adaptation depicted a nostalgic view of the past. They celebrated traditional values and placed the nuclear family on a pedestal. For six Sundays in a row, *Pollyanna* offered a nostalgic view of a utopian past that stood in stark contrast to changes going on both within and outside the family home.

A more recent British adaptation was the 2004 film *Pollyanna*, directed by Sarah Harding and starring Georgina Terry as Pollyanna and Amanda Burton as Aunt Polly, which sets the story in pre–World War I England. The film incorporates numerous shots of a stereotypically English countryside interwoven with shots of Pollyanna out and about in the community, allusions to English works of literature, through games of Pooh Sticks and recitations of Longfellow's *Song of Hiawatha*, as well as quintessentially English activities such as taking tea on the lawn after a game of croquet. Combined, these activities and scenes transport Pollyanna out of America and into an English setting. This also requires a downplaying of Irishness: Nancy the Irish maid, who in Porter's novel is the first to befriend Pollyanna and play the game, becomes English, and the Irish actress, Amanda Burton, loses all trace of her Irish accent. Despite its cross-Atlantic journey, *Pollyanna* remains otherwise unchanged and the film's plot very closely resembles Porter's novel, demonstrating how adaptable it is.

The novel also transcends its Anglophone origins, and has been adapted for film and television around the world. One of the earliest adaptations of *Pollyanna* to appear outside the English-speaking world was a Brazilian TV series that aired in 1956. It was soon followed by another series in 1958 entitled *Pollyanna Moça*, both starring Verinha Darci as the lead. Turkey also embraced the *Pollyanna* story, first in translation and then in film. *Hayat sevince güzel* [Life is beautiful when you love] (1971) adapts the story of Ayşe (Pollyanna) and sets her optimism in contemporary Turkey. The focus on love rather than optimism is also evident in the Nippon Animation anime version, *Ai shôjo Porianna monogatari* [The Story of Pollyanna: girl of love]. This series of twenty-four-minute anime films stretched Porter's story across a series of fifty-one episodes that aired from 1986 onward. They depict Pollyanna as a barefoot girl in dungarees making friends with all and sundry, but especially her animal companions. Her voice is provided by the singer Mitsuko Horie, and, like *Polly*, the series contains numerous songs and set pieces that focus on gladness and Pollyanna's brand of loving-kindness.

Pollyanna's gladness has also been received with some skepticism: the name of Porter's orphan girl has come to function around the world as a metaphor for undue optimism. Noting that Pollyanna (or pollyanna) functions as a noun or adjective, the *Oxford English Dictionary* defines the term as a "person able to find cause for happiness in the most disastrous situations; a person who is unduly optimistic or achieves happiness through self-delusion. . . . Resembling Pollyanna; naively cheerful and optimistic; unrealistically happy." This sense that Pollyanna's optimism is unfounded is picked up in a more ironic response to Porter's character in *The League of Extraordinary Gentlemen* comic books. The character named Pollyanna in this series is an exceedingly optimistic young woman who is victimized by a violent demon who does not respond to Pollyanna's message as positively as do the characters in Porter's novels.

First included in the 1982 Supplement, the *OED*'s definition emphasizes the pejorative connotations held by the term today, but it begins with the reason behind the novel's original and enduring popularity. In Porter's novels, Pollyanna's gladness seems more concretely rooted in the here-and-now, and she admits that there are times when it is difficult to be glad: "sometimes it's almost too hard—like when your father goes to heaven, and there isn't anybody but a Ladies' Aid left" (37). Porter admits that optimism is hard work, and she shows how much effort her young protagonist puts into finding things to be glad about.

Pollyanna's commitment to positive thinking captivated Porter's audiences and encouraged a trend as readers attempted to emulate the fictional character's outlook on life. "Although the story is sentimental to a degree," the American Library Association correctly predicted, "it will be enjoyed by a large number of adult and juvenile readers" (*ALA*). Describing the novel as only slightly less influential than WWI, Grant Overton points out that "White Mountain cabins, Colorado teahouses, Texan babies, Indiana apartment houses, and a brand of milk were immediately named for the new character; there were Glad Clubs and likewise there were Pollyannathematizers" (263). Psychological studies were named after her: "The Pollyanna Hypothesis asserts that there is a universal human tendency to use evaluatively positive words (E+) more frequently and diversely than evaluatively negative words (E–) in communicating" (Boucher and Osgood 1). Eventually extending even to the lexicon, *Pollyanna* influenced every area of American life and beyond.

As the popularity of the novel exploded, so too did the cultural production surrounding *Pollyanna*: hundreds of "Glad Clubs" surfaced around America (at least one still exists today, in Denver, Colorado), along with dolls, handkerchiefs, illustrated storybooks, as well as the films and TV series already mentioned. More oddly, she has been turned into a board game produced by Parker Brothers between 1915 and 1967. In this variant of Parcheesi, each player has four pieces of the same color. In the 1915 edition of the game, the four colors are associated with characters from Porter's novel: blue for Aunt Polly; green for Nancy; red for Jimmy; and yellow for John Pendleton. The object of the game is to be the first player to move all four of the color pieces around the board to the home space. During the course of the game, players may block one another or force other players to return their pieces back to the start. Nothing in the rules of the game recalls Pollyanna's Glad Game; on the contrary, the tactics of block and capture needed to win the game are antithetic to the community spirit endorsed in all the books, films, and TV series. The connection is forged solely through the use of Pollyanna's name.

When Porter created her heroine's name by blending the forenames of her maternal aunts, she did more than simply draw connections between the 11-year-old orphan and her partial namesake and reveal her mother's longing for her family of origin; Porter also added a name to the English language. Any child, fictional character, or even board game with the portmanteau name "Pollyanna" is an allusion to Porter's character. A contemporary example of the same phenomenon would be "Renesmee" from Stephanie Meyer's *Twilight* series (a portmanteau of her grandmothers' names: Renee and Esme). If we find cultural artifacts such as Parcheesi games and children being named Renesmee over the next few decades, we can assume an allusion to Meyer's character. (Gaming manufacturers might take note that the tasks of capture and block needed to play Parcheesi seem better suited to *Twilight* than they do to *Pollyanna*!) Parker Brothers' assumption that association with *Pollyanna* would boost the sales of their version of Parcheesi may have had nothing to do with Porter's optimistic character, but it attests to her popularity and their desire to harness the power of fandom. These are ways in which Pollyanna's story has continued to thrive.

Visualizing and Placing Pollyanna

As this brief overview attests, Pollyanna has travelled the world and taken on new identities, and yet remains a pervasive cultural referent (Burt 328). Clearly Porter's orphan character has had a profound impact on her readers as she continues to teach the glad game to each new generation. Nevertheless, when one looks at the products generated by the Pollyanna industry, including those produced outside the Anglophone world, one cannot help but notice how disparate her visual appearance is, while other features such as her status as an orphan remain constant. With the exception of the 1920 film starring the childlike Mary Pickford, Pollyanna is always a *girl* (as opposed to a woman, boy, or man). Her positive thinking, her engagement with the people in her community, her ability to forge friendships with people from different classes, and also her neediness and desire for affection are performed in highly gendered ways and draw heavily on the Romantic view of childhood. Indeed, when critics such as Clare Brown dismiss the adult Pollyanna in *Pollyanna Grows Up* as "not impressive" (247), it is largely because they feel that the qualities that define Pollyanna's character cannot be reworked to fit an adult. Age and sex are such integral aspects of the Pollyanna story that they cannot be altered without altering who Pollyanna is and what she does.

The other feature that remains constant is that Pollyanna (in all her varying manifestations, except the Parcheesi game piece) always comes from an impoverished background and gains riches as a result of her adoption. The message that wealth does not bring happiness is integral to Pollyanna's story as she brings happiness to those who have wealth but are unhappy because they do not know how to be glad and just live. It is more than a little ironic, then, that Pollyanna is rewarded with wealth for knowing how to live happily without the comforts money can bring. Pollyanna's movement from rags to riches, repeated in *Pollyanna Grows Up*, draws on the Cinderella trope as she is restored to the status of her mother's family.

That Pollyanna belongs to her aunt's social status is emphasized through her name. Pollyanna's mother named her daughter after her sisters, Anna (who has also died before the novel begins) and Polly. Pollyanna is thus the heir to the Harrington fortune, but can only regain that wealth by drawing on her father's moral values. The Harrington fortune is lost in *Pollyanna Grows Up*, and it is the formerly impoverished Pollyanna who must take on the task of providing a living for Aunt Polly. Both Pollyanna and her aunt must learn to be happy without riches, and ironically are once again rewarded with wealth.

If Pollyanna's gender, age, and class remain constant features in all variants of the story, the same is not true of her racial, ethnic, and national features. She transcends the borders of these categories in ways that characters such as Anne Shirley, Sara Crewe, and Carroll's Alice cannot. She is the only character in the Children's Classics at 100 series to date who has managed to overcome racial boundaries as she appears as an African American in *Polly*, a mountain Turk in the *Hayat sevince güzel*, and a dungaree-clad Japanese anime character. Even Pinocchio is not as racially or ethnically ambiguous!

Pollyanna's visual and racial dexterity is partly a response to the first images of her, contained in the original publication. The *Christian Herald* series and the 1913 novel were illustrated with black-and-white line drawings by Stockton Mulford. In the novel the pictures appeared on separate leaves of thin, waxy paper in between the rougher pages of the text. These pages have not stood up to the test of time, and many reissues do not include images at all. As a result, unlike images of Alice, which even in the most recent Hollywood film version allude to Tenniel's illustrations, Pollyanna's visual identity is more amorphous. In Porter's novel, she is described as a "slender little girl in the red-checked gingham with two fat braids of flaxen hair hanging down her back" with "an eager, freckled little face" (14). The only features of Pollyanna's appearance that remain constant are her long hair and skin that identifies that she has been outdoors. The cover of the omnibus edition of both Pollyanna books in the Wordsworth Classics series is illustrated with a figure dressed in a blue sailor dress and rosy cheeks, but she retains her flaxen braids. On other covers, her long hair is loose and varies from blond to brown to red; it can be curly, coarse, or wispy. On the covers of English versions of the novel, she is always white but, as noted above, in adaptation she is not bound to one racial identity. Pollyanna is thus an iconic figure without an icon; it is her gladness that remains symbolic, not her visual image. And since gladness is a quality that easily transcends nationality, class, and ethnic divisions, Pollyanna has been transformed (and perhaps diluted) to suit the varied needs of those who allude to Porter's original character. The question as to how much *Pollyanna* can be diluted and still remain Porter's character is more a matter of taste than critical deliberation.

Pollyanna: Critical Reception and Scholarship

When we began work on this collection of chapters, we were surprised by the paucity of scholarship on *Pollyanna*, particularly of studies that focus on Porter's novel. When *Pollyanna* is mentioned, it tends to be within a broader context such as in discussions of the history of children's literature (Avery; Hunt; Goulden), the construction of the child (Hillel; Brown), American identity (Griswold), girlhood, orphanhood (Sanders; Nelson), invalidism (Keith; Larner), and manipulativeness (Sanders; Mills). Rather than discussing *Pollyanna* as a special case, critics have tended to compare Porter's novel with other novels from the same era along thematic lines. The implication that *Pollyanna* does not merit closer scrutiny in its own right is challenged by the chapters in this volume.

Because *Pollyanna* has rarely received special treatment, no development in the critical discussion of the novel can be discerned, although certain themes reoccur as she is situated in publishing history. Peter Hunt notes that all of Porter's stories are influenced by the popular genre of the mid- to late nineteenth century that focuses on "a strong, often displaced, female hero"; traces of Louisa May Alcott's *Little Women* (1868–69) and Susan Coolidge's *What Katy Did* (1872) are easy to find throughout Porter's oeuvre (23). Other common points of comparison within the American tradition are Kate Wiggin's *Rebecca of Sunnybrook Farm* (1903) and the Gypsy Breynton series (1866–67) by fellow New Englander Elizabeth Stuart Phelps. Both these female authors crafted female characters who must create a sense of home for themselves through dedicated engagement with their community. In his study of the bildungsroman and American culture, Jerry Griswold places Pollyanna alongside not only female characters but also hyper-masculine boys such as Tom Sawyer and Huck Finn. These children's independence and tenacity can be connected to the image of America as a country where success is possible. They are part of the American Dream. The common thread Griswold identifies among these "audacious kids" is their capacity to change the world they inhabit. As they grow up, they change America; these are bildungsromans of the nation, not just of the child protagonist.

Observing Pollyanna's capacity to manipulate others into accepting her worldview, Alice Mills, in "Pollyanna and the Not So Glad Game," uses a psychoanalytic approach to analyze Pollyanna's ability to reframe situations in order to create a more positive outcome. Mills suggests that Pollyanna's ability to disguise unpleasant situations with gladness situates her as both victim and manipulator. A similar conclusion is reached by

Joe Sutliff Sanders, although his route to this conclusion differs markedly. Sanders situates *Pollyanna* within the tradition of the sentimental girl's story in a study that focuses on how orphaned girls "discipline" the adults around them. Sanders refers to the redeeming qualities of characters like Anne Shirley, Sara Crewe, and Mary Lennox, who enable the adults around them to develop and in so doing reorganize their own environment. Pollyanna Whittier manages to discipline not only her aunt but also half the town into taking a more optimistic view of the world (in much the same way that Anne teaches Marilla Cuthbert to laugh). Indeed, for Sanders, what makes *Pollyanna* stand out is that the orphan girl must discipline half the town in order to have an impact on the adult in whom she most desires change (Aunt Polly), who must then discipline the eponymous heroine into a return to her former self.

Pollyanna also bears comparison with orphaned girls outside America, most notably the Canadian Lucy Maud Montgomery's *Anne of Green Gables* (1908) and the Swiss Johanna Spyri's *Heidi* (1880 in German; 1885 in English). In *Little Strangers*, Claudia Nelson examines *Pollyanna* alongside other works to reveal changing attitudes toward adoption. Her study situates *Pollyanna* between Massachusetts's 1851 comprehensive adoption law and 1929, when all American states had an adoption law. In mid-nineteenth-century legislation and discourse, children were adopted in order to provide cheap labor. Anne Shirley is adopted for precisely these reasons and nearly returned to the orphanage because she is a girl and so cannot be expected to work alongside Matthew in the fields. By the time *Pollyanna* was published a shift had begun, and eventually adoption was to become a matter of emotion. *Pollyanna* contributed to this change in attitude by revealing both Pollyanna's and Jimmy Bean's vulnerability to the whims of those who bestow charity, as well as presenting the adoption of children as a cure for broken hearts.

Pollyanna not only cures several broken hearts, she also cures herself. First she cures herself of her grief over the deaths of every single member of her birth family; then she cures herself of paralysis, in another well-established trope in books of the era (Keith). By placing *Pollyanna* alongside other works, such as *What Katy Did*, *The Secret Garden*, and *Heidi*, as A. J. Larner does in his study of literary accounts of invalids, such studies focus on *Pollyanna*'s generic qualities at the expense of what makes the novel stand out. Larner, for instance, treats all four novels as equally valid representations of contemporary thinking about neuro-rehabilitation during that era. He makes no comment on Pollyanna's commitment to her own recovery or on how the particular quality of gladness not evident in Katy, Colin, or Clara contributes to Pollyanna's self-healing and continuing recovery in *Pollyanna Grows Up*. Pollyanna's similarities to these other displaced girl heroines do indeed mark her as being simply one of an established kind of literary figure. However, the reason that Pollyanna, and indeed all these other girl characters, have remained so popular are the individual characteristics with which she has been endowed. If Porter relied on sentimentality in *Pollyanna* almost as much as she had in the *Miss Billy* series, then she added something new with the glad game and Pollyanna's cheerfulness.

Pollyanna's positive outlook on life is central to her appeal, but as Claire Brown notes in "*Pollyanna*, Moral Sainthood, and Childhood Ideals," moral saints are rarely characters one would like to invite to dinner. Brown demonstrates that Pollyanna's particular brand of positive thinking is so tightly linked to romanticized ideals of childhood that it simply does not work for adults. Twenty-year-old Pollyanna in *Pollyanna Grows Up*, Brown argues, embodies the problems of adopting a specifically childlike form of positive thinking in one's adult years. The example she uses to illustrate her point is Pollyanna's response to her mistaken belief that John Pendleton wishes to marry her: she decides that she must accept (out of a sense of pity and the strange belief that she must atone for her mother's earlier rejection of his hand) even though she is in love with Pendleton's ward, Jimmy. For Brown, the adult Pollyanna we see in *Pollyanna Grows Up* is a failed character.

Margot Hillel, in her essay-length study of the child as a redeeming figure, does not comment on Porter's sequel but does situate *Pollyanna's* success within a context that foregrounds her childlike qualities and the Christian overtones of the novel. Pollyanna's form of evangelism draws not only upon the presumed saintliness of young children but also on a shift in public sentiment toward more practical forms of expressing Christianity.

In the critical purview, then, *Pollyanna* belongs to several long-standing traditions within children's literature scholarship, and it is only right that she should be considered alongside other novels of the era. However, when the novel is *only* considered in comparison, an understanding of Pollyanna's particularities is lost. This volume offers the first book-length study of Porter's work and her character. The paucity of *Pollyanna* scholarship may partly be explained by the novel's popular appeal. Early scholars of children's literature, for whom the legitimacy of their work was not established, tended to focus on more obviously literary texts, and only made reference to works such as *Pollyanna* in passing. It is only fairly recently that scholars of children's literature have risked focusing on popular books which may not stand the test of time (like Meyer's *Twilight* quartet).

On a more positive note, this incorporation of *Pollyanna* into wider discussions attests to the novel's iconic status: "everyone" is assumed to be acquainted with her story. In celebration of its centenary, this collection of thirteen original chapters examines those aspects of *Pollyanna* and the character that have contributed to her vitality. The focus is primarily on the novel itself, but attention is also paid to Porter's sequel, *Pollyanna Grows Up*, film versions, and translations. With backgrounds in children's literature, cultural and film studies, philosophy, and religious studies, our contributors bring a provocative and diverse set of readings of Porter's germinal work.

The Chapters

In Part I: Pollyanna's World, the authors examine what happens when Pollyanna engages with the world—her community and the natural environment—around her. The five chapters in this section focus on how Porter's heroine's interactions with her environment change the ways others engage with their environment. In "'Then just being glad isn't pro-fi-ta-ble?': Mourning, Class, and Benevolence in *Pollyanna*," Roxanne Harde engages with turn-of-the-century debates about benevolence and the orphan through a discussion of mourning and class in the novel. Using theoretical discourse analyzing mourning and loss, Harde explores Pollyanna's ability to work through the loss of her father by engaging with the citizens of Beldingsville through acts of benevolence and unwavering "gladness." As a novel in which nearly every main character suffers from loss, *Pollyanna* enacts a response to mourning that reconsiders Progressive-era benevolence even as it reinstates the socio-economic status quo.

Laura Robinson is also concerned with Pollyanna's capacity to reinstate the status quo, but uses queer theory to uncover "The Ambiguous Heteronormativity of *Pollyanna*." Robinson draws on the work of Humphrey Carpenter to regard Pollyanna as a character who displays an "aggressive femininity," a girl who changes her world and the people within it (98). Yet, for all her impressively subversive potential, Pollyanna's triumphs simply reinstate the established order: Aunt Polly, a powerful, single, rich woman, is returned to a traditional role as wife and mother. In more ways than one, Robinson reveals, Pollyanna functions as a mouthpiece for patriarchy: by literally and figuratively repeating her father and by being the narrative thrust that returns her aunt to heteronormativity. Nevertheless, as Robinson discovers, *Pollyanna* works toward exposing the fragility and constructedness of family, gender, and patriarchal power.

The third chapter, Anthony Pavlik's reading of ecophobia and the domestic in "'Matter out of place': Dirt, Disorder, and Ecophobia," points out that while the Victorian literary tradition took as an enduring motif nature, in the form of the garden as a healthy and healing space for children, in *Pollyanna* there is no such safe, enclosed garden space. Instead, the novel presents the cleanliness of the house in opposition to the encroaching chaos that is the natural world. Pavlik considers *Pollyanna* in view of recent ideas of ecophobia—an unreasonable but deeply conditioned reaction against nature—taking the idea of dirt and disorder (and by extension those things that are ecophobically considered as specific to dirty and disordered nature such as animals and even the freckle-faced Pollyanna herself) as matter out of place. But by creating her home, and thus a place, in Beldingsville, Pollyanna questions both readers' and Aunt Polly's sense of order.

Pollyanna also defies the established world order as she crosses class boundaries once in *Pollyanna* and twice in *Pollyanna Grows Up*. In "'Ice-cream Sundays': Food and the Liminal Spaces of Class in *Pollyanna*," Samantha Christensen begins her study with the early scene in which Nancy collects Pollyanna from the train. Intrigued by the impression that her aunt may be wealthy, Pollyanna asks, "Does Aunt Polly have ice-cream Sundays?" (20). Pollyanna equates wealth with luxurious foods such as ice cream sundaes and with Sunday afternoon spent relaxing together with loved ones. At this moment, Christensen notes, food transcends its prominent role as basic human sustenance and takes on a deeper social meaning. Pointing out the inextricable links between food and class structure, and how behavior surrounding appetite and food choice shows food as an extension of social structure, Christensen explores the link between food and the complex class relations in *Pollyanna* to reveal the subtlety with which Porter blurs the hierarchal divisions between rich and poor.

In a chapter that draws from girlhood and eco-feminist studies, Monika Elbert brings *Pollyanna* into conversation with Johanna Spyri's *Heidi* (1880). "At Home in Nature: Negotiating Ecofeminist Politics in *Heidi* and *Pollyanna*" discusses the resemblances between the two novels, particularly in the way that both emphasize social misfits and invalid patients. Noting that both authors seek to find a balance in people's diseased natures by finding an alternative to modern urban or consumer living,

Elbert argues that the antidote in both cases appears in the form of an idealized girl who nostalgically embodies the "natural" values of a bygone era. Their idealism and simplicity provide cures for the sick that not even the many doctors (in both books) can fathom or hope to achieve. Both Heidi and Pollyanna need to create their own sense of home and can do so through their affiliation with nature. However, both must learn the consequences of spiritual bankruptcy by either suffering directly or indirectly from physical paralysis. Both girls show a love of nature and of animals, and both refuse to participate in socially sanctioned practices of shunning the working class. In addition, both Pollyanna and Heidi "civilize" several disgruntled and angry boys, who pose a threat to harmonious communal values. And though both girls are averse to formal modes of discipline and pedagogy, they finally allow themselves to be educated on their own terms.

In Part II: Ideological Pollyanna, the authors expose the implicit philosophical, religious, and nationalist ideologies of the era in which they were written which underlie Pollyanna's engagement with her environment. In "The 'veritable bugle-call': An Examination of *Pollyanna* through the Lens of Twentieth-Century Protestantism," Ashley N. Reese positions *Pollyanna* at the tipping point between children's books that emphasize religion, particularly Christianity, and those endorsing the values of secular humanism. If *Pollyanna* contains Christian elements, Reese notes, then she saves her community and the corrupt adults around her with her optimism in the form of the glad game. Reese argues that God and the Protestant church are hidden behind this game; Pollyanna's role is implicit. However, she is portrayed as the inherently innocent and pure child who can save the world, or at least her own world.

Janet Wesselius also examines the ways in which Pollyanna changes her world, but reads these changes alongside the emergence of the only philosophy indigenous to America: pragmatism. In "*Pollyanna*, the Power of Gladness, and the Philosophy of Pragmatism," Wesselius reveals numerous similarities between Pollyanna's capacity to change her world by wishing it were different and William James's philosophical discussion of how re-conceiving one's environment can be a form of action. Although she draws connections between James's contemplations of how one can relieve pain by reconceptualizing it, the main thrust of Wesselius's chapter is to situate *Pollyanna* within a distinctively American philosophical context.

The other two chapters in this section also offer insights into the specifically American qualities of Porter's novel. Dorothy Karlin's "When

Pollyanna Did Not Grow Up: Girlhood and the Innocent Nation" places the quality of Pollyanna's childhood innocence within early-twentieth-century American identity politics. Rather than taking the well-trodden path established by Jacqueline Rose to draw attention to generalized adult desires for an "innocent" child, Karlin draws parallels between romance plots in Latin American novels and Porter's construction of girlhood innocence to show how both function in similar ways to heal regional and class differences and so foster patriotism. Karlin's reading of *Pollyanna* as part of a nation-building project initially foregrounds the conflicting notions of American identity evoked when Pollyanna arrives in Beldings-ville, and then demonstrates how the sunshiny qualities of the innocent girl are used to promote a harmonious vision of American identity in order to inculcate a national ideology.

Patricia Oman's "*Pollyanna*: Intersectionalities of the Child, the Region, and the Nation" furthers Karlin's argument by demonstrating how Polly-anna's unrelenting optimism reinforces national American identity by erasing signs of local identity. Unlike other American children's classics of this era, such as Twain's *The Adventures of Huckleberry Finn* and Baum's *The Wonderful Wizard of Oz*, *Pollyanna* reverses the trend to "Go West" and grows up with her country. In her movement to New England from the Western frontier, Pollyanna brings the clash of the frontier back to the already civilized New England. In this process, Oman argues, Porter's character not only changes the psychological mindset of the residents of small-town America, she also inscribes national identity over regional identity.

Despite her specifically American qualities, *Pollyanna* has travelled well as both a book and a film. Our third section, *Adapted Pollyanna*, examines Pollyanna's adaptations into film and in translation. The first two chapters explore the American film versions. In "The Gospel of Good Cheer: Innocence, Spiritual Healing, and Patriotism in Mary Pickford's *Pollyanna*," Anke Brouwers analyzes the first film adaptation of the novel, the 1920 black-and-white silent starring "America's Sweetheart," Mary Pickford. Brouwers notes that the Pollyanna character was a perfect fit for Pickford's well-established screen persona of the child-woman with a partly sassy, partly sensitive, fragile but morally flawless disposition. Polly-anna's instructive and obtrusive "glad philosophy" matched Pickford's public profile as a role model for American women and girls, one who was qualified to offer advice to the American public at large. Between 1915 and 1916, Pickford published syndicated advice columns in which she mused on personal, professional, philosophical and even "funny little thoughts" of a political bent. The star's advice was, much like Porter's text, dripping with rural nostalgia and optimism, and inspired by a sentimental social conscience. By focusing on Mary Pickford, her career and star image, the release of the film in a post-sacral, spiritual society, the post–World War I context, and institutional developments within the film industry regarding censorship and regulation, Brouwers provides the necessary context for *Pollyanna*'s success as a film, its cultural meaning, and its eventual critical opprobrium within the context of the Hollywood industry as well as within a broader socio-cultural context.

The second chapter in this section, K. Brenna Wardell's "'Almost a golden glow around it': The Filmic Nostalgia of Disney's *Pollyanna*," explores the next popular film version of the novel, produced in 1960 by Walt Disney Productions. Wardell discusses the film as a product of late 1950s nostalgia, and as an effort to recover a sense of childhood innocence and community coherence in a period in which social, economic, and cultural shifts led to national anxiety about the state of the nation and its families. The film departs in a number of ways from Porter's narrative, Wardell notes, but it aims to capture the charm and determination of Pollyanna and her transformational effects on the community that becomes her home. Focusing on nostalgia in the film, Wardell argues that this adaptation of *Pollyanna* may seem to represent the first decade of the twentieth century, but rather it truly speaks to the dreams and concerns, and to the nostalgic impulses, of the previous century.

Porter's irrepressibly optimistic character has affected the national literatures of countries her author never visited, and the final two chapters provide windows into two very different cultural adaptations of *Pollyanna* from Japan and Turkey. Mio Bryce's examination of *Pollyanna* within the context of Japanese children's literature notes similarities between early-twentieth-century American desires to combine didactic intent with idealized childhood innocence, and Japanese desires to do much the same. A key difference she observes between the two national literatures is the willingness to entertain their young readers rather than simply preaching moral values. Identifying a shift in attitudes toward the child reader in Japanese children's literature from the 1950s onward, Bryce argues that translated literature provided the main models for "entertaining" literature for children, especially stories for girls or stories featuring girls as the protagonist. Novels such as *Pollyanna*, Bryce suggests, played a vital role in shaping the concept of girlhood during this era, and the impact of Porter's character is evident in romantic girls' love comedies and other popular fiction since the 1970s.

In contrast, Pollyanna's adventures in Turkey have a more political bent. In "*Pollyanna* in Turkey: Translating a Transnational Icon," Tanfer Emin Tunç traces three phases in the history of *Pollyanna* in the Turkish context. The early translations of the novel in the 1930s and 1950s presented Pollyanna as an advocate for female children as she mimics the admirable qualities of the traditional boy-hero—honesty, trustworthiness, bravery, resourcefulness, rationality, and resilience (Goulden and Stanfield 193), and in doing so promoted the pro-Western sentiments of the era. However, Tunç argues, the novel has also been used as a vehicle for spreading Islamist ideologies in the early twenty-first century. Tunç's investigation of translations and other cultural adaptations (such as film) of *Pollyanna* in Turkey opens up the complexity of the politics of translating and adapting an American text (with Western, Christian values) in a predominantly Muslim country grappling with larger issues of modernity and identity.

While no collection of chapters could ever claim to offer a comprehensive overview of a classic as significant as *Pollyanna*, this study of Porter's creation, one hundred years after its publication in book form, offers readers varied insights into her continuing popularity and influence. Intersections between the chapters highlight the most significant aspects of the *Pollyanna* phenomenon—most notably the ideological and political implications of Pollyanna's gladness, the constructions of girlhood, the Christian motifs, and national identity—and by setting these issues in different contexts proffer richer insight into the varied cultural manifestations of *Pollyanna*. The distinctively different approaches offered by each of the contributors also bear testament to *Pollyanna*'s capacity to appeal to readers, children, and critics alike, on an individual level. It is this versatility that enables Pollyanna to "just live" on today (51).

Notes

1. We quote exactly from *Pollyanna*, which means that there is no period behind the abbreviations of personal titles like Dr. and Mr., as was the custom in Porter's time. Outside of quotations, we conform to contemporary practice.

2. The *Christian Herald* can be accessed in facsimile online at *Internet Archive*. There one can see *Pollyanna* in its original context along with the illustrations by Stockton Mulford. See archive.org/details/christianherald35unse for Volume 35 (in which *Pollyanna* appears from 27 November 1912) and archive.org/details/christianherald36unse for Volume 36 (until 19 Feb. 1913).

3. The Rauner Special Collections Library at Dartmouth College in Hanover, New Hampshire, has a collection of Porter's letters and papers (1889–1928).

4. See archive.org/details/pollyannagladgiroocush for the script.

5. These actresses played Rudy and Claire Huxtable in the television series *The Cosby Show* (1984–92), a landmark in African American TV not only for its portrayal of everyday life but also for the way in which it transcended racial boundaries among its viewers.

Works Cited

Ai shôjo Porianna monogatari [The Story of Pollyanna: girl of love]. 1986. Nippon Animation. DVD.

Alcott, Louisa May. *Little Women*. Boston: Roberts Brothers, 1868–69. Print.

American Library Association. *A.L.A. Booklist: A Guide to the Best New Books*. Chicago: ALA, 1913. Print.

Avery, Gillian. "Porter, Eleanor H." *Twentieth-Century Children's Writers*. 3rd ed. Ed. Tracy Chevalier and D. L. Kirkpatrick. Chicago: St. James, 1989. Print.

Borton, Eleanor. *Pollyanna in Hollywood*. New York: Grosset & Dunlap, 1931. Print.

———. *Pollyanna's Castle in Mexico*. Boston: L.C. Page, 1934. Print.

———. *Pollyanna's Door to Happiness*. New York: Grosset & Dunlap, 1936. Print.

———. *Pollyanna's Golden Horseshoe*. New York: Grosset & Dunlap, 1939. Print.

———. *Pollyanna and the Secret Mission*. New York: Grosset & Dunlap, 1951. Print.

Boucher, Jerry, and Charles E. Osgood. "The Pollyanna Hypothesis." *Journal of Verbal Learning and Verbal Behavior* 8 (1969): 1–8. JSTOR. Web. 2 May 2012.

Brown, Claire M. "*Pollyanna*, Moral Sainthood, and Childhood Ideals." *Philosophy in Children's Literature*. Ed. Peter R. Costello. Plymouth: Lexington, 2012. 235–50. Print.

Burnett, Frances Hodgson. *A Little Princess: The Story of Sarah Crewe*. New York: Warne, 1905. Print.

———. *The Secret Garden*. New York: Frederick A. Stokes, 1911. Print.

Burt, Daniel S., ed. *The Chronology of American Literature: American Achievements from Colonial Era to Modern Times*. New York: Houghton Mifflin, 2004. Print.

Carpenter, Humphrey. *Secret Gardens: A Study of the Golden Age of Children's Literature*. Boston: Houghton Mifflin, 1985. Print

Carroll, Lewis. *Alice's Adventures in Wonderland*. London: Macmillan, 1865. Print.

Chalmers, Margaret Piper. *Pollyanna's Protégée*. New York: Grosset & Dunlap, 1944. Print.

Coolidge, Susan. *What Katy Did*. Boston: Roberts Brothers, 1872. Print.

The Cosby Show. Dir. Jay Sandrich. 1984–92. First Look Studios, 2002. DVD.

Cushing, Catherine Chisholm. *Pollyanna: A Comedy in Four Acts*. 1915. Internet Archive. Web. 13 August 2013.

Dixon, Franklin W. (pseud.). *The Hardy Boys*. Series. New York: Grosset & Dunlap; Stratemeyer Syndicate, 1927–2005. Print.

Goulden, Nancy Rost, and Susan Stanfield. "Leaving Elsie Dinsmore Behind: Plucky Girls as an Alternative Role Model in Classic Girls Literature." *Women's Studies* 32.2 (2003): 183–208. Print.

Griswold, Jerry. *Audacious Kids: Coming of Age in America's Classic Children's Books*. New York: Oxford UP, 1992. Print.

Hayat sevince güzel [Life is Beautiful when you Love]. 1971. *Sinema Türk 2.0*. Web. 3 June 2012.

Hillel, Margot. "'A little child shall lead them': The Child as Redeemer." *Children's Literature and the Fin de Siècle*. Ed. Roderick McGillis. Westport: Greenwich, 2003. 57–70. Print.

Hope, Laura Lee (pseud.). *The Bobbsey Twins*. Series. New York: Grosset & Dunlap; Stratemeyer Syndicate, 1904–79. Print.

Hunt, Peter. *An Introduction to Children's Literature*. Oxford: Oxford UP, 1994. Print.

Keene, Carolyn (pseud.). *Nancy Drew*. Series. New York: Grosset & Dunlap; Stratemeyer Syndicate, 1930–2004. Print.

Keith, Lois. *Take Up Thy Bed and Walk: Death, Disability and Cure in Classic Fiction for Girls*. New York and Abingdon, UK: Routledge, 2001. Print.

Larner, A. J. "Voices From the Past: Some Literary Accounts of Possible Childhood Paraplegia and Neurorehabilitation." *Developmental Neurorehabilitation* 12.4 (2009): 248–52. Print.

Melody. "The Glad Books Part 1." 5 June 2007. *Redeeming Qualities*. Web. 1 October 2012.
———. "The Glad Books Part 2." 6 June 2007. *Redeeming Qualities*. Web. 1 October 2012.

Merriman, C. D. "Eleanor H. Porter." *The Literature Network*. Ed. C. D. Merriman. East Lansing: Jalic, 2004. Web. 3 May 2012.

Meyer, Stephenie. *Breaking Dawn*. London: Atom. 2008. Print.

Mills, Alice. "Pollyanna and the Not So Glad Game." *Children's Literature* 27 (1999): 87–104. *Project MUSE*. Web. 29 May 2012.

Moffit, Virginia May. *Pollyanna at Six Star Ranch*. London: George G. Harrap, 1948. Print.
———. *Pollyanna of Magic Valley*. New York: Grosset & Dunlap, 1949. Print.

Montgomery, Lucy Maud. *Anne of Green Gables*. 1908. New York: G. P. Putnam's Sons. 2008. Print.

Moore, Alan, and Kevin O'Neill. *The League of Extraordinary Gentleman Omnibus*. New York: DC Comics. 2011. Print.

Nelson, Claudia. *Little Strangers: Portrayals of Adoption and Foster Care in America, 1850–1929*. Bloomington: Indiana UP, 2003. Print.

Nesbit, Edith A. *The Railway Children*. London: Unwin, 1906. Print.

Overton, Grant Martin. *The Women Who Make Our Novels*. New York: Moffat, Yard, 1918. Print.

Phelps, Elizabeth Stuart. *Gypsy Breynton*. Series. New York: Dodd, Mead, 1866–67. Print.

Polly. Dir. Debbie Allen. 1989. Walt Disney Home Entertainment. 2008. DVD.

Polly: Comin' Home! Dir. Debbie Allen. 1990. Walt Disney Home Entertainment. DVD.

Pollyanna. Dir. David Swift. 1960. Walt Disney Video, 2002. DVD.

Pollyanna. Dir. June Wyndham-Davies. 1973. BBC Enterprises. 1992. VHS.

Pollyanna. Dir. Paul Powell. 1920. DVD.

Pollyanna. Dir. Sarah Harding. 2004. ITV Studios Home Entertainment, 2007. DVD.

"Pollyanna." *Masterpiece Theatre*. PBS. Web. 13 August 2013.

"Pollyanna." *Oxford English Dictionary*. *OED Online*. Web. 28 May 2012.

Pollyanna Moça. Dir. Júlio Gouveia. 1956 and 1958. TV Tupi. TV.

"Pollyanna of Littleton, New Hampshire." *GoLittleton*. Web. 29 May 2012.

Porter, Eleanor H. *Cross Currents: The Story of Margaret.* Holliston: W. A. Wilde, 1907. Print.

———. *Miss Billy.* Boston: Page, 1911. Print.

———. *Miss Billy's Decision.* Boston: Page, 1912. Print.

———. *Miss Billy Married.* Boston: Page, 1914. Print.

———. *Pollyanna.* 1913. London: Puffin, 2004. Print.

———. *Pollyanna Grows Up.* New York: Grosset & Dunlap, 1914. Print.

Reece, Colleen L. *Pollyanna Comes Home.* Philadelphia: Barbour, 1995. Print.

———. *Pollyanna Plays the Game.* Philadelphia: Barbour, 1995. Print.

Rose, Jacqueline. *The Case of Peter Pan: Or, the Impossibility of Children's Fiction.* Basingstoke: Macmillan, [1984] 1994. Print.

Smith, Harriet Lummis. *Pollyanna of the Orange Blossoms.* Boston: A.L. Burt, 1924. Print.

———. *Pollyanna's Jewels.* New York: Grosset & Dunlap, 1925. Print.

———. *Pollyanna's Debt of Honor.* New York: Grosset & Dunlap, 1927. Print.

———. *Pollyanna's Western Adventure.* Boston: A.L. Burt, 1929. Print.

Stratemeyer, Edward (as Arthur M. Winfield). *The Rover Boys: Series for Young Americans.* New York: Grosset & Dunlap; Stratemeyer Syndicate, 1899–1926. Print.

Sanders, Joe Sutliff. *Disciplining Girls: Understanding the Origins of the Classic Orphan Girl Story.* Baltimore: Johns Hopkins UP, 2011. Print.

Spyri, Johanna. *Heidi.* 1880. New York: Simon and Schuster, 2000. Print.

Wiggin, Kate Douglas. *Rebecca of Sunnybrook Farm.* Boston: Houghton Mifflin, 1903. Print.

Part 1

POLLYANNA'S WORLD

1

"Then just being glad isn't pro-fi-ta-ble?": Mourning, Class, and Benevolence in *Pollyanna*

ROXANNE HARDE

As early as the tenth short chapter of Eleanor H. Porter's *Pollyanna*, the novel's eponymous hero has moved from profound loneliness to being so thoroughly contented that she "often told her aunt, joyously, how very happy [her days] were" (86). Pollyanna's joy has come, in the main, from the effort she has put into her new community, from her benevolent actions on behalf of its less fortunate members, an effort born of the work of mourning. Even at this early stage of the novel, her glad game has made a difference to several people, and playing it has helped Pollyanna work through her grief over the recent death of her father and the earlier death of her mother. Aunt Polly—for whom benevolence is merely a duty and who has responded to her many losses with bitterness and isolation— replies to Pollyanna's declaration that her days were happy: "I am gratified, of course, that they are happy; but I trust that they are profitable as well . . . otherwise I should have failed signally in my duty" (86). Pollyanna, who already knows that she might come to hate the word *duty*, finally asks if it would not be enough that her days were happy, "They must be pro-fi-ta-ble as well? . . . Then just being glad isn't pro-fi-ta-ble?" (87). She seems to reach an intuitive understanding that both duty and profit are about personal investment and benefit, and are, at least from Aunt Polly's example, conjoined to class. Duty and benevolence, to Aunt Polly, both represent and entrench one's social standing. For Pollyanna, duty and benevolence require a wholehearted engagement with life that enables her to work through her mourning and come to terms with her orphanhood.

Considered alongside theoretical discourse that analyzes the operations of mourning and responses to absence, *Pollyanna* offers far more than the usual Progressive-era commentary on Christianity or sentimentalism or social institutions with which it is regularly credited. In *Writing*

History, Writing Trauma, Dominick LaCapra cautions that because of personal loss or general empathy, people may invest death with value to which they remain "dedicated or at least bound," which is both intolerable and no solution to loss (23). LaCapra argues that to work through mourning means articulating affect and representation in a way that precludes transcendence or withdrawal.[1] In *The Work of Mourning*, a collection of eulogies written on the deaths of his friends, Jacques Derrida suggests that recognizing death and working through grief is a supremely verbal act. Even as he notes the impossibility of speaking at times of mourning, Derrida considers silence "another wound, another insult" (50). Refusing to make of death, and therefore mourning, an allegory or even a metaphor, Derrida models mourning as a movement toward life, a kind of ongoing work: "In and of itself. Even when it has the power to give birth, even and especially when it plans to bring something to light" (142–43). For both LaCapra and Derrida, the work of mourning allows an engagement with loss and insists on a reinvestment in life.

As a novel in which nearly every character suffers from loss, mainly of loved ones who have died or moved on, *Pollyanna* enacts a response to loss and mourning that reconsiders Progressive-era benevolence and posits Pollyanna's "gladness," in the form of her engagement with life, as an appropriate means to work through mourning. In its discussion of mourning and class in *Pollyanna*, this chapter engages with turn-of-the-century debates about benevolence and the orphan. While Porter offers pointed commentary on private and public altruism—even as she lamentably reinstates the socio-economic status quo, by attaching philanthropic social action to the act of mourning—her novel enacts an outlook as hopeful as Pollyanna herself.

"Practically nothing": Mourning and an Orphan's Worth

In its comments on the social movement toward the institutionalization of benevolence, *Pollyanna* offers some insight into changing representations of the orphan in children's literature through the late nineteenth and early twentieth centuries. As Claudia Nelson points out, "the orphan's undeniable symbolic qualities change over time" (65). Where antebellum orphans adapt to their new circumstances rather than changing the adults around them, Reconstruction-era orphans, "like the ideal immigrant, are often represented as infinitely flexible, upwardly mobile, and potentially useful" (Nelson 65). After the turn of the twentieth century, Nelson argues, the dependent child is used "to illustrate and endorse important new approaches toward children as a group, especially the redefining of the child's value as emotional rather than practical. . . . Orphan fiction reca-pitulates the late-nineteenth-century debate about what to do with the dependent child, a debate in which the impulse to nurture the parentless slowly vanquished the impulse to hire them" (55). Even so, *Pollyanna* offers both sides of this debate about the value of a dependent child: Pollyanna's value is clearly emotional, but before Porter introduces her, she introduces her readers to Nancy, whose value is practical.

Miss Polly's new servant has been with her two months; this young woman, "had never 'worked out' before; but a sick mother, suddenly wid-owed and left with three younger children besides Nancy herself, had forced the girl into doing something towards their support in the kitchen of the great house on the hill" (2). Nancy's, and possibly Pollyanna's, worth may be practical to the adults in the novel, but it is emotional to Polly-anna. When Nancy expresses joy that a little girl, like "the sunshine her own little sisters made," will brighten up Miss Polly's home and life, Miss Polly replies: "Nice? Well, that isn't exactly the word I should use. . . . How-ever, I intend to make the best of it, of course. I am a good woman, I hope; and I know my duty" (3). Nancy's ensuing sense that "somehow she must prepare a welcome for this lonely little stranger" demonstrates the emotional value she will hold for Pollyanna (3). A dependent child forced by the death of her father into independence, Nancy also functions as a mirror and model for Pollyanna as she adumbrates Pollyanna's benevolent actions.

Both girls have recently lost their fathers, and while Pollyanna's father has taught her the glad game that will enable her to work through her mourning, Nancy draws on her own experience of loss to understand that Pollyanna needs her. Shortly after they meet, Nancy develops an "aching sympathy for the poor little forlornness beside her" (19). By the end of the first chapter, she declares to Timothy, "You couldn't hire me ter leave! . . . she'll be aneedin' some rock to fly to for refuge. Well, I'm a-goin' ter be that rock" (22). The grieving and compassionate Nancy thus sets the stage for Pollyanna and her glad game. LaCapra suggests that converting absence (an infinite site of pain) into loss (which ends with the thing or person lost and mourned), allows a "crucial distinction between then and now wherein one is able to remember what happened to one in the past but realizes one is living in the here and now with future possibilities" (46–47). Forced into service by her family's need, Nancy must grieve her father's death with the same efficiency she brings to cooking and cleaning for Miss

Polly. The novel may blithely accept the assignments and distinctions of class—one mourning girl moves into the domestic labor force while the other moves into privilege and a new wardrobe—but it also champions Nancy's active engagement with her present and future, particularly her growing friendship with Timothy. Nancy's practical approach to loss and change, to use LaCapra's terms, "opens up empowering possibilities . . . in the creation of a more desirable, perhaps significantly different . . . life in the here and now" (58).

Porter brings Nancy's liveliness, and her compassion for Pollyanna, into sharp contrast with Aunt Polly's view of the little girl. The language of worth and class-based duty surrounds Polly's view of her niece, and lacks the compassion Nancy expresses, which would mitigate Polly's focus on social standing and wealth. The letter that requests she take her niece invokes questions surrounding the value of an orphan: "I regret to inform you that the Rev. John Whittier died two weeks ago, leaving one child, a girl eleven years old. He left practically nothing else save a few books; for, as you doubtless know, he was the pastor of this small mission church, and had a very meagre salary" (4). Where the letter suggests that this child has emotional value, in that it suggests Pollyanna's belonging "among her own people," and that Polly might actually desire to raise the penniless orphan for her "sister's sake," Polly's response, "She *hoped* she knew her duty . . . disagreeable as the task would be," makes clear she sees the child as only a burden she is obliged by her social position to undertake (5). To her aunt, Pollyanna has no emotional or economic value. Even as Polly expresses her frustration at this unwelcome burden, she ruminates on the loss of her sister, "when Jennie, as a girl of twenty, had insisted upon marrying the young minister, in spite of her family's remonstrances. There had been a man of wealth who had wanted her—and the family had much preferred him to the minister but Jennie had not. . . . The break had come then" (5). The Harrington family's preference for the man of wealth and standing over the impoverished minister speaks to their place within the constrictions of class and social standing, in the same way that Polly meets social expectations about her duty as Pollyanna's last living relative. The early perspective of her, through Nancy's eyes, as an impossible-to-please, "stern, severe-faced woman . . . who never thought to smile," places Polly in an antagonistic position. She clearly sees the worth of the dependent child as only practical and tied to her class.

However, Porter also adds enough detail about Polly's past—the deaths of her parents and both sisters, and the loss of her lover—that readers should understand Polly as a figure who has retreated into absence and pain. In LaCapra's terms, she is bound to death and the past. Her focus on her money and possessions can be read as a focus on all that has been left to her, and her retreat into her house and solitude is complete: "For years now, she had been sole mistress of the house and of the thousands left her by her father. There were people who had openly pitied her lonely life, and who had urged her to have some friend or companion to live with her; but she had not welcomed either their sympathy or their advice. She was not lonely, she said" (6). If choosing solitude and a retreat into her wealth, absenting herself from the fullness of life, is Polly's response to loss, a response that offers safety and the means to defer the pain of mourning, then Pollyanna's presence understandably causes her aunt a good deal of anxiety. By simply living under the same roof, Pollyanna threatens Polly's comfortable retreat into absence and stagnation.

"The little attic room": The Site of Mourning

However, Pollyanna does more than simply live. As she explains to her aunt, living involves much more than breathing and should include a combination of playing, reading, climbing, talking, and finding things out (51). Living, to Pollyanna, means going out and engaging fully with her community, her surroundings, and her life. In so doing, she moves past absence and undertakes the work of mourning that, LaCapra contends, "brings the possibility of achieving a reinvestment in, or recathexis of, life, which allows one to begin again" (66). From their first meeting, Pollyanna's concentration of emotional energy defines her value as emotional and negates Polly's practical view of the child. When they meet, Polly does not consider it her duty to rise to greet her niece, so the child flings herself into "her aunt's scandalized, unyielding lap," just as she will fling herself into her new life (23). As in this scene, the narrative often stands clearly in judgment of Polly, particularly through Nancy. Nancy feels Polly should be ashamed for not meeting the child's train and for putting her in a room that is "like an oven for heat" (12). Nancy's rant, as she prepares the attic room for Pollyanna's arrival, initially suggests that she thinks Polly miserly with possessions, space, and affection: "The idea of stickin' that blessed child 'way off up here in this hot little room—with no fire in the winter, too; and all this big house ter pick and choose from! Unnecessary children indeed!" (7). Later, as Nancy helps Pollyanna move into the room, the younger girl fears that she may have taken Nancy's room, which then reduces Nancy to tears and emphasizes the connection between the two recent bereavements. When Nancy defines the attic room as "a pretty place this is ter put a homesick, lonesome child into!" she displays both empathy for the newly orphaned little girl and the crux of her criticism of Polly and the attic room: this is an inappropriate place for a child to undertake the work of mourning (8).

The narrative validates Nancy's conclusion as she brings Pollyanna home from the station, and the child mentions her father for the first time: "'What a pretty street! I knew 'twas going to be pretty; Father told me—' She stopped with a little choking breath. Nancy, looking at her apprehensively, saw that her small chin was quivering and that her eyes were full of tears" (17). Where Nancy sympathizes with the grieving girl, Aunt Polly expects her to ignore her loss, just as she has refused to acknowledge her own. When Pollyanna meets her aunt and mentions her father twice, Aunt Polly interrupts her both times, saying sharply "there is one thing that might just as well be understood right away at once; and this is, I do not care to have you keep talking of your father to me" (24). Forbidden to speak of her loss, to engage in the discourse of mourning Derrida posits as vital in the work of grieving around her aunt, Pollyanna must turn to her little attic room as the site of her mourning, a room where she can continue to play the glad game only when she looks outside through the window.

How, then, does this discourse of mourning function? In *The Work of Mourning*, Derrida contends that, ultimately, the living can only give the dead something in us: our memory. One must speak of the dead, in Derrida's terms, "to combat all the forces that work to efface or conceal not just the names on the tombstones but the apostrophe of mourning" (30). This apostrophe, the address to the living, the eulogy, meets a number of needs, as Derrida asks, "What are we doing when we exchange these discourses? Over what are we keeping watch? Are we trying to negate death or retain it? Are we trying to put things in order, make amends, or settle our accounts, to finish unfinished business?" (50). In mourning her father, Pollyanna keeps watch over his memory and negates death by keeping him with her through language. As his child, she is her father's unfinished business; only by living fully and through the example he has set, the glad game he taught her, will she perform the functions of mourning.

In denying Pollyanna discourse about her father, Aunt Polly effectively takes away one of the child's few remaining connections to her past, to the things and people that were hers. As they go up to the attic room, Pollyanna's "big blue eyes tried to look in all directions at once, that no thing of beauty or interest in this wonderful house might be passed unseen.

Most eagerly of all her mind turned to the wondrously exciting problem about to be solved; behind which of all these fascinating doors was waiting now her room—the dear, beautiful room, full of curtains, rugs, and pictures, that was to be her very own?" (26). Lori Ginzberg suggests that nineteenth-century benevolence laid the groundwork for the emergence of early-twentieth-century middle-class, conservative reform movements that placed more emphasis on social control (206–8). Aunt Polly blurs any distinctions between duty, benevolence, and acceptable behavior as she undertakes Pollyanna's training, one form of social control, but completely ignores Pollyanna's grief and misreads the child's need to have a home and family to call her own. Admiring the beauty around her, her aunt's luxurious black silk skirt, a soft green carpet, gilt picture-frames, and lace curtains as her aunt takes her upstairs to her new room, Pollyanna declares "what a perfectly lovely, lovely house! How awfully glad you must be you're so rich!" (25). Aunt Polly corrects her harshly: "I hope I could not so far forget myself as to be sinfully proud of any gift the Lord has seen fit to bestow upon me . . . certainly not of *riches!*" (25). Faced with Pollyanna's passion for life and desperate need to make Polly and the house her very own, Polly falls back on the social status quo and doctrines of sin. Her immediate thoughts are about controlling what she understands as Pollyanna's vices: "She was glad, now, that she had put the child in the attic room. . . . Now—with this evident 'strain of vanity showing thus early—it was all the more fortunate that the room planned for her was plain and sensible" (26). However, she also thinks, "Her idea at first had been to get her niece as far away as possible from herself, and at the same time place her where her childish heedlessness would not destroy valuable furnishings" (26). In so doing, Polly further negates the child's need to mourn and reaffirms her own retreat into absence and the denial of life. Later, when Polly finally relents and moves Pollyanna to a proper bedroom, she devalues the child's joy with further emphasis on her possessions, asking her niece for assurance that "if you think so much of all those things, I trust you will take proper care of them" (91). In both cases Polly, rather ironically, demonstrates her own vanity regarding her possessions. That vanity, however, might also be read as another sign of her refusal to come to terms with all the loved ones that she has lost. Instead of mourning and returning to the fullness of life, Polly turns to social codes and the trappings of class.

Pollyanna's reaction, when she sees the room, might seem to be anguish over its shabbiness. However, her reaction to the shabbiness of her clothes is matter-of-fact; she neither laments her decrepit wardrobe nor gets excited over the new clothing Aunt Polly buys her out of duty, because "Not one of your garments is fit for my niece to wear" (52). Pollyanna reacts to the attic room with tears, not for the lost trappings of wealth but for the isolation to which she is consigned, the further loss of family. Her tears reflect, in Derrida's terms "the disappearance itself" (107). She kneels to cry beside her trunk, which holds the remnants of her life with her father and stands as the symbol of all she has lost. Thinking the child distraught over the room, Nancy offers sympathy, but Pollyanna corrects her about the cause of her grief: "I just can't make myself understand that God and the angels needed my father more than I did" (28). This correction matters enough that Porter repeats it in the scene where Pollyanna teaches Nancy the glad game. The one problem with the game, Pollyanna explains, happens when "sometimes it's almost too hard—like when your father goes to heaven, and there isn't anybody but a Ladies' Aid left" (37). Nancy agrees and notes that the "snippy little room 'way at the top of the house" is also hard (37). Pollyanna, however, makes it clear that her sorrow over the room primarily was about location, "specially when I was so kind of lonesome" (37).

Even as she makes a friend and recognizes the hardship of her isolation, Pollyanna engages in the work of mourning, which at its core is an act of defiance. After bidding an affectionate good night to her aunt, Pollyanna ascends to the little attic room, where she "sobbed into the tightly clutched sheet: 'I know, Father-among-the-angels, I'm not playing the game one bit now—not one bit; but I don't believe even you could find anything to be glad about sleeping all alone 'way off up here in the dark" (40). Derrida calls the eulogy, part of the work of mourning, "a supplementary fiction," because with it we call out to "the others standing around the coffin": "because of its caricatured excess, the overstatement of this rhetoric at least pointed out that we ought not to remain among ourselves. The interactions of the living must be interrupted, the veil must be torn toward the other, the other dead in us though other still" (51–52). Speaking of her father and playing his glad game function as Pollyanna's eulogy for him and allows her to "tear the veil" toward him. Giving voice to and for him allows her to work through mourning, to move outside of herself, to call out to the others around his coffin. However, in forbidding Pollyanna to speak her father's name and in putting the child in the attic, Polly disrupts the work of mourning. Motivated by the constrictions of class (her brother-in-law is beneath her in death as in life, and she does not want a child harming her expensive possessions) and her own refusal to mourn, Polly cannot acknowledge the needs of the orphan and engage in benevolence in any meaningful way.

"I love different folks": Benevolence as the Work of Mourning

Unlike her aunt, Pollyanna demonstrates a thoroughgoing engagement with benevolent action throughout the novel. Moreover, Porter conjoins Pollyanna's benevolence to her mourning even as she undertakes a critique of private and public practices of benevolence in the early twentieth century. In considering various early-twentieth-century novels about orphans, Nelson suggests that "their task is nothing less than to heal the adult world" (54). "Although these novels, too, critique domesticity and respectability, they suggest that households that can accept the dependent child can transcend their original limitations," argues Nelson, and she points out that from the late nineteenth century these fictional children excavate the humanity in their benefactors and come to "embody a national myth of orphan as transformative force" (54). Pollyanna's glad game enables her to function as a "transformative force" from the early chapters of the novel when she teaches Nancy "the 'just being glad' game": "Father told it to me, and it's lovely. . . . We've played it always, ever since I was a little, little girl" (36). Pollyanna then tells Nancy the story she will repeat or allude to many times in the novel. In recounting the details of the wanted doll, the missionary barrel, and the unwanted crutches, she foreshadows the accident that will leave her unable to walk even with crutches and lays the foundation of a game predicated on optimism and hope, a game that suggests benevolence should be an act of love, not of social obligation.

Further, in retelling the story behind the glad game, Pollyanna enables her father's narrative, his voice, to be heard and reheard. As she visits Mrs. Snow, she brings a glad heart into the invalid's room. Rather than coming to Mrs. Snow with her aunt's burden of duty or Nancy's aversion to the invalid's complaints, Pollyanna brings instead a cheerful response to each complaint. Because of the glad game, she can end the visit declaring she's had a "lovely time" as she leaves the patient groomed and far more content in a sunlit room (72). It seems no coincidence that this visit and Pollyanna's move out of the attic are placed in the same short chapter, something its first audience, reading it in serial form week by week, would have appreciated. Pollyanna assumes her aunt is visiting in the same way that Pollyanna has visited Mrs. Snow and the outcome for both is a more cheerful, light-filled room.

Pollyanna's interactions with the cranky Mr. Pendleton similarly are informed by her father's voice. In her determination to brighten her neighbor's life—telling him the sun was shining so he would notice it until he is able to notice it on his own—she pursues benevolence in the form of her father's gladness even as her hopeful outlook insists she credit Mr. Pendleton for the best intentions. Pollyanna acts by allowing, in Derrida's terms, the dead to "speak, to turn speech over to him, his speech, and especially not to take it from him, not to take it in his place . . . to allow him to speak, to occupy his silence or to take up speech oneself only in order, if this is possible, to give it back to him" (95).

Pollyanna turns her speech over to her father most eloquently when she helps Reverend Ford. Their conversation in the woods, between the minister struggling with the text of a sermon meant to chastise his divided and discontent congregation and the child who gives him her father's "rejoicing texts," enables Reverend Ford to look to gladness to craft a sermon that "was a veritable bugle-call to the best that was in every man and woman and child that heard it" (196). She allows her father to speak again and be heard by another congregation in a way that allows her the fullness of memory and mourning.

In addition, Pollyanna's benevolence engages with wider questions about charity and class in the period. Porter asks her child reader, as R. Gordon Kelly puts it, "to become self-conscious about his own behavior and to see it in relation to a moral position dramatized in the stories" (37). In a study of late-nineteenth-century American children's periodicals, Kelly argues that publications for children provided a training ground for an American gentry class, and instilled "the code of the gentleman" in children who would have to address social threats to their class (37). While being less than explicit about the connections between the two, Kelly suggests that those social threats often come from the groups and individuals who need aid from the readers of these periodicals, who need them to take a moral position and behave accordingly. Nelson suggests that children's literature in the period frequently describes "the waif as belonging to a higher order than his or her adoptive parents," as having unusual talent, strength of character, or membership in a higher socioeconomic class (56). These exceptional children, like Pollyanna, are figured then as having a real ability to change the world, to address the challenges of those needing charity, particularly impoverished orphans like Jimmy Bean.

Porter thus undertakes the issue of benevolence through her orphans, and with them, the novel juxtaposes contemporary debates about public/institutional and private/individual charity. Responses to the problem of poverty were generally contested in terms of who should offer aid—individuals; churches and other benevolent societies; local, municipal, or federal governments—and even how the problem should be understood, since poverty, including child poverty, was widely seen as an issue of morality as much as of economics. Christine Stansell discusses the nineteenth-century American understanding of the vicious poor, the unworthy, idle or debauched poor, and the virtuous poor as arising from Calvinist doctrine and the tenets of English poor laws. She also makes clear the connections between prostitution and the female labor market, the means by which capital forced the poor to become "vicious." Anne MacLeod also traces how concepts of poverty and charity changed through the period, and how the concept of the vicious poor came to blur the simple act of charity as a Christian mandate: "the acute concern with the 'vicious poor' who deliberately deceived and dissembled to take advantage of Christian people was a new development in children's stories" (MacLeod 125).

Porter's Mrs. Payson, with her cheap finery and behavior, hints toward this cultural assumption. One of the many townsfolk who come to help Pollyanna be glad again after her accident, Mrs. Payson causes an internal conflict for Aunt Polly that reveals a good deal about early-twentieth-century attitudes toward the poor. After refusing to shake hands with her visitor, Polly hears how Pollyanna has helped the Payson family, which leads Polly to make the gesture as Mrs. Payson leaves. On the one hand, Polly's change of heart suggests that benevolent actions, even to the so-called vicious poor, may make a dramatic change, and Porter thus encourages her readers to offer kindness and charity to all. On the other hand, the description of Mrs. Payson, "with unnaturally pink cheeks and abnormally yellow hair; a young woman who wore high heels and cheap jewellery," her tearful reaction to Polly's proffered hand, and Polly's reaction to the visit, which "strained her nerves to the snapping point," reifies class divisions (242–43, 245). Because their parents' social class affects children's life experiences, sociologist Annette Lareau shows that in America—the land of opportunity and inequality—family practices and approaches to child rearing cohere and differ according to social class, and "lead to the *transmission of differential advantages* to children" (5). The handshake between Polly and Mrs. Payson does not breach social hierarchies, and Polly will not be surprised if the Paysons or their children need charity, from individuals or institutions in the future. The handshake—accompanied by Mrs. Payson's tearful acceptance of it as an act of benevolence, and Polly's strained nerves as evidence of the cost of benevolence to some members of the privileged class—functions as division rather than connection.

If *Pollyanna* offers an implicit commentary on private acts of benevolence, then the novel also considers benevolent organizations, both religious and governmental, particularly those focused on the alleviation of child poverty. LeRoy Ashby argues that child welfare systems in the United States have always been unable to overcome a "class-based propensity to find parents, typically working-class mothers, culpable for bad lifestyles and poor methods of childrearing," and he notes that even as political agencies introduced the modern welfare state, they "retained long-familiar judgments about poverty, the working class, and race" (80). Using as one example those activists in church organizations—such as Sunday School movements or Pollyanna's Ladies' Aiders—who "fretted that youngsters, particularly those in [or from] poor homes, were 'moral orphans,'" Ashby traces this propensity to the blurring of distinctions between misfortune and vice in nineteenth-century America (31).

With the story of the Paysons, Porter gestures toward the idea of the vicious poor in *Pollyanna*, and the subplot featuring Jimmy Bean makes a number of similar suggestions about child poverty and the dependent orphan. Porter implies, first, that places like Beldingville's Orphan's Home are overcrowded and inadequate for the raising of children. As Jimmy puts it, "they've got so many kids there ain't room for me, an' I wa'n't never wanted anyhow" (97). MacLeod notes that in a good deal of literature in the period, "community resources for the care of the poor . . . were dismissed quickly, leaving the impression that they were not only the last but the worst refuge for the desperate," and Porter's brief mention of the Orphans' Home does just that (59).

The novel also examines questions of morality and poverty where Jimmy is concerned, even as it offers a rather pointed critique of church organizations. In a study of reform discourses in philanthropic novels for adults in nineteenth-century America, Deborah Carlin argues that this "philanthropic literature resolutely avoided or denied the economic origins of difference between the working poor and the privileged" (211). Literature for children follows the same trend, including *Pollyanna*, as it elides entrenched class structures and makes the poor, even the impoverished orphan, morally suspect. In many ways, these texts function like the later ones Eric L. Tribunella argues use some form of trauma as a disciplinary force to turn children into the kinds of adults society desires (xxix). Fictional orphans tend to be figures of mourning, but Porter's orphans are hardly passive representatives of grief: Jimmy is particularly active as he deals with his grief by looking for a new family. When Jimmy explains to Pollyanna that he wants only a home that wants him, "jest a common one," she brings him to Aunt Polly (98). Polly's reaction to the "dirty little boy," like her reaction to the prospect of raising her orphaned niece, comes from social expectations about the class of the dependent child (100). In

Pollyanna's case, duty born of family ties and social class governs Polly's seeming benevolence; she can raise her niece because she knows where the child comes from. In Jimmy's case, perceptions of the poor lead her to declare him a "ragged little beggar from the street," akin to the "tramp cats and mangy dogs" her niece has brought home (101). Jimmy's response that he would not have come to Polly if Pollyanna had not convinced him that her aunt was "so good an' kind," that she would certainly adopt him, later rings in Polly's ears even as it reverberates with Porter's reader. Someone who was truly good and kind would understand, Jimmy and the novel imply, that the orphaned child matters more than his background. Porter offers a similar scene in *Pollyanna Grows Up*, when Pollyanna informs her aunt that she and Jimmy plan to marry. Polly refuses, saying that she does like Jimmy, "in his place," but he is a "rough little runaway urchin from an Orphans' Home! We know nothing whatever about his people, and his pedigree" (292).[2] When she rejects Jimmy in the first novel, Aunt Polly feels "a curious sense of desolation—as of something lost," but just as she has refused to mourn her losses, she rejects the idea of breaching social codes and effectively helping this child (105).

To properly mourn her father, however, Pollyanna needs to be both glad and benevolent, so she takes Jimmy's case to her church's Ladies' Aid. In a scene that calls benevolent organizations to account in the way that the scene with Polly and Jimmy questions class restrictions on private charitable activity, Pollyanna comes to realize that had she not been the child of a minister, her own "Ladies' Aiders" might have simply placed her in an orphanage. After she tells them about Jimmy's need for a "common kind" of home where he will work for his keep, "there was silence; then, coldly, one or two women began to question her. After a time they all had the story and began to talk among themselves, animatedly, not quite pleasantly" (110). When it becomes clear that no one will take the "mongrel" child into their home, the minister's wife suggests that they support him and send less money to India: "their society was famous for its offering to Hindu missions, and several said they should die of mortification if it should be less this year" (110). Commenting that "it sounded almost as if they did not care at all what the money *did*. . . . I should *think*, though, they'd rather see Jimmy Bean grow—than just a report," Pollyanna gestures to the appearances and social expectations motivating private and public benevolence (111).

The novel's critique of these motivations continues when she decides to write to her Ladies' Aiders out west to take Jimmy: "I'll write Mrs Jones. Mrs White has got the most money, but Mrs Jones gives the most—which is kind of funny, isn't it?" (122). That group rejects the idea of helping an American boy as well. MacLeod points out that while literature for children in the period worked to impart morality and motivate them to combat human suffering, the realities of American social problems were hard on this vision. These problems stayed and grew, as had human indifference to the needs of others (137). While changing social and political views of poverty predicated ever-increasing institutionalization of benevolence, Porter works to put charitable action back into communities, homes, and the hands of individuals. Just as she presents Aunt Polly as a poor example of individual benevolence, she focuses on the callousness of both church organizations.

However, Porter counters Polly's actions with those of Mr. Pendleton. Wealthier even than Polly, and depicted early in the novel as a miser, John Pendleton nonetheless ignores social codes and gives Jimmy Bean a home after Pollyanna brings them together. While Karen Sanchez-Eppler is correct in arguing that just as childhood is the period of gender and race identity formation, it is also when class identity is formed. Pollyanna (and Jimmy in his turn) will never identify herself with her aunt's class or act according to those restrictions when it would be morally wrong to do so. Instead, her worldview continues to be informed by her father, and her mourning for him governs her actions.

"I can be glad I've *had* my legs": Pollyanna's Work

Over the course of the novel, as Pollyanna's glad game gains momentum in her new community, it forms a core of hopeful optimism and benevolence that affects every character, even Aunt Polly. Through the work of mourning, through teaching people the game and thereby giving speech back to her father, Pollyanna brings grief into the semiotic order and enacts benevolence. She perfectly works with her contemporary fictional orphans, such as the ones Nelson studies, who work to heal the world. After Pollyanna's injury, when John Pendleton speaks with Polly about previously wanting to adopt the little girl, "she wondered if Pollyanna were old enough—and mercenary enough—to be tempted by this man's money and position," but when Pendleton explains that he "stood ready to give Pollyanna the love that had been twenty-five years in storage," Polly remembers "why *she* had taken this child in the first place" (213).

This scene is only one moment of a number when Porter delineates Pollyanna and her game as profoundly transformative. Because Pendleton sees loving and raising the child as the way to mourn and honor her mother, Polly is final able to see Pollyanna in the same way. Derrida writes that the work of mourning can be understood as the work of one who "engenders, produces, and brings . . . to the light of day and gives something to be seen, who enables or empowers, who gives the force to know and to be able to see . . . the one who takes the pains to help us see" (142). While he includes "to read and to think" as actions enabled by the one who does the work of mourning, Derrida's emphasis on seeing, on vision, suggests that effective mourning will make visible something that mattered to those who have died. While *Pollyanna* gestures, largely ineffectively if the sequel is any indication, toward a leveling of social and economic class structures, and while it offers a critical commentary on social and religious charitable organizations, it works most meaningfully at the personal level.

In a study of the politics of poverty in young adult novels, Miguel Ortiz argues that if they are writing about the poor, authors "must shed some light on the social and political forces that create poverty" (6). Porter simply does not satisfy that imperative. Instead, she alludes to those forces and offers a mild critique of social (the Orphans' Home) and religious (the Ladies' Aids) charitable organizations, and individual efforts (Aunt Polly). Porter's comments on the restrictions and codes of class are more pointed and negative (and even more so in *Pollyanna Grows Up*). However, when it comes to Pollyanna and her game, Porter offers one innovative approach. As America faced growing numbers of dependent children, as class structures became ever more economically and racially informed and entrenched, Pollyanna and her game greet loss and pain with hope and compassion. In a novel that went on to influence generations of readers, Porter posits the dependent child as an individual with a history, as someone who needs care and attention, even as she might have the capacity to enact social transformation.

The novel's denouement—a marriage, a cure—comes as a brief afterthought following Pollyanna's sickbed. The extended narrative describing the difference she has made to the citizens of Beldingsville makes clear what matters and what, in her mourning, Pollyanna has brought to light. Her pain and loss, her mourning and returning speech to her father, have allowed her to help her neighbors and friends to see more clearly. She has made a difference to Polly and Nancy, to Pendleton and Jimmy, to the Snows and the Paysons, to Reverend Ford and his congregation, to the recuperating Mrs. Tarbell and the widowed Mrs. Benton, to all the people who come to Polly to tell how Pollyanna changed things for them for the better. As they urge her to be glad about the differences she made in all those lives, she finds the strength to become glad that she has had her legs (252). Her many happy days, it turns out, were profitable after all, even in Aunt Polly's terms. In engaging fully with her grief for her father, in honoring him by living fully, Pollyanna reckons with the work of mourning and follows his example by offering care and attention to others even as her actions offer an implicit criticism on issues of class and benevolence.

Notes

1. Many languages, including German, Finnish, and Swedish, have a term or verb for working through mourning, but English lacks such a neat expression, implying it is not fully thought through in the Anglophone world.

2. As *Pollyanna Grows Up* makes clear, Jimmy is not originally from the "vicious poor" class or from the streets, but—like Pollyanna—has descended to this state as a result of family disagreements in which he has played no part. He is returned to the status he should have held, as is Pollyanna. Jamie is the only one who is actually raised from his start in life.

Works Cited

Ashby, LeRoy. *Endangered Children: Dependency, Neglect, and Abuse in American History.* New York: Twayne, 1997. Print.

Carlin, Deborah. "'What Methods Have Brought Blessing': Discourses of Reform in Philanthropic Literature." *The (Other) American Traditions: Nineteenth-Century Women Writers.* Ed. Joyce W. Warren. New Brunswick, NJ: Rutgers UP, 1993. 203–25. Print.

Derrida, Jacques. *The Work of Mourning.* Ed. Pascale-Anne Brault and Michael Naas. Chicago: U of Chicago P, 2001. Print.

Ginzberg, Lori D. *Women and the Work of Benevolence: Morality, Politics, and Class in the Nineteenth-Century United States.* New Haven, CT: Yale UP, 1990. Print.

Kelly, R. Gordon. *Mother Was a Lady: Self and Society in Selected American Children's Periodicals, 1865–1890.* Westport, CT: Greenwood, 1974. Print.

LaCapra, Dominick. *Writing History, Writing Trauma.* Baltimore: Johns Hopkins UP, 2001. Print.

Lareau, Annette. *Unequal Childhoods: Race, Class, and Family Life.* Berkeley: U of California P, 2003. Print.

MacLeod, Anne Scott. *A Moral Tale: Children's Fiction and American Culture, 1820–1860.* Hamden, CT: Archon Books, 1975. Print.

Nelson, Claudia. "Drying the Orphan's Tear: Changing Representations of the Dependent Child in America, 1870–1930." *Children's Literature* 29 (2001): 52–71. Print.

Ortiz, Miguel. "The Politics of Poverty in Young Adult Literature." *The Lion and the Unicorn* 2.2 (1978): 6–15. Print.

Porter, Eleanor H. *Pollyanna*. 1913. London: Puffin, 2004. Print.

———. *Pollyanna Grows Up*. New York: Grosset & Dunlap, 1914. Print.

Sanchez-Eppler, Karen. "Playing at Class." *ELH* 67 (2000): 819–42. Print.

Stansell, Christine. *City of Women: Sex and Class in New York, 1789–1860*. Urbana: U of Illinois P, 1987. Print.

Tribunella, Eric L. *Melancholia and Maturation: The Use of Trauma in American Children's Literature*. Knoxville: U of Tennessee P, 2010. Print.

2

"Aggressive femininity": The Ambiguous Heteronormativity of *Pollyanna*

LAURA M. ROBINSON

In *Secret Gardens: A Study of the Golden Age of Children's Literature* (1985), Humphrey Carpenter laments the appearance of Louisa May Alcott's *Little Women* on the literary scene, not because it is inferior in his eyes, but because it begot a generation of "happy happy" girls' stories. He suggests that the later writers created "a kind of aggressive femininity, which allowed their heroines to charm hearts and get their own way without playing traitor to their sex. This produced the 'Pollyanna' or 'glad girl' school of writing, featuring girls of unbearable cheerfulness" (98). In a footnote to this sentence, he cites Eleanor H. Porter's 1913 *Pollyanna* as one of these novels (*Rebecca of Sunnybrook Farm* and *Anne of Green Gables* are the other two). Carpenter's dismissive approach reflects a general critical trend in the recent past toward Porter's relentlessly optimistic book. Indeed, "Pollyanna" appears more frequently in psychological, psychiatric, and business analyses than in literary ones because of the title character's cognitive powers to recast her own personal narrative, and perhaps this active agency is what Carpenter regards as aggressive.[1]

Two facets of Carpenter's scathing dismissal stand out for me. One is the delightful contradiction "aggressive femininity," suggesting that these girls are putting on or performing femininity to a degree that just might reveal the constructedness of the very gender they are performing. The other is that, in Carpenter's eyes, the heroines' feminine performances enable them to stay true to their sex. Thus, the over-the-top performance or aggressive femininity allows the heroines of these post-Alcott novels to adhere to, rather than betray, gender roles. This raises the question, of course: what are the heroines up to that requires them to masquerade as they do? Exactly how might they be betraying their sex? Unfortunately,

Carpenter relegates them to a footnote and does not explore the intriguing implications of his apt phrase "aggressive femininity." I agree with Carpenter on one issue: Porter's novel is discomfiting, and her heroine is often bewildering. *Pollyanna* both purveys and disrupts patriarchal ideology through its simultaneous lauding and critiquing of father figures, the family, and traditional marriage. By suggesting that these institutions and authorities are constructed—and therefore inherently vulnerable—the novel invests its heroine with an ambiguous power even when she appears most disabled, thus allowing for a reassessment of traditional gender roles. Arguably, the voice of conformity is necessary to allow the voice of rebellion.

Demonstrating how Pollyanna has agency, Joe Sutliff Sanders in *Disciplining Girls* suggests that the orphan girls, such as Pollyanna, are the ones doing the disciplining in the classic orphan tale for children. Sanders argues that Pollyanna is an empowered character whose greatest triumph is the transformation of her rigid unloving spinster aunt into a happily wedded woman. While Sanders's argument is intriguing, his focus on the discourse of individuality that Pollyanna embodies overlooks another competing disciplinary regime, that of heteronormativity. While Pollyanna may challenge traditional power roles by placing transformative possibilities into the mouth and actions of a child, the transformation that Pollyanna causes is one that re-establishes the heterosexual norm. Her aunt, a powerful, single, rich woman, assumes a traditional role as a married woman by the end of the narrative.

Furthermore, as Sanders points out, Pollyanna's empowered narrative of "the glad game" is her patriarchal inheritance. Each time she repeats the story, she invokes her dead father. Sanders writes: "By stripping away the body of the father but retaining his power, these novels make conceivable a way of placing some agency in the hands of the imaginary child" (112). In more ways than one, then, Pollyanna becomes a mouthpiece for patriarchal authority: by literally and figuratively repeating her father, and by being the narrative thrust that restores her aunt to heteronormativity. Indeed, this might be why scholars such as Gillian Avery suggest that Pollyanna seems "cast from an older mold" (18) than similar novels from that era. Arguably, however, Porter's manipulations of the marriage conventions of domestic romance and her placing patriarchal (and ministerial) authority into the body of a girl child create enough ambiguity to disrupt the very constructs of gender and sexuality that the novel ostensibly and aggressively endorses. *Pollyanna* comes across queerly because of this ambiguity, which potentially destabilizes her readers.

Aggressive Femininity: On Productive Ambiguity

There is something troubling about this novel and its heroine, and that disruption is precisely where Porter's novel overturns the very gender and sexual ideology it seems to uphold. Scholars of *Pollyanna*, such as Carpenter, echo Aunt Polly's sense of being "vaguely disturbed" by the girl (Porter 106). The comparative dearth of scholarship about *Pollyanna* might speak to readers' discomfort with this novel.[2] Many volumes about classic girls' stories simply overlook *Pollyanna*, such as Shirley Foster and Judy Simon's *What Katy Read*. One agreement in scholarly examinations of Porter's allegedly optimistic novel is that it is deeply ambiguous. Alice Mills argues that *Pollyanna* is not as cheerful as it appears, for example. She highlights the novel's ambiguity: "Porter's Pollyanna is both victim and expert manipulator, under the guise of the innocently loving child" (103). Similarly, Claire M. Brown's philosophical investigation of this novel suggests that readers are not fully comfortable with the kind of saintliness that Pollyanna displays: "philosophers have come to see what fiction has long recognized: that however useful, praiseworthy, and even inspiring moral saints may be, many of us would think twice before inviting them to our dinner party or trying in earnest to become them ourselves. The moral saint accordingly occupies an uneasy position in our hearts" (236). Brown provides one explanation for some readers' discomfort with the relentlessly happy heroine. In an article on *Pollyanna*, Sanders picks up on the uneasiness to argue that this novel is part of a literary tradition that "limits and ambiguously empowers fictional girls" ("Spinning Sympathy" 41).

Through its over-performance, *Pollyanna* destabilizes the femininity it outwardly endorses. First in *Gender Trouble* and then in *Bodies That Matter*, Judith Butler argues that our identity is performative, not in the sense that we perform ourselves consciously, but in the sense that our self-hood is repeated in iterations of itself. She uses the example of drag to point out that the drag queen is not imitating heteronormative gender, but rather that drag exposes that all gender is a construction; all gender is performed. For Butler, understanding gender through performativity is liberatory because, in the endless repetitions of identity, there is necessarily and inevitably change and transformation. One cannot repeat oneself constantly without new iterations creeping in. That Carpenter, Avery, Claudia Nelson, Janis Dawson, and Sanders ("Spinning") each identify Pollyanna as one iteration in a tradition of orphan girls' stories demonstrates one type of repetition that can happen. That Pollyanna is a strange iteration, an aggressive, albeit feminine one, indicates that the repetitions are always and necessarily open to change. In *Undoing Gender*, Butler writes, "it is important not only to understand how the terms of gender are instituted, naturalized, and established as presuppositional but to trace the moments where the binary system of gender is disputed and challenged, where the coherence of the categories are put into question, and where the very social life of gender turns out to be malleable and transformable" (21).

Every facet of Porter's novel resonates with ambiguity. Binary systems of all kinds are disrupted, and Pollyanna herself, while engaged in endless repetitions of her story and her identity, never replicates herself exactly. This slippage creates discomfort about identity, gender, and sexuality, opening space for a queer reading of Pollyanna that suggests that Porter's novel undermines the very heterosexual normativity that it endorses.

I am not attempting to argue that Porter consciously created a "queer" text, as that would be an anachronism. In their introduction to *Over the Rainbow: Queer Children's and Young Adult Fiction*, Michelle Ann Abate and Kenneth Kidd trace the etymology of the word *queer*, showing that it became connected to sexuality specifically from around 1914 onward. Rather, I regard Pollyanna as the oft-described "extraordinary child" she is (60, 70, 72), one who disrupts complacency, normativity, and the status quo even as she labors to re-establish a naturalized heterosexuality with its concomitant gender role inequality. Abate and Kidd write: "'Queer' defies definition, indeed is the antidote to definition in any easy or clear sense. The term at once fortifies and dismantles the notion of a stable or knowable self, in relation to gender and sexuality especially but not exclusively" (4). That Pollyanna must work so adamantly and that her body is required as a sacrifice to reassert the primacy of patriarchal rule and the heterosexual family that supports it has the very effect of allowing readers to see how constructed and deeply fragile, how unnatural, those institutions are.

The Ambiguity of the Patriarchal Glad Game

As critics such as Mills have pointed out, Pollyanna's glad game is a vehicle of patriarchal power. From the first moment that Pollyanna explains the game, the reader clearly sees how the patriarch uses the "game" to shut down the girl's legitimate disappointment (Mills 91). Instead of a doll in the mission barrel, as Pollyanna had requested and her father had "written them so," Pollyanna received crutches (43). The game is, famously, "to just find something about everything to be glad about" (43). The young girl has difficulty with this task, and "Father had to tell it to me" (43). She can be glad that she does not need the crutches, her father points out. The maid Nancy's response might reflect the ordinary reader's: "'Well, of all the queer doin's!' breathed Nancy, regarding Pollyanna with almost fearful eyes" (44). The queerness and the fearfulness are telling here; Porter is not suggesting that the glad game is recuperative or to be celebrated. It is a strange invention of the patriarchal authority; Pollyanna's insistent repetition of the game with each new person she meets reasserts, queerly and fearfully, the power of the father.

However, the invention of the glad game, and its obsessive repetition, underscores Porter's sleight of hand in diminishing patriarchal power altogether. First, the father who is continually resurrected through the story of the game is significantly absent because he is dead; he is not fulfilling his fatherly obligations to his family. Second, while the father was alive, he was not ideal. Pollyanna's mother's family rejected him as a potential suitor. Of course, they do so for unjust economic reasons I will discuss shortly. When Pollyanna's mother elopes with him regardless, the Harrington family refuses to acknowledge the marriage, their daughter, and her offspring. Thus, the patriarchal figure—the poor minister— is responsible for dismantling rather than upholding a family structure. Third, the impoverished father is consistently unable to provide. He writes away to request a doll and receives crutches for his daughter instead. As Mills points out, the father cannot confront his own failings, which is why he teaches his daughter the glad game. While the entire narrative appears to be an endorsement of Rev. John Whittier because his words, through the mouth of his daughter, transform the community of Beldingsville, Pollyanna's tale actually undermines the patriarch.

Moreover, the novel similarly disrupts the authority of many other patriarchal figures. For example, Pollyanna inadvertently challenges the Rev. Paul Ford's prepared sermon when she comes across him in the woods. As a result of his conversation with the girl, he changes his sermon and sees positive results from his parishioners. Wealthy and cantankerous John Pendleton similarly becomes better acquainted with Pollyanna when she assists him with his broken leg; the wounded patriarchal figure needs the child rather than the other way around. Demonstrating ineffectual power, the family doctor, Dr. Warren, cannot cure Pollyanna after her debilitating car accident. When masculine, broad-shouldered Dr. Mead, the "very famous doctor from New York," arrives, he also proves unable to help (250). Pollyanna insists that the only doctor who can help her is Dr. Chilton, and her assertion proves to be accurate.

The novel's challenge to patriarchal authority also works to question the traditional family. While the trajectory of this novel seems to move in the direction of creating a traditional family structure by beginning with an adoption and ending with a marriage, like many girls' stories, such as *Anne of Green Gables* and others, it does so by "queering" the family. For example, the orphan Anne is adopted by an elderly brother and sister, not a heterosexual couple. While Aunt Polly and Dr. Chilton are reunited by the end of Porter's novel, thus upholding marriage as the important ideological endpoint, the novel entrenches disturbances to traditional family. First, because her parents have died, Pollyanna is an orphan in need of a home. Her aunt takes her in only through a sense of duty: "I am a good woman, I hope; and I know my duty" (3). The reader early learns that "the [Harrington and Whittier] families were not on the best of terms," which proves to be a bit of an understatement as the Harringtons outright rejected the Whittiers (5). After her adoption by her aunt, Pollyanna becomes obsessed with rescuing similarly disenfranchised "orphans": a bedraggled kitten, a stray dog, and a ragamuffin boy.

While Aunt Polly puts her foot down at adopting the orphaned boy, the figure of Jimmy Bean underscores the novel's critique of the family. A runaway resident of the oversubscribed Orphans' Home, Jimmy explains: "I'd like a home—jest a common one, ye know, with a mother in it, instead of a Matron. If ye has a home, ye has folks; an' I hain't had folks since—dad died" (113). Jimmy, too, is a victim of an absent patriarch. Even persistent Pollyanna has difficulty finding Jimmy a home. Her petition to the Ladies' Aid for someone to adopt him is fruitless, for they "decided that they would rather send all their money to bring up the little India boys than to save out enough to bring up one little boy in their own town" (125). Most importantly, in articulating his desires, Jimmy identifies a family organization that does not have much presence in the novel. He wants a "common" family with a mother, father, and children. This family is, in fact, rare in Porter's Beldingsville. The town is populated by heartbroken bachelors (Mr. Pendleton and Dr. Chilton), widows (Widow Benton, Mrs. Snow, Nancy's mother), and other individuals in nontraditional families. The traditional married families that Porter describes are not particularly happy or flourishing. Pollyanna's family was not only rejected by the extended family, but, one by one, they all died off, leaving only Pollyanna. The ill-reputed Mrs. Payson's family is poor and beset with troubles, not the least of which is the threat of divorce. So, Porter's novel at once pines for and undermines the possibilities of an idealized family structure. In doing so, it exposes the extent to which the family rests on capricious and ineffectual patriarchal authority.

The Economics of Romance

While the novel offers a challenge to patriarchal authority and the traditional family structure that upholds that authority, the dominant narrative counters this challenge by asserting the supremacy of heterosexual
romance. Porter's domestic romance requires Aunt Polly to relinquish her
spinster status and embrace Dr. Chilton and marriage at the end. Arguably, this generic imperative could be regarded as trumping the challenge
to patriarchy that has preceded it. The happy end of the story is, of course,
a heterosexual pairing; the so-called natural order is restored, largely due
to Pollyanna's game-playing.

Aunt Polly's transformation is the climax of the novel, but its ideological message is multiple and contradictory. Miss Polly Harrington blossoms from "a stern, severe-faced woman who frowned if a knife clattered
to the floor, or if a door banged—but who never thought to smile even
when knives and doors were still" (3) to a blushing bride-to-be after
accepting Dr. Chilton: "At twilight a wonderfully *tremulous*, wonderfully
different Aunt Polly *crept* to Pollyanna's bedside" (307, emphasis added).
The crux of Miss Polly's sudden transformation is not simply the conservative message of embracing the heterosexual imperative. Polly is first
associated with knives and doors, symbols of power and impenetrability,
and then alters to become a shaking, creeping woman. The Polly Harrington plotline—and Miss Polly arguably is really the main character of
the novel—is a cautionary tale against women's economic independence.
The problem with Polly is her status. She is "the mistress of the old Harrington homestead, and one of the wealthiest residents of the town" (2).
Her independence, particularly her economic independence, establishes
her as the unloving but dutiful aunt, as a woman in need of transformation. Other spinsters populate the novel unproblematically. Beloved and
faithful servant, single Nancy must work out in order to support her family. She is not economically independent. Nor is Milly Snow, the belea-
guered and obviously economically dependent daughter of Mrs. Snow;
ironically and without explanation, Miss Polly regards this young woman
as "queer" (275).

Those other spinsters are not in need of change. The problem with
Polly is that she is a woman living independently from a man *by choice*
and because she has the means to do so. Porter makes clear that Miss Polly
holds the cards in the failed romance between herself and Dr. Chilton.
The doctor explains to Mr. Pendleton why he cannot visit Pollyanna: "the
mistress of that house told me that the *next* time she *asked* me to enter

it, I might take it that she was begging my pardon, and that all would be as before—which meant that she would marry me" (296). Pollyanna cannot get the treatment she needs because Miss Polly refuses to brook the notion of marriage to the doctor.

Porter writes her novel in an era and about a time period in which women's independence from marriage was regarded with great suspicion. Writing about women's friendship and love both across history (*Surpassing*) and in America (*Odd Girls*), historian Lillian Faderman underscores patriarchal society's fear of the independent woman. In the late nineteenth and early twentieth centuries, American and British Commonwealth women were increasingly agitating for rights: suffrage, education, access to employment, rights within marriage. Faderman regards women's push for independence as eliciting a backlash from a society that expected docility and dependence from them. The work of the sexologists—nineteenth-century doctors who specialized in sexuality—in particular worked to frighten women back into their traditional gender roles. Faderman cites a passage from a novel written by American psychiatrist William Lee Howard in 1901: "The female possessed of the masculine ideas of independence, the viragint who would sit in the public highways and lift up her pseudo-virile voice, proclaiming her sole right to decide questions of war or religion . . . and that disgusting anti-social being, the female sexual pervert, are simply different degrees of the same class—degenerates" (qtd. in Faderman, *Odd Girls* 47). The sexologists established a connection between lesbianism, pathology, and women desiring independence. Any woman seeking independence might thus stay silent to avoid being regarded as lesbian or diseased.

Furthermore, at this time period, the role of marriage was shifting. In the nineteenth century, marriage was regarded as an economic necessity and duty for women, rather than a union of love. Historian Nancy Cott explains that "under the common law, a woman was absorbed into her husband's legal and economic persona upon marrying, and her husband gained the civic presence she lost" (Cott, Introduction). Cott shows that while many American states created laws that supplanted the common law, most Americans in the late nineteenth and early twentieth centuries still believed in this hierarchy. Joyce W. Warren similarly explains, "for most of the nineteenth century, if a woman did have money of her own (through inheritance or through her own labor), legally and by tradition her money belonged to her husband" (147). While Porter was born in New Hampshire and lived in Massachusetts, her novel is set in Vermont, one of the last American states to pass a married women's property act (1881) ensuring that women retained their property upon marriage; women still did not have the legal right to control any money they made while married. Warren suggests that even after the law changed, "tradition and social pressure made women slow to take advantage of their rights" (147). In depicting a wealthy woman who is unmarried by choice, Porter's novel engages with myriad tensions around women's economic independence and role in marriage. It is telling, therefore, that Porter's sequel, *Pollyanna Grows Up*, shows Polly losing her wealth after the death of her husband, Dr. Chilton. The sequel emphasizes women's economic vulnerability.

Pollyanna highlights economics on every page, echoed by Aunt Polly's insistence that Pollyanna's mere existence be "pro-fi-ta-ble," something that the girl has difficulty understanding (100). Scholars have picked up on this theme of profitability and economics; Sanders discusses the representation of consumer culture in this novel, for instance, and Nelson shows how Pollyanna is an example of American society's transformation from focusing on the use-value of the orphan to the value of child as a commodity for itself (66–67). In many ways, Porter's emphasis is even more basic. From the first pages of the novel, economic inequities form the centerpiece of the story. Pollyanna's family is desperately poor; Aunt Polly is excessively rich. Potentially, the Whittiers' hardship contributed to the multiple deaths in that family. Pollyanna consistently paints a picture of her dire poverty. Her family received framed pictures in the mission barrel, she twice relates; her father sold the one unbroken one for money to purchase Pollyanna shoes (25, 102). Similarly, Pollyanna repeats the Ladies' Aid's desire for a red carpet several times with the effect of emphasizing the ladies' hypocrisy in valuing appearances over providing an orphan with necessities (19, 21, 56). In this world of inequality, Miss Polly is a woman with money. The novel seems to suggest that, for the natural order to be restored, she must become "tremulous" and "creeping" in acquiescence to male authority. Her stern competence has quickly become a shaky submissive weakness. The narrative encourages the reader to experience this ending as fit and ideal.

What is fascinating here is that Porter links economics and the transformation of Aunt Polly to freedom of movement. As other scholars have noted, the crutches in the mission barrel that Pollyanna does not need become a key trope in a novel that is all about mobility. Mr. Pendleton needs crutches after he breaks his leg; Mrs. Snow is bedridden; Pollyanna's father sells a picture he received in the mission barrel to buy shoes for his daughter, allowing her mobility. Pollyanna loses her ability to walk because of an accident with a car, a signifier of even greater mobility. The novel's anxious focus on mobility works as a metaphor for social mobility. Through his adoption by John Pendleton, Jimmy Bean moves from poverty to wealth, as does Pollyanna through her adoption. The very fact that the plot requires Pollyanna to lose her mobility in order to facilitate the reunion of her aunt and Dr. Chilton suggests that the heterosexual romance, rather than liberating, is immobilizing. Aunt Polly's metamorphosis, her alteration from independent spinster to tremulous fiancée, mirrors Pollyanna's own change from active girl to bedridden invalid: both characters are forced to curtail their previous freedom of independence and movement. Thus, the novel arguably exposes the cost of marriage for the independent woman by equating it with losing the power of mobility.

Porter's novel shakes up of the depiction of heterosexual marriage even further. Instead of Miss Polly becoming the object of exchange in the marriage as women have traditionally been, Dr. Chilton is. Aunt Polly says to Pollyanna: "I'm going to give Dr. Chilton to you for your—uncle" (307). Dr. Chilton becomes the goods, overturning his earlier characterization of Pollyanna: "I wish I could prescribe her—and buy her—as I would a box of pills" (149). By placing Dr. Chilton as the object of exchange, the novel exposes not only the economic operations of traditional marriage but also how it "delineat[es] relationships of power and meaning" (Sedgwick 27). In *Between Men*, Eve Kosofsky Sedgwick draws on the work of anthropologist Claude Lévi-Strauss and Gayle Rubin's reassessment of his theories to explain the exchange of women to forge homosocial bonds between men: "Rubin has argued that patriarchal heterosexuality can best be discussed in terms of one or another form of the traffic in women: it is the use of women as exchangeable, perhaps symbolic, property for the primary purpose of cementing the bonds of men with men" (Sedgwick 25–26). *Pollyanna*'s reversal of the traditional exchange of women emphasizes the bond between aunt and niece, effectively rewriting patriarchal power relations.

Offering even more of a challenge to the ostensible endorsement of heterosexuality is the fact that Aunt Polly and the doctor are reunited by the previously disenfranchised orphan, Jimmy Bean, and by Pollyanna's condition. The orphans, the life-sized symbols of family gone awry, are the vehicles for the domestic union, the creation of a new family. While outside in the garden, Jimmy overhears Dr. Chilton telling Jimmy's adoptive guardian, Mr. Pendleton, that he believes he can help Pollyanna. A symbol of the outsider begrudgingly taken in, Jimmy proves his worth by daring to betray propriety and pleading with Aunt Polly to let Dr. Chilton examine her niece. Similarly, orphaned Pollyanna's immobility is the key to the formation of a romantic union. The figure of Pollyanna as conduit of traditional marriage is even more ironic considering that she represents the choice of a companionate marriage over duty. Pollyanna's mother ran away to marry for love rather than money. She made the ultimate sacrifices for marriage: her family of origin, her wealth, her social standing and, arguably, her life. It is hard not to see Porter's "cheerful" novel as an indictment of marriage, even if Pollyanna, the product of a companionate marriage, is presented as a positive figure.

Feminine Aggression: Destabilizing Gender

Pollyanna's challenge to traditional marriage, the family, and patriarchal authority destabilizes the gender roles that work in tandem with these other institutions, and leads back to Carpenter's delightful phrase about Pollyanna's "aggressive femininity." Cott states, "The whole system of attribution and meaning that we call *gender* relies on and to a great extent derives from the structuring provided by marriage. Turning men and women into husbands and wives, marriage has designated the ways both sexes act in the world and the reciprocal relation between them" (Introduction). While Pollyanna's story could be regarded as merely a "happy happy" girls' story, and Pollyanna herself as an agent of patriarchal authority, Porter's novel upends gender expectations through its challenge to heteronormativity.

In addition to spreading gladness and good cheer in her community, Pollyanna's internalization of subservient gender roles emerges in her apparent penchant for masochism. As Aunt Polly metes out punishment to the girl, she is troubled: "For the third time since Pollyanna's arrival, Miss Polly was punishing Pollyanna—and for the third time she was being confronted by the amazing fact that her punishment was being taken as a special reward of merit" (71). This pleasure in one's submission is the girl's strategy in the face of the poverty, grief, and loneliness she endures. That her "punishment" brings enjoyment exposes the hardship she previously encountered. The result is that Aunt Polly feels "curiously helpless" (71). Pollyanna aggressively performs traditional femininity to a degree that is discomfiting and which reveals the expectations of submission.

However, Porter's ending disrupts the notion of submissive girlhood by displacing the heterosexual marriage and eradicating the third-person narrator. In the final moments of the novel, Miss Polly and Dr. Chilton disappear from the action; the reader hears that they tied the knot at Pollyanna's bedside, but that event occurs offstage. The words of the wounded girl supplant the romance plotline in Pollyanna's letter. That the final words are Pollyanna's firmly places the girl in a position of independence, even as she is immobilized. She has progressed from being a child without a voice, indeed without a story of her own as she consistently repeats her father's words and ideas, to having her own voice. Pollyanna's words herald her increasing mobility and reiterate her gladness, but significantly without mention of the patriarchal glad game: "Oh, I'm so glad," she exclaims in her letter to her aunt and uncle: "I'm glad for everything" (310). Being on her own in the hospital for ten months, she is also surprisingly independent of a family structure, given that orphan tales are usually about the waif finding a home; instead, this distance from family necessarily facilitates her healing.

Porter provides the requisite happily-ever-after ending by having the stern spinster marry the warm-hearted doctor, but her novel points an accusing finger at the reader. Because the final chapter is Pollyanna's letter, the reader occupies the same position as Miss Polly and Dr. Chilton, reading the missive. The reader becomes the representative of extreme wealth (Aunt Polly) and patriarchal authority (Dr. Chilton), as well as the traditional heterosexual couple at a far remove from the heartbroken child who finds it difficult to be mobile, socially and otherwise, in this type of world. By troubling the institutions of patriarchy, the family, marriage, and gender, Porter's novel allows for a happy ending, but one that is rife with misgivings, if the reader looks closely enough. Not many happy families live in Beldingsville; Aunt Polly's transformation appears sudden and problematic, a direct result of Pollyanna's immobility. The glad game of this novel is the reader's in overlaying on top of a tragic tale a joyous ending. Porter's novel thus discomfits the reader thirsty for a happy-ever-after romantic climax, even when it requires the disfigurement of a beloved heroine.

The novel's consistent ambiguity exposes the inefficacy and vulnerability of some of society's most unquestioned institutions—family, father, marriage, gender roles—at the same moment that it appears to endorse them. Pollyanna is indeed an "extraordinary child" who potentially leaves all her readers, like Aunt Polly, "vaguely disturbed" and "curiously helpless." It is precisely in that discomfiture, in the blending of aggression and femininity, that the girl's power rests. Those few shaky steps that Pollyanna takes from the bed to the window arguably symbolize the shaky steps that women in early-twentieth-century America were taking toward greater rights and independence. Significantly, the hospital appears to be populated by immobilized women learning to walk: "A lady in the next ward who walked last week first, peeked into the door, and another who hopes she can walk next month, was invited in to the party" (310). Pollyanna expresses her determination to become increasingly independent: "I'm going to take eight steps tomorrow" (310). Only removed from the institutions of heterosexuality, the family, and patriarchy, Porter's novel suggests, can Pollyanna truly learn to walk by herself. Pollyanna may be taking baby steps, but the reader knows with certainty that, because of her determination, Pollyanna will become independent. By giving Pollyanna a voice in the final page, and eradicating all the other players, the novel establishes the possibility for the girl-child to speak for herself and puts the power directly in the hands of the most traditionally disenfranchised.

Notes

1. See Margaret Matlin and David Stang, *The Pollyanna Principle: Selectivity in Language, Memory, and Thought* (1978), for a classic psychology text. See also Daniel A. Helminiak, *Sex and the Sacred: Gay Identity and Spiritual Growth* (2006), for a sub-chapter entitled, "The Pollyanna Effect: Focus on the Human Family and the Cosmos." "A lover is a Pollyanna," Helminiak states (70). As intriguing as Helminiak's four-page subchapter sounds, he does not make reference to Porter's text (or the film, for that matter). Instead, he refers to a 1960s song, "Everybody Loves a Lover," made famous by first Doris Day and then the Shirelles. The lyrics read:

Everybody loves a lover
I'm a lover, everybody loves me
Anyhow, that's how I feel
Wow, I feel just like a Pollyanna (www.lyricsdepot.com)

2. Compare with the relative wealth of scholarship on novels such as *Little Women* or *Anne of Green Gables*.

Works Cited

Abate, Michelle Ann, and Kenneth Kidd. Introduction. *Over the Rainbow: Queer Children and Young Adult Literature*. Ann Arbor: U of Michigan P, 2011: 1–14. Print.

Adler, Richard. "Everybody Loves a Lover." *Lyrics Depot*. Web. 13 August 2013.

Avery, Gillian. "'Remarkable and Winning': A Hundred Years of American Heroines." *The Lion and the Unicorn* 13.1 (June 1989): 7–20. Print.

Brown, Claire M. "*Pollyanna*, Moral Sainthood, and Childhood Ideals." *Philosophy in Children's Literature*. Ed. Peter R. Costello. Lanham MD: Lexington Books, 2012: 235–50. Print.

Butler, Judith. *Bodies That Matter: On the Discursive Limits of "Sex."* New York: Routledge, 1993. Print.

———. *Gender Trouble: Feminism and the Subversion of Identity*. New York: Routledge, 1990. Print.

———. *Undoing Gender*. New York: Routledge, 2004. Print.

Carpenter, Humphrey. *Secret Gardens: A Study of the Golden Age of Children's Literature*. Boston: Houghton Mifflin, 1985. Print.

Cott, Nancy F. *Public Vows: A History of Marriage and the Nation*. Cambridge MA: Harvard UP, 2000. E-book.

Dawson, Janis. "Literary Relations: Anne Shirley and Her American Cousins." *Children's Literature in Education* 33.1 (March 2002): 29–51. Print.

Faderman, Lillian. *Odd Girls and Twilight Lovers: A History of Lesbian Life in 20th-Century America*. New York: Penguin, 1992. Print.

———. *Surpassing the Love of Men: Romantic Friendship and Love between Women from the Renaissance to the Present*. New York: William Morrow, 1981. Print.

Foster, Shirley, and Judy Simons. *What Katy Read: Feminist Re-Readings of "Classic" Stories for Girls*. Iowa City: U of Iowa P, 1995. Print.

Helminiak, Daniel A. *Sex and the Sacred: Gay Identity and Spiritual Growth*. New York: Harrington Park Press, 2006. Print.

Matlin, Margaret, and David Stang. *The Pollyanna Principle: Selectivity in Language, Memory, and Thought*. Cambridge MA: Schenkman, 1978. Print.

Mills, Alice. "*Pollyanna* and the Not So Glad Game." *Children's Literature* 27 (1999): 87–104. Print.

Nelson, Claudia. "Drying the Orphan's Tear: Changing Representations of the Dependent Child in America, 1870–1930." *Children's Literature* 29 (2001): 52–70. Print.

Porter, Eleanor H. 1913. *Pollyanna: The Glad Book*. New York: Grosset & Dunlap, 1946. Print.

Sanders, Joe Sutliff. *Disciplining Girls: Understanding the Origins of the Classic Orphan Girl Story*. Baltimore MD: Johns Hopkins UP, 2011. Print.

———. "Spinning Sympathy: Orphan Girl Novels and the Sentimental Tradition." *Children's Literature Association Quarterly* 33.1 (Spring 2008): 41–61. Print.

Sedgwick, Eve Kosofsky. *Between Men: English Literature and Male Homosocial Desire*. NY: Columbia UP, 1985. Print.

Warren, Joyce W. "Fracturing Gender: Women's Economic Independence." *Nineteenth-Century American Women Writers: A Critical Reader*. Ed. Karen L. Kilcup. Cambridge, MA and Oxford, UK: Blackwell, 1998. Print.

3

"Matter out of place": Dirt, Disorder, and Ecophobia

ANTHONY PAVLIK

At first glance, *Pollyanna* might not seem like fertile ground for an eco-critical reading. The novel's focus is very domestic, and "writing nature" as such is conspicuously absent. The literary motif of nature, however, is often seen in novels of the latter part of the nineteenth century and into the early twentieth century. Novels such as Frances Hodgson Burnett's *The Secret Garden* (1911) foster an idealized representation of the countryside as being a "natural" space for the child, utilizing an idyll of the cultivated garden as a safe and controlled space, a space of healing for children and adults alike, a space that is contrasted with images of urban living as a source of threat to human health. In *Pollyanna* (1913), however, there is no obvious ascription of a healing power to the force of "nature," and the protagonist, Pollyanna, is not cultivating, or being cultivated by, the novel's garden; in fact, Aunt Polly's garden is scarcely mentioned. Missing from *Pollyanna*, too, are the elements of nature writing of the kind found in other contemporary novels, such as Gene Stratton-Porter's *Freckles* (1904) and *A Girl of the Limberlost* (1909), with their often long, descriptive passages of the natural world. As this chapter will show, the seemingly muted presence of the natural world in *Pollyanna* reveals contemporary perceptions of dirt as disorder and the natural world as intrusions into the domestic but ultimately reveals the value of different kinds of embodied engagement with the world in all its forms.

Urbanization and Cleanliness

The publication of *Pollyanna* came at a time of ongoing changes in the American landscape, changes that reveal themselves in Porter's creation. During the latter part of the nineteenth century, the United States transformed from being a largely rural and agrarian society into a modern, industrialized nation and, with the development of an urban middle class, social attitudes began changing in many areas of life.[1] One such change was an alteration in the way Americans related to nature and the environment. By the time of the writing of *Pollyanna*, a rather dichotomous approach to nature had emerged. As Adam Rome puts it, "[w]hile many Progressive-Era Americans loved certain aspects of nature . . . they hated others" ("Nature" 448), and this ambivalence also plays out in *Pollyanna*.

Contemporary writers such as the amateur naturalist and conservationist Mabel Osgood Wright were concerned with how the expansion of industrial areas was affecting the natural habitats of animals (and, in Wright's case, birds in particular).[2] Wright's books often seek to extol the natural in the urban, and to create an emotional connection between readers, young and old, with the natural world.[3] As she writes,

> [i]n every town or country village there is some one who takes more than passing interest in the life outdoors, who has a keener eye and more responsive ear than his neighbor, coupled with a heart that has a bit of Eden still lodged in it, so that it keeps tender and yearning toward the simple, direct affections of life, as expressed in childhood and the lives of the timid wild brotherhood, whether foot or wing. (xi)[4]

Urbanization had brought with it a separation from nature, but also a concomitant desire to preserve the wild places. In the period around the turn of the century, "middle class women provided critical support in almost every campaign to preserve wild places and wild creatures" (Rome, "Political" 442); yet, at the same time, nature in many forms (particularly the natural products of bodily functions) and the dirt and detritus of urban life became a matter of scientific and social concern.

The reforms of the Progressive Era (roughly between 1890 and 1920) sought to improve urban working conditions, slum housing conditions for the poor (especially immigrants), food hygiene, sanitation systems (which were hidden from view in respectable houses) and the pollution that was emerging from industrial centers.[5] This included strict attention to household cleanliness, not simply to keep the dirt and pollution out, but also because, as Suellen Hoy notes, "without a certain degree of cleanliness and order, those feelings and values that the emerging middle class associated with a good home and family and with genteel living and respectability could not have developed" (16). Whereas, in the mid-nineteenth century, for "hardworking New England or mid-western farm families, dirt was seen as something positive, even healthy" because "it gave life and livelihood in the form of crops" (Hoy 3), the turn of the twentieth century saw ideas about dirt as unwelcome and of "the critical role of women as agents of cleanliness" (Hoy xiv). Although Aunt Polly may not do the actual work of cleaning herself, her attention to domestic cleanliness and her obsession with dirt mark her as a woman of her time.

While nature was being held up as a place of escape from a dirty and polluted urban existence, this only seems to have held good as long as nature in its various forms was not close by or, even worse, encroaching in its less appealing form on the domestic. In an 1885 text, entitled *Women, Plumbers, and Doctors; or, Household Sanitation*, author Harriette Merrick Plunkett felt able to declare that "[t]he nineteenth century, with all its marvellous subjugation of the subtile and titanic forces of Nature, shows nothing more wonderful than the vast body of sanitary science now in existence" (241). Plunkett's choice of words suggests a battle royal between the forces of good (in the form of the dutiful housewife maintaining a clean and pure home) and those of "bad" nature that must be brought under strict control.

Dirt and Disorder

Concern about cleanliness and the safeguarding of one's home against pollutants from outside are not new ideas, but in *Pollyanna* this focus is an essential element in how Aunt Polly maintains her home. Indeed, it is with a domestic cleaning scene that the novel opens, with the hired help, Nancy, washing dishes in the kitchen of a house that seems to be a paradigm of order and cleanliness. When Aunt Polly issues instructions to Nancy about preparing Pollyanna's room, the primary focus is on cleanliness rather than comfort: "Sweep the room and clean it, of course, after you clear out the trunks and boxes" (3), says Aunt Polly, and with attention to detail and perfection she adds, "See that you clean the corners, Nancy" (4). The task done, after much sweeping and scrubbing, the room is ready and, as Nancy observes, "There ain't no dirt here—and there's mighty little else" (10). Although Nancy refers primarily to the lack of creature comforts in the room, her remark suggests that something more than just dirt and dust have been removed from the room.[6]

Home, for Aunt Polly, represents distance from the chaos of nature, and is symbolic of order and cleanliness compared to the dirtiness of the outside, within which the social practices of cleaning and being clean mark a culturally constructed boundary between the natural and cultural, nature and the domestic. Dust is simply one of the undesired elements of the natural. The clean and tidy home is a powerful point of separation of the inside from the outside, a barrier against the encroaching wildness that is the natural world in all its forms, including dirt.

Aunt Polly's desire for a well-cleaned and orderly house, and her need to maintain the purity and order of the inside of her house against the outside (particularly as signified by the presence of dirt and dust) can also be considered in terms of Mary Douglas's discussions of the notions of dirt and pollution and how these relate to social structures and norms (and even moral values, since cleanliness, as the saying goes, is next to godliness).[7] For Douglas, "[o]ur idea of dirt is compounded of two things, care for hygiene and respect for conventions" (7).[8] Douglas shows that, in societies around the world, dirt equates danger and, more specifically related to Aunt Polly's home, Douglas notes that "dirt is essentially disorder" (2). Douglas continues, "[u]ncleanness or dirt is that which must not be included if a pattern is to be maintained" (41) because, says Douglas, dirt "offends against order" (2) and organization of one's environment (in this case, the home) requires "rejecting inappropriate elements" (36).[9] Thus, dust and dirt both confirm and deny the system, for the presence of dust represents a failure of control over the environment and allows for a focus on what it is around us that pollutes. In the social, urban environment, dirt is found as dust, garbage, bodily excretions, and other pollutants; and, in nature, dirt can be found as soil and, by taking the system to extremes, untamed nature and its non-human inhabitants as well. Thus, cleanliness and good housekeeping become intrinsic to maintaining the social space of the home by instituting a cultural boundary whereby the clean and ordered house marks the difference between culture and the "other," the natural world.

Indeed, the narrative gives a contrast to this controlled environment in its descriptions of John Pendleton's house. With its "big neglected lawn" (133) outside, suggesting the risk of nature taking back control, the inside is untidy and disorganized, with "a littered floor, an untidy desk, innumerable closed doors (any one of which might conceal a skeleton), and everywhere dust, dust, dust" (134). Later, Pendleton's house is seen after having been cleaned and, although the windows are wide open (presumably there are screens here too), "there was no litter on the floor, no untidiness on the desk, and not so much as a grain of dust in sight" (150); some sense of order has been restored through cleanliness and tidiness.

Classifying dirt in this way, as disorder, as outside, marks the limit of domestic order and constitutes a boundary between the good/inside and the bad/outside. Such a notion conforms to what David Sibley calls the "dominant message of environmental psychology," which is that "the private domain of the home is a benign, controllable, personal space standing in contrast to the exterior, public domain which is uncontrollable, uncertain and riven with conflict" (129). The inside becomes safe, familiar and independent not only as a private space separate from the public space, but also as a means of excluding the elements of the natural world and the dirt and pollution associated with it.

This way of conceiving of dirt provides a way to order human lives and, for Aunt Polly (and for urban women at the time the novel was published), the fear is that that the undifferentiated mass that is the outside will force its way into the controlled order of the household. In essence, Aunt Polly is fighting an outside enemy that has no place in the home (and her desire for strict, clear boundaries against the threat from outside is, to a large degree, what gives her life stability). In sum, as Douglas says, dirt is "matter out of place" (36), and what is dirty or impure is that which is out of place or disordered. Over and above material dirt, however, the novel also has other forms of dirt or matter out of place that Aunt Polly reacts against: children and non-human creatures, forms of dirt and disorder to which my discussion turns next.

Matter out of Place

Of course, in a literal sense, Pollyanna herself can also be seen as a kind of "matter out of place"; she is an orphan, displaced, and no longer in her own home. For Aunt Polly, Pollyanna's unwelcome arrival is not only a disruption to the domestic routine, it is also an intrusion from the outside which, although unpreventable, is something Aunt Polly clearly intends to control and keep out of the way, removed from anywhere she might bring contamination. In this desire Aunt Polly's intent is clear, for "[h]er idea at first had been to get her niece as far away as possible from herself, and at the same time place her where her childish heedlessness would not destroy valuable furnishings" (30). Pollyanna is to be placed as far away from domestic order as possible. Her room is "the little room at the head of the stairs in the attic" (3), and Nancy refers to it as a "snippy little room 'way at the top of the house" (44). However, it is not only the furnishings that are in danger from Pollyanna's entry into the home. It seems that there is also an identification of the child figure with wild abandon and chaos in Aunt Polly's mind.

To overcome this threat, Aunt Polly decides on a strict routine for Pollyanna in order to instruct her in the ways of domesticity, all things to be done inside the house. For Pollyanna, however, this "endless round of duty" can only be "existence" (61); it is not living properly. Aunt Polly is working with a notion that is seen in many nineteenth-century (and later) writers, where attention to duty and self-control (in effect, abandoning one's natural desires) are essential to the formation of a child's character, part of the process of maturation and eventual entry into adult society through putting aside childish things and ideas. Pollyanna, by contrast, operates with an unfettered and natural desire "just to—to live" (59), and this desire includes the environment outside the house, which she sees as a "lovely picture out the window" (44), and to which she wants to belong or with which she wants to engage. Thus, although dutifully remaining indoors in compliance with her aunt's rules, Pollyanna's constant desire is to be out and about: "Almost every pleasant afternoon found Pollyanna begging for 'an errand to run,' so that she might be off for a walk in one direction or another" (73), although she is just as likely to be out on rainy days as well. In this respect, Pollyanna is doubly matter out of place, for she wants to be outside and feels trapped inside.

While Aunt Polly strives to keep the outside firmly in its place, the narratorial voice gives Pollyanna's alternative perspective, with the inside as bad and the outside now good. When Pollyanna first opens the window in her new room she leans "far out, drinking in the fresh, sweet air" (36), as though the air outside is a tonic. Tellingly, these same descriptors, "fresh and sweet," are used more than once to describe the air. The next morning, when Pollyanna wakes up, she finds that her "little room was cooler now, and the air blew in fresh and sweet" (49). The outside is coming in through the window but, again, it is not depicted as bad; rather, it is the inside where Pollyanna finds "the air was all the more stifling after that cool breath of the out of doors" (70) when she creeps out from the confines of her hot, stuffy attic room. There is "fresh, sweet air" outside (68), and "Pollyanna quite danced up and down with delight, drawing in long, full breaths of the refreshing air" (68). For Pollyanna, nature outside the house holds no fears; it is invigorating and uplifting, life-giving. The systems and practices that Aunt Polly employs define nature and the natural as dirty and disordered and, by extension, uncontrolled, wild, and savage. Through Pollyanna's quite different responses to the world outside the walls of the house and beyond the screens that keep things out, the narrative offers a contrasting perspective that asks the reader to consider the nature-culture binary.

This dual consideration is largely reflected in the attitudes taken by both Aunt Polly (with her science-based response to nature as unclean) and Pollyanna, whose ignorance of the perceived dangers allows her to relate to nature on a different, less troubled level. Pollyanna's connection to the natural world is developed in terms of the way she exhibits an empathic response to animals, recognizing non-human creatures' inherent subjectivity, as she reveals in a comment to John Pendleton: "It's funny how dogs and cats know the insides of folks better than other folks do, isn't it?" (135). Pollyanna confirms the agency of the animals, just as she did on the first morning after her arrival, when she awoke to the sounds of nature outside her room, "the birds were twittering joyously, and Pollyanna flew to the window to talk to them" (49), much like a bird herself.

While this connection may argue for figuring the child as being more fanciful of mind, more primitive and more in touch with their emotions, and while it may be true that, as Stuart Aitken writes, "two hundred years after the publication of *Émile*, young people are still thought to be naturally closer to nature" (36), the narrative does not labor this point as other "nature as cure" novels do; and it does not explicitly make such assumptions. Pollyanna is not so much a fantasy figure of the Romantic child of nature as she is simply a natural child. She may be untainted by adulthood and uncorrupted by society, but Pollyanna is identified as and with dirt, as material out of place from the sanitized house and, unknowing though she may be, she is natural in her acceptance of the dirt and disorder of nature and her desire for embodied placement within it. As Stephen and Rachel Kaplan have observed, an organism "must prefer those environments in which it is likely to thrive" (147), and Pollyanna is not a domestic creature. Animal imagery is used to describe Pollyanna, thus furthering the connection between Pollyanna and wild nature and, therefore, as matter out of place. She not only "flies" to greet the birds, but she is also presented as "clinging like a monkey" (37) as she climbs down the tree outside her window. Later, Nancy is described as "shooing Pollyanna into the house as she would shoo an unruly chicken into a coop" (51) and, later still, Nancy describes Pollyanna as a "blessed lamb" (252). This imagery does seem to argue for Pollyanna being directly connected with nature, and her empathetic attitude to other "creatures," both human and non-human, is also a cause of dirt and disorder entering Aunt Polly's house, thereby threatening the established order in which Aunt Polly is "at home." This theme is aptly demonstrated in the case of the houseflies (and other non-human beings) that enter the house through Pollyanna's actions.

Flies, Other Unwanted Creatures, and Little Boys

Even though, by the time of *Pollyanna*, germs had been identified as the cause of illnesses, as Naomi Rogers notes, "the popular association of dirt and disease lingered" (600), especially because women "were taught to assume that where there was dust there were germs" (Tomes, *Gospel* 144).[10] The idea of germs as the agents of disease, however, was not confined to the microscopic; agents of transmission were also given due attention. In *Pollyanna* one such agent of transmission is the housefly and, even prior to Pollyanna's arrival, there is a telling scene as Aunt Polly inspects Pollyanna's room and specifically the windows: "A big fly was buzzing angrily at one of them now, up and down, up and down, trying to get out. Miss Polly killed the fly, swept it through the window (raising the sash an inch for the purpose), straightened a chair, frowned again, and left the room" (15–16). Even flies, it seems, want to escape Aunt Polly's house. At the same time, the matter-of-fact description of Aunt Polly needlessly killing the fly (she could, perhaps, simply have shooed it safely out of the slightly open window) can be seen as part of a process of her regaining order and control over the natural by cleansing the domestic environment and removing the matter out of place. The sash window is not opened too far lest other unwanted intruders should try to get in from the outside, for screenless means defenseless against intrusion: "'Nancy,' she said a few minutes later, at the kitchen door, 'I found a fly up-stairs in Miss Pollyanna's room. The window must have been raised at some time. I have ordered screens, but until they come I shall expect you to see that the windows remain closed'" (16). Flies clearly constitute an element of nature that is not to be tolerated within the house, and even a single fly, it seems, can invoke Aunt Polly's concerned displeasure.

The next morning, however, worse is to come as the purity of the house has clearly been sullied by unwelcome intruders: "Breakfast, for the first five minutes, was a silent meal; then Miss Polly, her disapproving eyes following the airy wings of two flies darting here and there over the table, said sternly: 'Nancy, where did those flies come from?'" (52–53). Nancy does not know how the flies have entered the house uninvited, but Pollyanna certainly does: "'I reckon maybe they're my flies, Aunt Polly,' observed Pollyanna, amiably. 'There were lots of them this morning having a beautiful time upstairs'" (53). Pollyanna clearly feels a sense of joy in the naturalness of the flies simply flying around as nature intended. Sensing a confrontation, however, Nancy wisely leaves the room, leaving Aunt Polly to express her consternation:

"Yours!" gasped Miss Polly. "What do you mean? Where did they come from?"

"Why, Aunt Polly, they came from out of doors of course, through the windows. I *saw* some of them come in."

"You saw them! You mean you raised those windows without any screens?"

"Why, yes. There weren't any screens there, Aunt Polly." (53)

Without suitable protection, the house has been invaded, and Aunt Polly immediately orders Nancy to remove all the flies in the house: "when your morning work is done, go through every room with the spatter" (53) because, as she points out, "Flies, Pollyanna, are not only unclean and annoying, but very dangerous to health" (53). As with the idea of keeping a clean house, the intrusion of flies as matter out of place is an affront to the idea of cleanliness and purity of the household. Here, too, Aunt Polly's responses are also very much in keeping with ideas prevalent at the time.

With germs as invisible as the miasma that had preceded them as the believed agent of illness and disease, animals, particularly the house fly, quickly became identified as visible and targetable carriers of germs.[11] Rogers observes that public health officials at the time had denoted flies as "germs with legs" (601), and the pamphlet on the subject that Aunt Polly gives Pollyanna to read is clearly one of the many advisory publications "warning the lay community and the medical profession of the habits of houseflies," conflating "dirt and germs through the medium of the fly" (610). From the scientific work and the publications that emerged, the housefly "was transformed from a friendly domestic insect into a threat to health and hearth" (Rogers 601).[12] It was made clear that flies in the house were signs of bad housekeeping and part of nature's efforts to force itself into the home. On this, Rogers quotes a contemporary entomologist, Ephraim Felt, as stating that "the malevolent house fly is a constant menace to the integrity of the home" (612). Consequently, says Rogers, "a careful housekeeper could ensure her family's health by guarding her home from the housefly, now known to be a dangerous element of the outside environment" (601). Aunt Polly's attitude clearly emerges from this kind of thinking about flies and, as later events show, other creatures as well.

Pollyanna's attitude toward flies (and to other creatures), however, is quite different from that of her aunt. Pollyanna is not immune to the information she has read, and she tries to follow Aunt Polly's rules, shutting the window behind her when she goes out onto the sun-parlor roof to sleep, "so the flies couldn't carry those germ-things in" (Porter 70).

However, she does so with a very different understanding of flies: "Polly-anna had not forgotten those flies with the marvellous feet that carried things" (68). That Pollyanna's approach here should still be presented as seeing the positive is significant, for although it would seem that she has taken on board the science of the pamphlet, she still sees something else in the natural world; flies' feet are not simply bearers of germs and disease, true as that may be, but are "marvellous" constructions for carrying things, a natural wonder that deserves appreciation.

Although Pollyanna may have an openness to non-human beings, this was not necessarily the case at the time, and certainly not for Aunt Polly. In addition to the raised awareness of insects as carriers of disease at the time, other animals were also identified as potential carriers of germs. Nancy Tomes quotes home economist Martha Van Rensselaer's 1913 statement that not only have the "hum of the mosquito and the buzz of the house fly . . . become fraught with a new significance," but "[e]ven the dog and the cat, with their burden of fleas, have taken on a new aspect" (*Gospel* 145). Consequently, just as Aunt Polly abhors the presence of flies, her reaction is one of disgust when Pollyanna brings germs into the house in the form of another potential carrier of disease, a stray kitten: "Miss Polly did not care for cats—not even pretty, healthy, clean ones. 'Ugh! Pollyanna! What a dirty little beast! And it's sick, I'm sure, and all mangy and fleay'" (108). Aunt Polly's immediate association, beyond even her entrenched dislike of cats, is that the animal from the outside, dirty as it is, brings disease and illness with it. The next day, however, Pollyanna brings home "a dog, even dirtier and more forlorn, perhaps, than was the kitten" (109), but her aunt "abhorred dogs even more than she did cats" (109).[13] Although Pollyanna is eventually able to keep Fluffy and Buffy, as she names them, their initial arrival clearly upsets the strict order of Aunt Polly's household.[14]

Pollyanna's disruption is also figured through the arrival of another dirty and unwelcome intruder to the house in the form of Jimmy Bean, described as "a small, ragged boy" (109). For Aunt Polly, this is another dirty invasion from the outside, much as Pollyanna was, and her response to Jimmy's arrival at her door a few days after the arrival of the stray animals is telling. She immediately defines him by his state of cleanliness, and describes him as "this dirty little boy" (115). She also equates the dirty boy with the dirty animals that Pollyanna has already brought to the house: "As if tramp cats and mangy dogs weren't bad enough but you must needs bring home ragged little beggars from the street" (116). Pollyanna agrees with her aunt's assessment, but responds to the dirt differently: "And he is dirty, too, isn't he?—I mean, the boy is—just like Fluffy and Buffy were when you took them in. But I reckon he'll improve all right by washing, just as they did" (116). Clearly, the only way for the outside to have been allowed in was through the animals being cleaned (and the same must be true for human beings).[15]

This exchange shows that, while Pollyanna and her aunt both equate the child Jimmy with the stray animal strays that have come in from outside, they do so from very different perspectives. With Aunt Polly's reaction to Pollyanna in particular, and children in general, one could assume that she does indeed consider children to be nasty, brutish, short, untamed and unclean, wild things. Whereas Pollyanna is innately aware of the intrinsic connectedness of human beings with the rest of the natural world, and thus more able to connect empathetically with the natural world, Aunt Polly has become disconnected from real nature and seeks to maintain her distance from it. This disconnection can be seen in the brief depictions of her garden and how it is tended.

Order in the Garden

Although it features little in the story, the garden in *Pollyanna* cannot be overlooked, especially given my earlier discussions. Aunt Polly sees nature, in the form of the garden, as both a place to control and of control, of nature and her self.[16] It is clear that this is a cultivated and manicured garden, with "orderly rows of green growing things" (36); green and growing, they may be, but they are ordered in neat rows. The gardener, Old Tom, who is almost always to be found in the garden, "had pulled the weeds and shovelled the paths about the place for uncounted years" (10), reinforcing the idea of the control of natural growth since the natural, as a disordered place, is inimical to the cultivated and threatens to subvert good order.

On the morning after she arrives, Pollyanna sees her aunt from the window of her room, "out among the rosebushes" (49). Being "among" the roses suggests she is pruning them, restricting natural growth to ensure that the cultivated rose grows as humans want, rather than as nature intended. In that context, Mary Douglas's image of the garden as metaphor is apt here: "a garden is not a tapestry; if all the weeds are removed, the soil is impoverished" (164). Perhaps, too, this is as true of people and dwelling places as it is of gardens. The acts of weeding and pruning can, of course, be seen as acts of aggression against the natural, and garden pests, weeds, and the like are all ascribed as such because they are not useful or provide a threat by their presence. Thus, as Zygmunt Bauman suggests,

gardening is the act of *"separating and setting apart useful elements des-*
tined to live and thrive, from harmful and morbid ones, which ought to be
exterminated" (70).[17] Pollyanna, perhaps, is seen as something of a "weed"
herself, at least at the start of the novel.

Unsurprisingly, Aunt Polly's manicured garden holds little interest for
Pollyanna. When she escapes from her hot attic room by climbing down a
tree whose branches are, for Pollyanna, animated because they "looked like
arms outstretched, inviting her" (36), her desire is not for the cultivated,
but the unkempt and the wild: "Beyond the garden a little path through
an open field led up a steep hill, at the top of which a lone pine tree stood
on guard beside the huge rock. To Pollyanna, at the moment, there seemed
to be just one place in the world worth being in—the top of that big rock"
(36). It is untamed nature that Pollyanna wants to be a part of, outside the
boundaries of the house and the overly ordered garden, where Pollyanna
knows "there was a wide world of fairy-like beauty" (68). The narrator also
confirms that Pollyanna "was used to climbing trees" (37), indicating that
she had spent much time out in nature prior to her arrival in Aunt Polly's
house, and Pollyanna herself is seen to recognize the benefits of a relationship with the natural world. After learning that the local Ladies' Aid group
would not help the orphan, Jimmy Bean, "Pollyanna was sure that nothing
would do her quite so much good as a walk through the green quiet of
Pendleton Woods" (128), one reason being that "[i]t was very beautiful in
the Pendleton Woods, as Pollyanna knew by experience" (128), which suggests that visiting the wood, being in a natural environment, is a regular
event for Pollyanna. Pollyanna's desire for embodied placement in nature,
and her response to other creatures, contrasts markedly with that of her
aunt, whose attitudes in general can be considered in terms of the notion
of ecophobia, "a subtle thing that takes many forms" (Estok, "Shakespeare"
34); it is to this broader consideration that I now turn.

Ecophobia

Aunt Polly's attitudes represent a sentiment that, although its roots go
much further back, was entrenched within the processes of modernization and the outcomes of the industrial age: a dissociation of human
beings from the natural world.[18] As Simon Estok argues, "[h]uman history is a history of controlling the natural environment" ("Theorizing"
210), a history founded on what he terms *Ecophobia*, an "irrational (often
hysterical) and groundless hatred of the natural world, or aspects of it,"

and a "fear of a loss of agency and control to Nature" ("Shakespeare" 34, 17). This idea very much resonates with Mary Douglas's consideration of dirt, but also takes the argument further by considering elements of nature as possessing agency, in much the same way that Pollyanna can be seen to do. In short, for Estok, "anything that amputates or seeks to amputate the agency of nature and to assert a human order on a system that follows different orders is, in essence, ecophobic" ("Shakespeare" 34), and this amputation is exactly what Aunt Polly attempts. Her killing of houseflies is a particularly apt exemplification of the basis for ecophobia, which Estok says is based on "maintaining personal hygiene to protect ourselves from diseases and parasites that can kill us, of first imagining agency and intent in nature and then quashing that imagined agency and intent. Nature becomes the hateful object in need of our control, the loathed and feared thing that can only result in tragedy if left in control" ("Theorizing" 210). Aunt Polly could, therefore, be called ecophobic in all of her actions to preserve the sanctity of her domestic environment against the forces of nature outside.

Significantly, it is only when Pollyanna is knocked down by a car (and the association of the automobile with the industrial and urban should not go unnoticed here) that Aunt Polly is moved to do as much as she can to help Pollyanna, now totally confined to the house, the very place she had been keen to escape from before. Her actions show a change in attitude, albeit a small one, for as Nancy tells Old Tom, "if 'tain't more than ter let in the cat—an' her what wouldn't let Fluff nor Buff up-stairs for love nor money a week ago; an' now she lets 'em tumble all over the bed jest 'cause it pleases Miss Pollyanna!" (252). Now, the animals are not only inside the house, but they are even in Pollyanna's bedroom regardless of any diseases or vectors of disease they might carry with them (clean as they may be at this point), although they still bring disorder as they "tumble" around. Notably, nature is also brought into the house in another way, for Nancy relates that Aunt Polly has also "sent Timothy down ter Cobb's greenhouse three times for fresh flowers—an' that besides all the posies fetched in ter her, too" (252). That Nancy feels the need to remark on this suggests that Aunt Polly did not normally admit flowers of any kind inside before and, although the fresh flowers may be cultivated, the posies are more likely to be wildflowers, so there is a combination of the cultivated and the natural now inside the house.[19] This small turn hints at how the novel can be considered within a twenty-first-century context and our own approach to the natural.

Twenty-first-century Aunt Pollys

It should be noted that Aunt Polly's example of moving away from her ecophobia, small though it may be, has not always been taken up as an example by later generations. Sadly, as Estok observes, "[t]he romanticization of Nature as a space of simplicity, innocence, and peace . . . no more slowed the progress of ecophobia than did the notion of 'the Noble Savage' slow the genocide of colonized people" ("Shakespeare" 18). This ecophobic position holds steadfastly in society, despite the fact that, as John Stephens notes, "[t]here is now, in most parts of the world, a recognition that the continued survival of human beings depends on a harmonic balance between human subjects and natural environments" (209). Germs still feature heavily as targets of human beings' need to eradicate that which is outside and, as Tomes points out, "current obsessions with germs have some striking parallels with [the] period of intense anxiety about disease germs that occurred between 1900 and 1940" ("Making" 191). As for home cleanliness, even with today's modern household gadgets to ease the burden, the elimination of dirt and dust (and, therefore, disorder) remains a primary component of housework. Cleaning product companies and their anti-dirt advertising campaigns promote cleaner, whiter, brighter lives and bodies, all underpinned by degrees of ecophobia:

> The personal hygiene industry relies on it, since capital driven notions about personal cleanliness assign us preference for perfumes (for some more than others) over natural bodily odors; the cosmetic industry (in its passion for covering up nature's "flaws" and "blemishes") uses it; beauticians and barbers (in their military passion for cutting back natural growths) are sustained by it; city sanitation boards display it in their demands that residents keep grass short to prevent the introduction of "vermin" and "pests" into urban areas. (Estok, "Shakespeare" 34)

The ugly and the dirty, it seems, exist in all areas of life, and must be eliminated, or at least covered over, and one hundred years after the publication of *Pollyanna*, developed societies still operate in large measure with the same nature/culture binary that affects Aunt Polly's domestic behavior and her attitude toward nature and the outside.

The modern practice of cleanliness has gone far beyond carbolic soap and a scrubbing brush; but, ironically, this over-emphasis on cleanliness has probably brought with it some unforeseen consequences, particularly for children. As Scott Weiss explains, "[a] gradual change in the frequency of childhood infection has been occurring for a long time, affected by the introductions of indoor plumbing in the 19th century, antibiotics in the middle of the 20th century, and cleaner, more energy efficient homes at the end of the 20th century" (930). The "hygiene hypothesis" suggests this over-cleanliness might actually be a negative factor in human well-being by arguing that the "increase in the prevalence of autoimmune and allergic diseases ... results from a decrease in the prevalence of childhood infection" (Weiss 930). Ironically, then, the modern obsession with cleanliness may well have had a negative effect on human health in that children and adults have become more prone to certain allergies and illnesses precisely because they are not exposed to dirt and natural, biotic pathogens early in life.[20]

Even though late-nineteenth-century notions of nature as an antidote to the ill effects of society and urban existence persist in contemporary social thinking, the counterargument that existed then can also still be observed today. Nature is demonized as culture's less appealing other, in an ecophobic reaction that argues that the space of nature can and must be mastered and controlled for the benefit of humankind. Indeed, the idea of nature as unclean and impure has been taken up by some as a rationale.[21] In fact, it could be argued that the prevalence of ecophobic attitudes may well be stronger now than it was at the time of *Pollyanna*'s first publication.

Conclusion

In a broad sense, *Pollyanna* might be said to share some kinship with those novels that characterize the natural environment as a space of growth and exploration, for the natural world clearly plays a part in characters' development over the course of the narrative. Importantly, however, the novel does not work within the limits of the garden trope by depicting nature in a safe, controlled form, nor does it posit the space of the garden as one of healing. However, by reading *Pollyanna* in terms of dirt, disorder, and ecophobia, it is possible to, as Anthony Lioi suggests, "consciously construct a symbolic place in ecocriticism for dirt and pollution, an alias or icon that allows us to give dirt its due" (17). Pollyanna's more natural contact with the physical world, dirty as it may be in its different forms, contrasts with Aunt Polly's disgust with it and withdrawal from it (and, at the same time, reveals something of Polly's mental state).

Aunt Polly manages to maintain a sense of domestic cohesion (however artificial), order, and purity by keeping out "others" in the form not only of animals and nature in the form of dirt and weeds in the garden, but also loved ones on an emotional level, intrinsically connecting these elements.[22] It is the moment when Aunt Polly accepts (but does not show a desire to control or remove) the "matter out of place" that is Pollyanna and the animals that marks her transformation and move, albeit a small one, away from an ecophobic position.

Pollyanna still relates to modern readers and environmental concerns, for, reading with an ecocritical eye, it is possible to recognize that little has changed in the hundred years since the novel was first published. Developments in hygiene and disease control have come as part of an often ambivalent relationship that human beings have with the natural world of which they are inherently a part. Although the development of better sanitary provisions has brought health benefits for human beings, it has done so by reinforcing a desire to maintain a distance from material nature. As such, *Pollyanna* reveals as false the idea that the best context for raising a child is a clean and controlled home, and that the banishing of the natural (and the natural within the child) in order to maintain a separation from the social and cultural is not living, as Pollyanna herself recognizes.

Through the eyes of Pollyanna, the novel shows that human well-being can never really exist outside the full, unmediated context of nature, and while the novel does not go so far as to present non-human life as having genuine agency, it does show that hierarchical boundaries between one creature and another, human and animal, human and nature (in all its supposedly dirty and disgusting forms) should be seen as arbitrary impositions. Thus, while modern human beings might not wish to fling open doors and windows to all that is outside, *Pollyanna* shows that a safe and anthropocentrically controlled nature, one that is apart from human existence, is actually inimical to human well-being. In this regard, Lawrence Buell is right when he argues that personhood today "is defined for better or for worse by environmental entanglement" (23), and this remains as true today as it was in the early twentieth century of *Pollyanna*.

Notes

1. For information on the shift to urban dwelling in the United States of the period, see Mohl.

2. Much of this attitude had been foreshadowed in 1850s and 1860s in the writings of Thoreau and Emerson, presenting the natural world as a space where human beings could try to reconnect with what was perceived as lost innocence, although Friedrich Froebel had earlier argued that an "out-door life, in open nature, is particularly desirable for young people" because "it develops, strengthens, elevates, and ennobles. It imparts life and a higher significance to all things" (309).

3. Wright's output includes fiction for adults and children (originally published anonymously), illustrated (using her own photographs) field guides, and other semi-narrativized accounts of gardens, nature, and animals. Her books for children were intended to both entertain and educate about nature.

4. In *Pollyanna*, of course, this "some one" is very much Pollyanna herself.

5. Many of the unsanitary urban conditions and practices were famously dramatized at the time in Upton Sinclair's novel *The Jungle* (1906).

6. There is, too, the underlying notion of dirtiness related to notions of class (as a working-class immigrant, Nancy is much closer to dirt than her mistress), race, and, of course, gender (the "uncleanness" of menstruation, for example).

7. Douglas's main concern is to describe ideas of ritual pollution and how, in turn, rituals and other practices develop to manage that pollution and restore and/or maintain order.

8. As an aside, here, it is worth noting literary depictions of characters that are dirty—street urchins, for example—where the dirtiness represents illegality, criminality, or chaos in varying degrees.

9. This links, of course, to Julia Kristeva's notion of *the abject*—which itself draws on Mary Douglas—whereby, for society or the individual to maintain control, the abject is that which must be expelled or repressed, an act that simultaneously reveals the anxieties and fears that threaten the security of that culture or person.

10. This also touches on the notion of "material ecocriticism," referring to "the well-being of our material bodies—both as agents and as small-scale, mobile environments in their own right" (Phillips and Sullivan 446).

11. For a general overview of the development of germ theory, see Waller.

12. Rogers notes that, prior to the turn of the century, the fly had been seen in a far more positive light and had even figured as a delightful, albeit anthropomorphized character in an 1865 poem for children in a book by Theodore Tilton called *The Fly*.

13. Aunt Polly's initial reaction to the animals in the novel also lends itself to an Animal Studies reading that space does not allow for here. Certainly, and alongside ideas of the domination in general, this episode can also be read in terms of recognizing the social subjugation of non-human beings.

14. The cat and the dog appear to have become feral when Pollyanna finds and accepts them. Aunt Polly's need for them to be sanitized is a form of re-domestication, and their names now suggest they are sufficiently clean to remain indoors (Fluffy, cleaned and

brushed; Buffy, as in buffed or polished), although presumably they still retain something of the feral.

15. Physically, Pollyanna herself may not have been in need of such cleansing, but her old clothes certainly did—they all were thrown away and new, clean ones were purchased.

16. On this idea of control, see also Harde's essay in this volume.

17. Bauman's image here is specifically related to the Nazi regime's desire to weed out (and thereby cleanse society of) those individuals seen as undesirable in German society.

18. Aunt Polly's attitude also inverts the standard notion that women have some inherent affinity with nature.

19. Clearly, the point holds for adults as well as for children, perhaps more so. Aunt Polly only really begins to flourish emotionally when dirt and disorder are allowed into the house.

20. It should be noted, however, that these ideas still rest on hypothesis rather than conclusive evidence.

21. As Frederick Buell has argued, "modern day anti-environmental attitudes in America have happily taken up the idea of the impurity of nature and trumpeted the claim" that "nature-lovers' notions of the pure and pristine were delusions" (127).

22. Interestingly, Old Tom describes Aunt Polly's temperament since her broken love affair as being "as if she'd been feedin' on wormwood an' thistles ever since—she's that bitter an' prickly ter deal with" (13). Although it is not clear which type of wormwood is referred to here, presumably reference is made because wormwood plants have "profoundly bitter tasting leaves" but, interestingly, they are also "strong pest repellents" that "will also discourage moles and cats" and can also deter the growth of weeds (Garland 53–54). These latter properties are appropriate to a well-ordered, cultivated garden (one that keeps wild, untamed nature firmly outside the boundaries) and, of course, to Aunt Polly herself.

Works Cited

Aitken, Stuart C. *Geographies of Young People: The Morally Contested Spaces of Identity.* London: Routledge, 2001. Print.

Bauman, Zygmunt. *Modernity and the Holocaust.* Ithaca, NY: Cornell UP, 1989. Print.

Buell, Frederick. *From Apocalypse to Way of Life: Environmental Crisis in the American Century.* New York: Routledge, 2003. Print

Buell, Lawrence. *The Future of Environmental Criticism.* Oxford: Blackwell, 2005. Print.

Douglas, Mary. *Purity and Danger: An Analysis of the Concepts of Pollution and Taboo.* 1966. New York: Routledge, 2002. Print.

Estok, Simon C. "Shakespeare and Ecocriticism: An Analysis of 'Home' and 'Power' in *King Lear*." *AUMLA* 103 (2005): 15–41. Print.

———. "Theorizing in a Space of Ambivalent Openness: Ecocriticism and Ecophobia." *Interdisciplinary Studies in Literature and Environment* 16.2 (2009): 203–25. Print.

Fröebel, Friedrich. *The Education of Man.* 1826. Trans. W. N. Hailmann. New York: D. Appleton, 1887. Print.

Garland, Sarah. *The Herb Garden*. London: Frances Lincoln, 1984. Print.

Hoy, Suellen. *Chasing Dirt: The American Pursuit of Cleanliness*. 1995. New York: Oxford UP, 1996. Print.

Kaplan, Stephen, and Rachel Kaplan. *Humanscape: Environments for People*. Ann Arbor, MI: Ulrich's, 1982. Print.

Kristeva, Julia. *Powers of Horror: An Essay on Abjection*. Trans. Leon S. Roudiez. New York: Columbia UP, 1980. Print.

Lioi, Anthony. "Of Swamp Dragons: Mud, Megalopolis, and a Future for Ecocriticism." *Coming into Contact: Explorations in Ecocritical Theory and Practice*. Eds. Annie Merrill Ingram, Ian Marshall, Daniel J. Philippon, and Adam W. Sweeting. Athens: U of Georgia P, 2007. 17–38. Print.

Mohl, Raymond A. *The New City: Urban America in the Industrial Age, 1860–1920*. Arlington Heights, IL: Harlon Davidson, 1985. Print.

Phillips, Dana, and Heather I. Sullivan. "Material Ecocriticism: Dirt, Waste, Bodies, Food, and Other Matter." *Interdisciplinary Studies in Literature and Environment* 19.3 (2012): 445–47. Print.

Plunkett, H. M. *Women, Plumbers, and Doctors; or, Household Sanitation*. New York: D. Appleton, 1885. Print.

Porter, Eleanor H. *Pollyanna*. 1913. Boston: Page, 1919. Print.

Rogers, Naomi. "Germs with Legs: Flies, Disease, and the New Public Health." *Bulletin of the History of Medicine* 63.4 (1989): 599–617. Print.

Rome, Adam. "Nature Wars, Culture Wars: Immigration and Environmental Reform in the Progressive Era." *Environmental History* 13.3 (2008): 432–453. Print.

———. "'Political Hermaphrodites': Gender and Environmental Reform in Progressive America." *Environmental History* 11.3 (2006): 440–63. Print.

Sibley, David. "Families and Domestic Routines: Constructing the Boundaries of Childhood." *Mapping the Subject: Geographies of Cultural Transformation*. Eds. Steve Pile and Nigel Thrift. London: Routledge, 1995. 123–37. Print.

Stephens, John. "Impartiality and Attachment: Ethics and Ecopoeisis in Children's Narrative Texts." *International Research in Children's Literature* 3.2 (2010): 205–16. Print.

Stratton-Porter, Gene. *Freckles*. 1904. Radford VA: Wilder, 2008. Print.

———. *A Girl of the Limberlost*. 1909. Radford VA: Wilder, 2008. Print.

Tomes, Nancy. *The Gospel of Germs: Men, Women, and the Microbe in American Life*. Cambridge: Harvard UP, 1998. Print.

———. "The Making of a Germ Panic, Then and Now." *American Journal of Public Health* 90.2 (2000): 191–98. Print.

Waller, John. *The Discovery of the Germ: Twenty-Five Years That Transformed the Way We Think About Disease*. New York: Columbia UP, 2002. Print.

Weiss, Scott. "Eat Dirt—The Hygiene Hypothesis and Allergic Diseases." *New England Journal of Medicine* 347.12 (2002): 930–31. Print.

Wright, Mabel Osgood. *Gray Lady and the Birds; Stories of the Bird Year for Home and School*. New York: Macmillan, 1907. Print.

"Ice-cream Sundays": Food and the Liminal Spaces of Class in *Pollyanna*

SAMANTHA CHRISTENSEN

At the beginning of *Pollyanna*, Nancy is sent to retrieve Pollyanna from the train station and, intrigued by the impression that her aunt may be wealthy, Pollyanna asks Nancy, "Does Aunt Polly have ice-cream Sundays?" (20). Pollyanna equates wealth with luxurious foods such as ice cream sundaes, and at this moment, food transcends its prominent role as basic human sustenance and takes on a deeper social meaning. Pollyanna's understanding of socio-economic status is interconnected with aspects of food, and these social aspects of food continually surface throughout the novel. *Pollyanna* is a text that is rather restrained in terms of food— admittedly, it does not engage with representations of food as overtly as other texts emerging from the period, such as those by Susan Coolidge and Sarah Orne Jewett—but throughout the text, food is intertwined with issues of class in early-twentieth-century America. *Pollyanna* narrates the experiences of two classes—the upper middle class and the immigrant lower class—yet Pollyanna's ability to cross the boundaries between these two classes allows these two social spheres to enmesh, blurring the strict hierarchal divisions between rich and poor. Polly and Mr. Pendleton have vastly different understandings of food and eating from those of Nancy and Jimmy, and food is used to signal characters' positions within a decidedly hierarchal American culture. Pollyanna, who develops close relationships with both upper- and lower-class characters in the novel, consistently blurs the boundaries of this hierarchy through her ability to transcend and obscure class divisions, and her own complex class status (as the daughter of a poor minister and adopted niece of a wealthy upper-class woman) shapes her attitudes toward food. While hierarchal class boundaries are drawn rigorously throughout Porter's novel—boundaries that are held firmly in place through representations of food and the characters' relationships to it—Pollyanna herself works against social expectations surrounding food and creates a sort of liminal space between rich and poor, the privileged class and poor immigrants. This chapter explores this complex relationship by analyzing food's impact on the differing classes in the text in terms of memory, eating spaces, immigrant identities, and the development of an appropriate appetite.

"I don't see how she can help liking ice-cream": Food, Memory, and Familial Relationships

Pollyanna's original young readers would have been steeped in literary lessons stemming from the popular classics of the period. Along with many other early-twentieth-century children's authors, Porter was undoubtedly influenced by nineteenth-century children's authors, and *Pollyanna* falls into the girl's coming-of-age genre established by women authors such as Louisa May Alcott, Susan Coolidge, and Elizabeth Stuart Phelps. As in many of these mid-to-late-nineteenth-century texts, issues of food and eating permeate *Pollyanna*, and Porter's novel offers an insightful exploration of food as it interweaves with social behavior. After Pollyanna's discovery that Aunt Polly not only does not have "ice-cream Sundays," but does not actually like ice cream at all, she tells Nancy, "I don't see how she can help liking ice-cream. But—anyhow, I can be kinder glad about that, 'cause the ice-cream you don't eat can't make your stomach ache like Mrs White's did" (20–21). Aunt Polly's distaste for ice cream is consistent with her unpleasant personality, and Pollyanna's genuine and unfaltering optimism makes this aspect of her aunt's personality completely unfathomable. Upon discovering that Aunt Polly does not share her taste for ice cream, Pollyanna accepts that *she*, herself, will not be eating ice cream in the Harrington household, and the notion of indulging in the luxurious dessert alone does not cross her mind. "Ice cream Sundays" take on dual meanings here—not only is Pollyanna referring to ice cream itself, but she is also alluding to traditional Sunday afternoons, when families take time to be with one another during the day of rest, a ritual with which Pollyanna, a minister's daughter, would be all too familiar. Sweet foods, including ice cream sundaes, encourage camaraderie—they are meant to be shared with loved ones in familial spaces.

While the child reader may be expected to make connections between Aunt Polly's aversion to ice cream and her sour personality, Polly's distaste for sweets runs deeper than her general unpleasantness. Sweet foods are typically a comfort—a luxury meant to evoke pleasure and complement existing happiness—and they create a premise for bonding not only with others but with oneself. In *Pollyanna*, a novel that, as mentioned previously, is rather constrained when it comes to food, confectionary is rarely mentioned, and when Pollyanna does refer to indulgent foods, such as the fudge and fig cake she has been taught to bake, she is scolded by her embittered aunt. Discussing the politics of sweetness, Andrew Dix and Lorna Piatti draw connections between sweetness and nostalgia, and suggest "sweet foods are conceived as privileged vehicles for the preservation and mobilization of remembrances" (56). The food of childhood—beloved, sweet, indulgent food—functions as a sort of "language of memory," and Aunt Polly's aversion to ice cream and cake is embedded in her refusal to work through her difficult past. Early in the novel, the narrator reveals that the Harrington family had shunned Jennie, Polly's sister and Pollyanna's mother, after she rejected a wealthy suitor and ran away with a poor minister: "The break had come then. Miss Polly remembered it well, though she had been but a girl of fifteen, the youngest, at the time. . . . To be sure, Jennie herself had written, for a time, and had named her last baby Pollyanna, for her two sisters, Polly and Anna—the other babies had all died. This had been the last time that Jennie had written" (6). Polly's inability to make peace with her estranged sister and the pain attached to her memory keeps her in a constant state of emotional distress. Her resistance to any sort of confectionary or indulgent food, which may stir up buried memories of her late sister, suggests latent and unresolved trauma—trauma that prevents her from sharing ice cream sundaes on a Sunday afternoon with her niece.

What is more, Pollyanna *herself* evokes memories of Polly's own childhood—a childhood surrounded by young girls and close sisterhood. As Polly rereads the letter announcing her niece's arrival, "her thoughts [go] back to her sister Jennie," and she reflects on her childhood with her two sisters in the Harrington household (Porter 5). Pollyanna is named after Polly and her middle sister, Anna, and therefore embodies Polly's childhood—a childhood steeped in resentment and broken bonds: "She was forty now, and quite alone in the world. Father, mother, sisters—all were dead" (6). As Pollyanna makes a swift and unexpected appearance in her lonely aunt's life, Polly is forced to reevaluate her identity as a spinster and "sole mistress of the house"—as a lone woman who "[is] not lonely," but who "like[s] being by herself" (6). This new way of living includes a new way of eating, and Polly's precisely structured food schedule collapses in response to Pollyanna's free spirit. Early upon her arrival, Nancy explains to Pollyanna, "that bell means breakfast—mornin's, . . . and other times it means other meals. But it always means that you're ter run like time when ye hear it, no matter where ye be"—she is to be at supper by six o'clock and to breakfast at half past seven (43). An ever-present anxiety in Pollyanna's life with her aunt is Polly's enforcement of these strict mealtime schedules, as any deviation from them leads to stern consequences. In the fourth chapter, Pollyanna is determined to climb a rock at the peak of a large hill and, underestimating the distance to her destination, misses Aunt Polly's scheduled supper. Fifteen minutes after Pollyanna embarks on her climbing adventure, the clock strikes six, and "[a]t precisely the last stroke Nancy [sounds] the bell for supper" (31). For Aunt Polly, Pollyanna's unexplained absence is not so much a cause for concern (as it is for Nancy) as much as it is a nuisance, and Pollyanna's heedless behavior leads to the disruption of Aunt Polly's austere domestic order. Pollyanna's deviation from her aunt's eating ordinances draws Polly closer to her own girlhood, steeping her in nostalgia with which she is uncomfortable. As Svetlana Boym suggests, "Nostalgia tantalizes us with its fundamental ambivalence; it is about the repetition of the unrepeatable, materialization of the immaterial" (xvii). Through Pollyanna, Polly is immersed in the memory of her childhood, and she is forced to work around the eating habits of a young girl who consistently rejects the social constraints surrounding food and eating behavior.

"No matter where ye be": Pollyanna's Eating Spaces

While Polly regulates eating times in the Harrington household, she also maintains control over appropriate eating spaces for Pollyanna and her servant staff. Throughout *Pollyanna*, meals are eaten indoors, and each meal eaten with Aunt Polly is eaten in the dining room—with the exception, of course, of Pollyanna's punishment supper with Nancy in the kitchen. After Pollyanna's outdoor adventure causes her to miss the supper bell, Polly informs Nancy, "I told her what time supper was, and now she will have to suffer the consequences. She may as well begin at once to learn to be punctual. When she comes down she may have bread and milk in the kitchen" (31–32). Polly works to ensure that Pollyanna's eating takes place strictly within the private sphere, and even while being punished, she is never permitted to eat any food outdoors. Rather, her punishment involves a simple, undecorated meal of bread and milk in a space outside of the dining room but within the confines of the domestic sphere. Eating is considered an entirely private action throughout nineteenth-century and early-twentieth-century American culture, and Hannah Arendt's theories of power structure in the private and public spheres supplement an exploration of public and private food behaviors.

Arendt argues that throughout history, certain behaviors have been condoned only within the private sphere, and it has been the "bodily part of human existence that needed to be hidden in privacy" (qtd. in Hartsock 212). Power relations, according to Arendt, exist on distinctions between public and private behavior that are inherently separate, yet are necessary to one another (Hartsock 212). Functioning properly in the public sphere relies on partaking in meals in the private, and Aunt Polly's insistence on Pollyanna eating within the confines of the home works to develop Pollyanna's eating habits in accordance with nineteenth-century social expectations surrounding food and bodily nourishment. Polly is shocked, though, to discover that not only has Pollyanna enjoyed her time with Nancy in the kitchen, but has also enjoyed her meal. Regarding her punishment, Pollyanna explains to her aunt, "I was real glad you did it, Aunt Polly. I like bread and milk, and Nancy too" (39). While Polly expects her niece's temporary displacement from her conventionally suitable eating space—the dining room—to be an unpleasant experience, Pollyanna instead recognizes her punishment as an opportunity to bond with Nancy over a basic, staple meal, and Polly is "confronted with the fact that her punishment was being taken as a special reward of merit" (61). Where she lacks opportunities to build a close relationship with her aunt over shared ice cream or even daily meals in the dining room—during meals Polly often "did not speak, indeed, until the meal was over" (45)—she is able to build a friendship with Nancy over a simple shared meal, and thereby crosses the class boundaries of proper eating spaces in the upper-class home.

Throughout the novel, Polly avoids eating in areas other than dining room, leaving the servant staff to adapt the kitchen as their own eating space, and her reluctance to deviate from the dining room extends to outside of the home as well. Each week Polly sends food to Mrs. Snow, an impoverished elderly woman in.the parish, and while she does take on this charitable duty, she does not actually enter the poor woman's eating space. Mrs. Snow's well-being is an obligation taken on by the members of the church, and "Miss Polly did her duty by Mrs Snow usually on Thursday afternoons—not personally, but through Nancy" (Porter 65). Polly does not physically contact Mrs. Snow, but rather sends Nancy to donate meals on her behalf. Despite her lack of contact with the impoverished woman and her sickroom-turned-dining area, Polly gains a sense of self-satisfaction through the charitable transactions. In "Charitable (Mis) givings," Monika Elbert explores issues of charitable action in nineteenth-century children's texts, and discusses the superficiality of giving on the part of the wealthy. She notes that "[f]or the wealthy, this charity helps assuage a guilty conscience, or promises more reward in another realm" (31). In the charitable transactions between Polly and Mrs. Snow, Polly is able to gain a sense of satisfaction without ever entering the eating space of the poor, allowing her to remain within the confines of her upper-class home while still feeling that she is feeding the hungry.

Upon learning about Mrs. Snow, Pollyanna "beg[s] for the privilege" to deliver the calf's-foot jelly, and while she is greeted with ingratitude on Mrs. Snow's part (she informs Pollyanna, "my appetite isn't very good this morning, and I was wanting lamb" [Porter 68]), she works to transform Mrs. Snow's sickroom into a more comfortable eating space. Rather than simply leaving the donation in the sickroom, Pollyanna "[places] the calf's-foot jelly on the stand and [seats] herself comfortably in the nearest chair" (68). Pollyanna invites Mrs. Snow to share her mealtime, hoping to establish a relationship with the unhappy woman, and food acts a vehicle of friendship between the newly upper-class child and poor elderly woman. Pollyanna transforms the practice of sending food to the sick, a technique adapted to distance the giver from the struggling individual, into a meaningful opportunity to provide meals in a comfortable eating space. She continues working to convert the sickroom into an appropriate eating space, and during her second visit to Mrs. Snow, she "arranges three bowls in a row on the table" (83). Pollyanna's own meal spaces are restricted to the dining room and, if she has misbehaved, the kitchen, and she attempts to make Mrs. Snow's bedroom look more like a dining room in order to create a more appropriate atmosphere based on her own understandings of upper-class eating spaces and mealtime customs. While Mrs. Snow does belong to the lower class, she *is* somehow a member of the deserving poor; unlike their refusal to help Jimmy and Mrs. Payson, the church members feel they must support Mrs. Snow through charitable offerings. Like Pollyanna, she has a complex class status, and Pollyanna draws from both her background as a minister's daughter and her aunt's privileges as an upper-class woman to build a relationship that transcends hierarchal class divisions. On the surface, Pollyanna and Mrs. Snow represent two distinctive class statuses—Mrs. Snow being "poor [and] sick" and Pollyanna being the niece of an incredibly wealthy woman—yet the two women blur conventional boundaries between rich and poor, subverting orthodox representations of appropriate eating spaces. The sickroom functions as a bourgeois dining room in a lower-class environment where a mealtime space is nonexistent (65).

While Mrs. Snow does belong to the lower class, she is not denied an eating space within the confines of the private sphere, and like the impoverished "cantankerous" woman (Porter 65), so too must Nancy convert a domestic space into an appropriate eating area. Nancy spends the majority of her time in the kitchen, and therefore immersed in quotidian aspects of food and eating, yet she is not an authoritative figure in terms of food choice and mealtimes in the household. She maintains the closest relationship to food throughout the novel, as she prepares, serves, and cleans up after meals in the kitchen; her connection with food in the domestic cooking space plays a significant role in her social position. While food and kitchen work consumes her life, she does not indulge in the fruits of her labor, and is not welcome in the dining area of the home. Faye Dudden, in her work on serving women in the nineteenth century, notes that "[a]lthough she ate separately, [the working girl] did not enjoy the privileges of privacy. Her food was chosen for her" (195). Nancy is apologetic in the fact that Pollyanna "will have ter have bread and milk in the kitchen with me" (Porter 35). She is reluctant to inflict the unpleasantness of eating staple foods in the kitchen that she faces daily. Just as the dining room creates possibilities of companionship and meaningful conversation between Polly and Pollyanna—possibilities that, due to Polly's reluctance, are left untapped—its redemptive features are undermined by the fact that Nancy, who works to ensure the flow of meals to the eating space is uninterrupted, is banished to the kitchen during mealtimes. Nancy's identity as an immigrant servant prevents her not only from taking part in shared meals between Polly and Pollyanna, but also in achieving any sort of social mobility; her relationship to food is closely intertwined with her class position. While Nancy is hesitant to inform Pollyanna of her punishment, referring to her as a "[p]oor little lamb," Pollyanna retorts, "Why, I like bread and milk, and I'd like to eat with you, I don't see any trouble about being glad about that" (35). Pollyanna is a newly introduced member of the upper class—she spent the majority of her childhood in the care of her financially struggling father. For her, bread and milk is nostalgic—the sort of food she would have shared with her father. Pollyanna's complex class relationship to the meal allows her to create a liminal space—a space between the prestigious dining room and the deplored kitchen—where she and Nancy can nourish both their bodies and their friendship.

Not only is Polly horrified by her niece's positive attitude toward her punishment, but she is also bewildered by Pollyanna's lack of basic cooking skills. As Pollyanna confesses that she has "only learned chocolate fudge and fig cake," Polly's repulsion toward the rich, frivolous recipes in Pollyanna's knowledge base is as strong as her distaste for her niece's lack of kitchen experience. Pollyanna's learned skills in the kitchen prove to be an asset in *Pollyanna Grows Up*, where Pollyanna's ability to "cook and keep house" allows her aunt to convert their home into a boarding house in order to solve their financial difficulties (Porter, *Pollyanna Grows Up* 193). Food plays a crucial role in the inner workings of the domestic realm, and girls are expected to be skilled in preparing meals from a young age.

Susan Bordo recognizes the tendency for young women to be shown in advertisements as spending a great deal of time in the kitchen, a depiction found in some nineteenth-century children's literature, and notes that "[o]nly occasionally are little girls represented as being *fed*; more often, they (but never little boys) are shown learning how to feed others" (124). She observes that in advertisements young women rarely eat, much as in *Pollyanna*, and the contact that they do have with food is through meal preparation in the kitchen. The texts she identifies often encourage the early development of future housewives, and idealize the wife as "she who stands . . . famished before her husband, while he devours, stretched at ease, the produce of her exertions" (qtd. in Bordo 118). While women are required to repress their own appetites, they are also expected to provide food in order to satisfy the male eater, and young women are pressured into domestic destinies from an early age. Pollyanna experiences these pressures in the novel, and after she admits to Aunt Polly that she is only familiar with recipes for chocolate fudge and fig cake, her aunt retorts, "Chocolate fudge and fig cake indeed . . . I think we can remedy that very soon" (Porter, *Pollyanna* 50). Polly understands Pollyanna's scarce kitchen experience as an inherent flaw in her upbringing, and in order to remedy this problem she schedules cooking lessons in the kitchen with Nancy twice every week to ensure she can cook nutritious, hearty meals. Pollyanna, who consistently refrains from voicing complaints throughout the novel, is displeased with her new education arrangements, and exclaims, "Oh but Aunt Polly, Aunt Polly, you haven't left me any time at all just to— to live. . . . I mean *living*—doing the things you want to do" (51). Through her enforced cooking lessons, Pollyanna feels cheated out of childhood activities and is uncomfortable with abandoning her identity as a child in order to prepare for an adulthood of domestic servitude. Although she is initially uncomfortable with her kitchen duties, Pollyanna soon learns to cherish Wednesday and Saturday afternoons in the kitchen, and both she and Nancy benefit from these cooking experiences.

Throughout *Pollyanna*, Nancy is constantly anxious and restless in her domestic duties, and is often portrayed "hurrying with her belated work, [jabbing] her dish-mop into the milk pitcher" (40). Her constant domestic labor is burdensome in her life, in part because she spends the majority of her days in solitude. Nancy Hartsock, in her work on feminism and historical materialism, discusses the alienation of women in the domestic sphere, and argues, "the isolation of women from each other in domestic labor . . . mark[s] the transformation of life into death, the distortion of what could have been creative and communal activity into oppressive toil" (245). Nancy's domestic labor prevents her from functioning in a healthy community, and in turn extinguishes any possibility of establishing relationships outside the private sphere. She is isolated in the kitchen, working to create meals appealing to the refined tastes of a class she will never belong to, and it is not until Pollyanna's arrival that she is able to establish a connection with another young woman. With Pollyanna's biweekly cooking lessons, "Nancy, in the kitchen, fared better. She was not dazed nor exhausted. Wednesdays and Saturdays came to be, indeed, red-letter days to her" (Porter 62–63). The two girls build a meaningful relationship during their time in the kitchen, and rather than mechanically working to serve others in the household, Nancy partakes in creative expression through cooking in a female communal environment. Both of the girls benefit from shared experiences in the kitchen, and are able to treat cooking as a creative outlet rather than an enforced burden. Food preparation becomes an opportunity for meaningful, relationship-building experiences in situations when women are able to cook without pressures of satisfying the male appetite, and although preparing meals can become a source of resentment and oppression when it is simply expected of women in the domestic sphere, it can also function as an empowering cooperative activity in close-knit female communities.

The relationship that Pollyanna and Nancy create in the kitchen is indeed one that celebrates creativity and female companionship, but it is also one that transcends the class boundaries implicit in the relationship between the servant and the served. Nancy, an immigrant domestic servant, is suddenly Pollyanna's superior, at least in the kitchen, and, as Kim Cohen suggests in her discussion of servant and class reform in the nineteenth century, "the servant's skill as teacher opens up the possibility for . . . hierarchal slippages" (113). Through Polly's constant berating of Nancy, she creates a firm hierarchy in the household—one that identifies the domestic Nancy as a subordinate—but this hierarchy dissolves in the kitchen, where Nancy is the culinary superior and Pollyanna is the student. By aligning the reader with Pollyanna, the learner, Porter questions the "hier-archal relationship between housewife and servant, native and immigrant, as well as middle and lower class" (Cohen 113). Nancy's rank as an immi-grant Irish domestic servant in America disintegrates while she teaches Pollyanna in the kitchen, and the practical, well-balanced meals they create together epitomize Nancy's brief class liberation. Food functions as an emancipator, blurring the class boundaries implicit in the relation-ship between Nancy, the servant, and Pollyanna, the served, and although Nancy does not permanently transcend her identity as a lower-class Irish immigrant, food allows her temporarily to break free of her marginalized identity and become a teacher to a newly upper-class young woman.

Toward the latter half of the nineteenth century and the beginning of the twentieth, as the middle class became entrenched in American cul-ture, there emerged a certain expectation in terms of the working rela-tionship between upper-class women and their servants (Stansell 161). Polly's treatment of Nancy is callous, at best, and the resentment between the two women is overtly expressed throughout the novel. Immediately in the first chapter, Polly charges into the kitchen—Nancy's workspace—and while Nancy attempts to finish with the dishes as quickly as possible, Polly chides, "'Nancy'—Miss Polly's voice was very stern now—'when I'm talk-ing to you, I wish you to stop your work and listen to what I have to say.' . . . Nancy stifled a sigh. She was wondering if ever in any way she could please this woman" (1–2). Christine Stansell, in her work on women in the American workforce in the late nineteenth century, notes:

> Serving girls were "universally complained of" and "generally and unhesitat-ingly denounced, even in their very presence [as] pests and curses." In one sense, the servant problem was an element of class-consciousness: One could not really *be* a lady if one did not have a problem with servants. For ladies who were not entirely confident in their own class identity, asserting judg-ment over the immigrant poor affirmed their position and status. (161)

Polly's constant reprimanding of Nancy and her inability to be pleased with the young cook works to constantly remind Nancy of her place as a second-class member of the household. While Nancy spends the majority of her time in the kitchen, cooking meals and ensuring the household has proper food on the table daily, Polly constantly reminds her that she has no sort of ownership or status within the walls of the kitchen. As the rela-tionship between Polly and Pollyanna grows, so too does Polly's patience with Nancy; just as Pollyanna is able to break down the class boundaries between herself and Nancy while in the kitchen, she is also able to foreground a more sincere relationship between her aunt and her servant. After Mr. Pendleton, the richest man in town, offers Pollyanna a place in his home, Pollyanna wonders whether or not her aunt would miss her, to which Nancy replies, "Would she miss ye if ye wa'n't here? ... It's little ways she has, that shows how you've been softenin' her up and mellerin' her down—the cat, the dog, *and the way she speaks ter me*" (emphasis added, 180). Nancy recognizes that Pollyanna's more liberatory attitude toward food and the social expectations surrounding it creates a liminal space where the boundaries of class no longer exist, and in this liminality Polly grows to treat Nancy with patience and gratitude for her kitchen duties.

"The pertater on t'other side of the plate": Immigrant Relations to Food

Nancy's identity as a young Irish woman is an important aspect of understanding the social attitudes toward immigrants in late-nineteenth-century and early-twentieth-century America, and Nancy's relationship with food is (re)constructed by her identity as an Irish woman living in America. Porter is meticulous in ensuring that her readers are aware of Nancy's Irish background, ascribing to her an exaggerated, oftentimes distracting Irish accent and placing her in a typical career environment for Irish immigrants in nineteenth-century children's literature: the kitchen of a wealthy household. The literary link between Irish immigrant women and the upper-class kitchen is shaped, though, by its surrounding culture, and by the end of the nineteenth century, 75 percent of Irish women in America were employed as domestic servants (Stansell 156). As the Famine in Ireland continued to spread throughout the mid-nineteenth century, Irish immigrants poured into American urban spaces searching for work, and kitchen positions began to be recognized as "work for those just off the boat" (Stansell 155). Kitchen staff was "comprised of young Irish women in their teens and early twenties," attempting to procure steady employment to support often struggling families (Stansell 156–57). At the beginning of the novel, the narrator reveals Nancy's familial background: "a sick mother, suddenly widowed and left with three younger children besides Nancy herself, had forced the girl into doing something towards their support, and she had been so pleased when she found a place in the kitchen of the great house on the hill" (2). Her skill in the kitchen, along with her ability to quietly tolerate Polly's constant scolding and general unpleasantness, secure Nancy's identity as a working woman, and while she is faced with a young adulthood of domestic drudgery and long hours in the kitchen, she remains passionate and grateful in her work—the ideal immigrant cook.

While not Irish, an overstated working-class accent is attributed to Jimmy Bean, and he is designated in the role of the orphaned street child. He does have a space in the local orphanage, but he prefers to earn his own meals by working from the streets and is reluctant to receive any sort of charity, including that which is offered to him by the orphanage. As is revealed in *Pollyanna Grows Up*, Porter's only sequel to *Pollyanna*, Jimmy is the child of a wealthy woman and a man who "came from good stock, but was not much himself" (18), and his father raised him in the working class before his death. Jimmy's relationship to food and eating is strongly influenced by his working-class identity, and this relationship is embedded in aspects as ubiquitous as language. In his frustrations with the Ladies' Aiders, Jimmy explains to Pollyanna the tendency for charitable organizations to aid children overseas before those in their own country, and notes, "the pertater on t'other side of the plate is always biggest" (Porter, *Pollyanna* 121–22). Readers recognize in Jimmy's expression the Western colloquial equivalent— "the grass is always greener on the other side"—and his reference to the potato, along with his working-class accent, reflects his descent into poverty after the death of his father, and his adoption of lower-class speech patterns.

In her theories of food's relationship to social structure, Lorna Piatti-Farnell suggests, "through shared practices, identifiable dishes and cultural representations of 'preparing the dinner,' food continues to be inextricably linked to immigrant and ethnic sensibilities in contemporary American culture" (105). While Jimmy himself is not an immigrant, he is a member of the lower class, and his relatively new identity as street orphan surfaces through language and its relationship to foodways. "Cultural history, immigrant consciousness and individual experience," Piatti-Farnell suggests, "are successfully synthesized through discourse of food" (148). Like Pollyanna, Jimmy has a complex relationship to food that blurs the boundaries of the lower and upper classes. He made his descent into severe poverty after the death of his father, and later in the novel is adopted by the wealthy Mr. Pendleton; rather than being firmly grounded in a lower-class identity, he fluctuates between classes—and, therefore, between relationships to food and eating—and exposes the fluidity of class consciousness.

Like Pollyanna, Jimmy is able to blur the boundaries between upper and middle class, and subverts social expectations surrounding his own eating behaviors by rejecting charitable offers. Throughout the novel, Porter critiques contemporary charitable institutions through the actions of the Ladies' Aiders, and her social criticisms convey a particularly poignant statement regarding charitable organizations in late-nineteenth- and early-twentieth-century America. Elbert discusses the shifting outlook of the poor in postbellum America and explores the strengthening dichotomy between the deserving and undeserving poor that developed throughout the last half of the nineteenth-century. Elbert suggests that "[t]wo movements toward the end of the nineteenth-century succeeded in dehumanizing, even demonizing, the poor, and in distancing the financially solvent individual . . . from the poverty stricken individual" (21–22). Both Social Darwinism and the institutionalization of charitable organizations created a perverse distaste for the poor, and a particularly negative outlook on the impoverished individual in postbellum America.

Assuming Polly, a dedicated member of the Ladies' Aid group, would be welcoming of Jimmy, Pollyanna brings him into the Harrington residence assuming that her aunt will be willing to adopt the orphaned child. Upon being introduced to Jimmy, Aunt Polly exclaims, "That will do, Pollyanna. This is . . . the most absurd thing you've done yet. As if tramp cats and mangy dogs weren't bad enough but you must needs bring home ragged little beggars from the street" (101). Jimmy is horrified to be referred to as a beggar, and responds with dignity: "I ain't a beggar, marm, an' I don't want nothin' o' you. I was cal'latin' to work, of course, fur my board an' keep" (Porter, *Pollyanna* 101). As a poor orphan, Jimmy is expected to receive charity from the upper classes, but his refusal to take any sort of charitable donation allows him to transcend his identity as a "ragged little beggar" as he attempts to enter the working class. As the narrator reveals in *Pollyanna Grows Up*, Jimmy is the son of an immigrant man and a wealthy woman, whose name can be traced "straight back to the crusades" (*Pollyanna Grows Up* 299). Upper-class American blood flows through Jimmy's veins, and his negative attitude toward the "undeserving poor" separates him from the lower class to which he is assumed to belong. His namesake, "Bean," characterizes the staple food of the working class, and his appetite leans toward the hearty, practical food he can earn as opposed to food given to him by members of the upper class.

"Beans and fishballs": Negotiating the Appropriate Appetite

Jimmy's refusal to accept charitable offerings grounds him in an appetite that is suitable for his social position. Developing an appropriate appetite in relation to social standing is a crucial component to food behavior. While throughout the novel, Pollyanna often associates wealth with refined, luxurious foods, Mr. Pendleton's habitually modest meals work against the tendency for the rich to indulge in expensive food, and instead expresses the importance of adhering to a modest and nutritious menu. As Pollyanna expresses interest in Mr. Pendleton, she learns that he "comes down [to] the hotel for his meals three times a day," and merely requests the most inexpensive meal on the menu (Porter 77). Pollyanna, assuming Mr. Pendleton to be poor, pities the man and reminisces about her experiences eating "beans and fishballs" with her financially struggling father (77). She is shocked, then, to discover that Mr. Pendleton is in fact the wealthiest man in town. As Nancy puts it, "[h]e could eat dollar bills, if he wanted to—and not know it" (77). Nancy recognizes the link between wealth and food, and at this moment actually interweaves the two and criticizes the man for his public displays of frugal meals. Because Pendleton is wealthy, he is able to cross boundaries between the food of the rich and the food of the poor, and although he is viewed with mystery and confusion within the community, his tendency to eat inexpensive food varieties is assumed to derive from miserliness rather than obscene impropriety. Discussing food trends emerging with the middle class in America, Dix and Piatti suggest that fine foods "[fetishize] food's decorative quality without regard for the labor involved in preparation helping to inhibit consumers from awareness of the differentiated social structure in which they live" (59). While Pendleton could be indulging in expensive luxuries, such as the European delicacies he would typically be expected to eat, he chooses simple, practical meals. He chooses not to "eat dollar bills," and rather than take part in culinary frivolity and eating as primarily a social practice, he paves the way for moral and practical food choices by eating simple, nutritional food.

For Pollyanna, much like Nancy, the notion of eating lower-class foods while having the means to indulge in rich luxuries is incomprehensible, and she assumes that his restraint stems from an inherent selflessness, noting, "'That's denying yourself and taking up your cross'" (Porter 79). Pollyanna, who is the embodiment of morality and the antithesis of the superficial wealthy in the novel, assumes that Pendleton donates his excess money to "the heathen," and naïvely creates in him a Christ-like identity (79). In discovering that he does not, in fact, donate his saved money to any sort of charitable organization, Pollyanna asks, "Say, *do* you like beans?—or do you like turkey better, only on account of the sixty cents?" (132). The thought of a wealthy man taking pleasure in a lower-class staple food is perplexing to Pollyanna, and although Pendleton admittedly does not donate his excess funds to any sort of charitable cause, Pollyanna still considers his eating habits to be moral.

As Roland Barthes argues in his 1957 essay "Ornamental Cookery," there is undoubtedly a moral quality to the "working-class public that is careful not to take for granted that cooking must be economical" (79). Pendleton recognizes the middle-class obsession with expensive, "ornamental cookery," and rejects the frivolous eating habits of the wealthy. Barthes looks deeper into the wealthy's fascination with extravagant dishes, and suggests that fine food "is for ever trying to extenuate and even to disguise the primary nature of foodstuffs, the brutality of meat or the abruptness of seafood" (78). Ornamental cookery functions as a means of removing the eater from the "brutality" implicit in satisfying the carnal appetite, and rejecting the social obsession with lavish meals also removes the eater from the conventional image of immoral rich. For Pendleton, though, denying oneself delicious foods and partaking in more staple, substantial meals is not simply about rejecting the frivolity of the upper class, it is about developing and adhering to an appropriate appetite—an appetite embedded in nutrition and functionality as opposed to social prestige. Just as Pollyanna paves the way for the appropriate appetite—through her early recognition that too much ice cream "[makes] your stomach ache like Mrs White's" and her genuine appetite for bread and milk (Porter 21)—Pendleton chooses the nutritious food of the working class over the superficial and unwholesome meals of the upper class to which he belongs.

Just as Mr. Pendleton develops and adheres to an appropriate appetite—an appetite that rejects the superfluity of upper-class delicacies—so too does Mrs. Snow, the impoverished bedridden woman, but her meals are chosen for her and appropriated to suit her ill state. As an invalided and impoverished individual, Mrs. Snow is unable to make decisions regarding what and where she eats, though she is vocal in regard to her preference. Being offered the calf's-foot jelly that Pollyanna brings to her, Mrs. Snow exclaims, "Dear me! Jelly? ... Of course I'm very much obliged, but I was hoping 'twould be lamb broth today" (Porter 67). Mrs. Snow's finicky appetite is viewed with repugnance in the novel, and Pollyanna works both to please the old woman's unsatisfied palate and feed her meals that are appropriate for the sick. The foods offered to Mrs. Snow—calf's-foot jelly, lamb broth, plain chicken—are nutritious, easily digestible staples, and while their indecorous and inexpensive nature is befitting of a woman of Mrs. Snow's social position, they are also appropriate food choices for a bedridden elderly woman.

Pollyanna's experiences with Mrs. Snow parallel a particular episode in another children's classic, Elizabeth Stuart Phelps's *Gypsy Breynton*, as the benevolent protagonists in each novel struggle with not only class expectations surrounding food, but also health expectations. Published in 1866, *Gypsy Breynton* was a best-seller popular among American Sunday schools, and has gone through many reprints over the past century. Gypsy, a kind, rambunctious tomboy, hears a strange groan emanating from a run-down building on her walk home one evening, and upon entering the dismal abode finds Mrs. Littlejohn, a bedridden elderly Irish woman. Mrs. Littlejohn explains that she does not have many opportunities to eat, and relies on others to "brings me up a cup of cold tea when they feels like it, and crusts of bread, and I with no teeth to eat 'em. I hain't had a mouthful of dinner this day, and that's the truth, now!" (Phelps 134). Gypsy immediately pities the old woman, and agrees to bring her the meal she has requested: white sugar for her tea and "some fresh salmon and green peas" (135). Gypsy conveys Mrs. Littlejohn's request to her mother, and is shocked by her mother's suggestion that "the old woman seems to like to complain" (139). Mrs. Breynton must explain to Gypsy that it is inappropriate to donate white sugar to the woman, and "to spend several dollars on fresh salmon—a delicacy which we have had on our own table but once this season" (139).

While Gypsy's experiences with Mrs. Littlejohn seem to be primarily embedded in issues of class—as Mrs. Breynton points out firm divisions between what is appropriate for the poor to eat and what is appropriate for the upper classes—the larger issue seems to be in the old woman's choice of rich, processed foods. Mrs. Littlejohn, like Mrs. Snow, is bedridden, and therefore must adhere to an appetite that is conducive to inactivity and illness. Like Pollyanna, Gypsy struggles to satisfy the needy woman while remaining not only within class boundaries, but also within appropriate divisions between the foods of the sick and of the healthy. Mrs. Littlejohn is ultimately condemned as immoral and unworthy of charity, and Gypsy's dilemma remains unresolved as she no longer makes visits to Mrs. Littlejohn's sickroom.

Whereas Gypsy is unable to please her charitable interest, Pollyanna does come to a satisfactory solution regarding Mrs. Snow. In order to please her finicky palate, Pollyanna brings her a small portion of each of Mrs. Snow's typical hankerings, explaining, "I was just bound you should have what you wanted for once; . . . there's only a little of each —but there's *some* of all of 'em" (Porter 82). Pollyanna is able to come to a resolution that Gypsy could not, and provides her charitable interest with a variety of food that not only satisfies her finicky palate, but also properly nourishes her disabled body. While Mrs. Snow does make requests for various foods, her choices, unlike Mrs. Littlejohn in *Gypsy Breynton*, always reflect an appropriate appetite for a woman in her condition.

Conclusion

Exploring literary aspects of food as an extension of social structure creates a particular vantage point from which to ground deeper under-standings of cultural understandings of food, class, and their relationship to nineteenth-century American society. Each character in *Pollyanna* expresses complex relationships to food, ones that are embedded in class structure in some form or another, but it is Pollyanna who is able to tran-scend its boundaries and create a liminal space where food and appe-tite are not constrained by social expectations. Pollyanna's own complex class status—being raised by her working-class father, yet belonging to a wealthy maternal family—intertwines with her own relationship to food and eating, and she, like Jimmy Bean and Mrs. Snow, complicates the con-ventional roles of food in nineteenth-century American culture. Polly-anna consistently rejects the social ordinances surrounding food and the appetite, and by upsetting the social order of eating schedules, spaces, and food choices, she changes the ways characters from both the upper and lower classes deal with food and appetite. While Polly understands food as a vehicle of social propriety and attempts to train Pollyanna to have a socially appropriate relationship with food, she must also face food's role in conjuring her painful past while attempting to keep it at bay. Whereas Polly's eating behavior functions primarily as a social practice, Pollyanna rejects the food rituals of the upper class and builds relationships with Nancy, Jimmy, and Mr. Pendleton—relationships that rely on shared eat-ing spaces and/or corresponding behaviors surrounding meals and food choice. As an Irish immigrant living in America, Nancy's understandings of food are embedded in her marginalized class position, and therefore her attitudes toward preparing, eating, and cleaning up after meals differ greatly from those of her wealthy mistress. While for Nancy, food most often functions as an oppressive force, grounding her in the servant class, she is able to transcend her lower-class identity by passing her skills onto Pollyanna while developing a meaningful relationship with the young girl—a relationship that goes beyond that of the typical servant-served dynamic. Pollyanna's presence in the kitchen, along with her enthusiasm for learning to cook and building a friendship with the cook, creates a liminal space where Pollyanna and Nancy can exist as equals in regard to food and eating. Pollyanna's rejection of the social constraints placed on food also allows her to pave the way for appropriate relationships to the appetite—relationships that Mr. Pendleton and Mrs. Snow each emulate. While the social forces acting upon food in the novel work to ground the characters in particular class divisions, Pollyanna's humanistic approach to food—an approach that shakes off social ordinance—creates a community of eaters based on nutrition, meaningful friendship, and an overall "glad" community.

Works Cited

Barthes, Roland. *Mythologies*. 1957. Trans. Annette Laverse. New York: Noonday, 1972. Print.

Bordo, Susan. *Unbearable Weight: Feminism, Western Culture, and the Body*. 2nd ed. Berkley: U of California P, 2004. Print.

Boym, Svetlana. *The Future of Nostalgia*. New York: Basic, 2001. Print.

Cohen, Kim. "True and Faithful in Everything: Recipes for Servant and Class Reform in Catherine Owen's Cookbook Novels." *Culinary Aesthetics and Practices in Nineteenth-Century American Literature*. Ed. Monika Elbert and Marie Drews. New York: Palgrave MacMillan, 2009. 107–22. Print.

Dix, Andrew, and Lorna Piatti. "Bonbons in abundance: The Politics of Sweetness in Kate Chopin's Fiction." *Culinary Aesthetics and Practices in Nineteenth-Century American Literature*. Ed. Monika Elbert and Marie Drews. New York: Palgrave MacMillan, 2009. 53–69. Print.

Elbert, Monika. "Charitable (Mis)givings and the Aesthetics of Poverty in Louisa May Alcott's Christmas Stories." *Enterprising Youth: Social Values and Acculturation in Nineteenth-Century American Children's Literature*. Ed. Monika Elbert. New York: Routledge, 2008. 19–38. Print.

Foucault, Michel. *The History of Sexuality Volume 1: An Introduction*. London: Penguin, 1979. Print.

Hartsock, Nancy. *Money, Sex, and Power: Toward a Feminist Historical Materialism*. Boston: Northeastern UP, 1985. Print.

Hayes-Conroy, Alison, and Jessica Hayes-Conroy. "Taking Back Taste: Feminism, Food, and Visceral Politics." *Gender, Place & Culture* 15.5 (October 2008): 461–73. *Canadian Research Knowledge Network*. 21 June 2011. Web.

Phelps, Elizabeth Stuart. *Gypsy Breynton*. 1866. New York: Dodd, Mead, 1875. *American Libraries Internet Archive*. 20 June 2011. Web.

Piatti-Farnell, Lorna. *Food and Culture in Contemporary American Fiction*. New York: Routledge, 2011. Print.

Porter, Eleanor H. *Pollyanna*. 1913. New York: Penguin, 2003. Print.

——. *Pollyanna Grows Up*. New York: Grosset & Dunlap, 1915. Print.

Stansell, Christine. *City of Women: Sex and Class in New York, 1789–1860*. Chicago: U of Illinois P, 1987. Print.

5

At Home in Nature: Negotiating
Ecofeminist Politics in *Heidi* and *Pollyanna*

MONIKA ELBERT

There is a tradition in children's literature of connecting orphan girls to redemptive and healing qualities to effect positive social change. Johanna Spyri's Heidi as the progenitor of such a character is often ignored, perhaps because of the privileging of Anglo-American girls' texts in the canon of children's literature.[1] But there is a tradition spanning Western literature, from the Swiss *Heidi* (1880) forward, including, in addition to the American *Pollyanna* (1913) by Eleanor H. Porter, such famous orphan heroines in the girls' classics as *Rebecca of Sunnybrook Farm* (1903) by American author Kate Douglas Wiggin, *Anne of Green Gables* (1908) by the Canadian author Lucy Maud Montgomery, and Mary Lennox in *The Secret Garden* (1911) by British author Frances Hodgson Burnett. I think it telling that there is a preponderance of these redemptive orphan girl figures in the period following 1880 and, most noteworthy, an entire cluster between 1903 and 1913 when all the horrors of modern consumer life, the angst of working-class alienation, and fears of corporate bureaucracy were emerging.

Clearly, these orphan girls seek a surrogate mother in various aunt-like figures, whether they are actual aunts or servant figures acting as such, even if they prove unsatisfactory. When a substitute mother is found in a male figure, such as Grandfather in chapter 2 of *Heidi* (tellingly titled "At Home with Grandfather"), or such as stodgy old Pendleton in chapter 18 ("Prisms") of *Pollyanna*, that Edenic moment is fleeting.[2] Ultimately, the orphan girls must find or create their own sense of home, and unlike the heroines of sentimental novels of the mid-nineteenth century, where the orphan's goodness leads her to the arms of a wealthy suitor, late-nineteenth-century novels allow the girl orphan to grow into womanhood with a sense of independence learned in nature (and often a calling to nurture, or to teach, even informally).[3] The vestige of the sentimental novel is, of course, the desire to find a home—but often that home is made in nontraditional ways or through the formation of nontraditional families. What is most significant to my study is that the missing link to a bygone sense of motherhood is found in nature, a quest which, in itself, is a vestige of the Romantic period, where nature was seen as a panacea to the world's evils.[4]

The orphans' quests culminate in alternate ways of perceiving the family within different non-oppressive and cooperative structures, but always in harmony with nature, so that a true ecofeminist perspective emerges. Using an ecofeminist lens, one sees that Heidi and Pollyanna are not redemptive because they are female children but rather because they are unspoiled, female, *orphan* children, still innocent until their rude awakening and confrontation with the evil of the material realm—seen in the wealth of urban centers (like Frankfurt) or embodied in that emblem of Modernist angst, the automobile. That said, these girl orphans are not averse to positive change: both Heidi and Pollyanna become excellent students, despite their initial expressions of fear of or aversion to formal (indoor) schooling, and their measured approach to life brings them and their loved ones a sense of balance in the most difficult situations.

Through their goodness, suffering, and wisdom, the girls are able to help and heal the many disabled characters they encounter, whether that disability is physical or spiritual. In the process, they, too, must learn what it means to feel disabled. Heidi is able to touch her Grandfather's soul so that he becomes part of the community; she becomes figuratively the eyes for Peter's blind grandmother; she brings the workaholic Herr Sesemann to his senses; she helps educate the goatherd Peter, who has resisted his studies; she brings the weary but wise doctor back to life in the Alpine landscape; and, of course, she restores health and vitality to the erstwhile crippled Clara, who can ultimately walk on her own, without use of the wheelchair. Similarly, Pollyanna can restore hope to her lovelorn and bitter Aunt Polly, happiness (and good health) to the jaded, old miser Pendleton, mobility to the bedridden Mrs. Snow, a sense of family to Jimmy Bean, self-respect to Mrs. Tom Payson, companionship and love to the isolated Dr. Chilton, and a sense of conviction to a doubting Reverend Paul Ford. Both Heidi and Pollyanna thrive, not as idyllic children or sentimental vestiges of the past, but as girls who become aware of their truths through their initial proximity to nature, which gives them a sense of courage and independence as they later find their voices in the most trying of circumstances (when they are removed from nature).

In a striking vignette that begins the third chapter of *Pollyanna* (1913), we see a stern Aunt Polly pondering the unwelcome arrival of her orphan niece Pollyanna and musing upon the very bare attic room, where she plans to sequester Pollyanna. Noting a "big fly . . . buzzing angrily," trying to escape through the shut screenless window, Miss Polly Harrington promptly kills the fly and methodically dispenses with it: "she "swept it through the window (raising the sash an inch for the purpose)" (11). She then proceeds to admonish the hired help, Nancy, for allowing the fly to enter the room and gives her strict orders to keep the windows closed: "I found a fly upstairs in Miss Pollyanna's room. The window must have been raised at some time. I have ordered screens, but until they come I shall expect you to see that the windows remain closed" (12). In this manner, Aunt Polly will attempt to use a modern invention, screens, to create a barrier to nature, wrought by a squeamish modern sensibility associating ugliness with naturalness.

Aunt Polly represents the type of paralyzed inhabitant of Beldingsville, Vermont, a town Pollyanna succeeds in rejuvenating through her affinity with nature. The child literally offers Aunt Polly a breath of fresh air, when she enters the aunt's mansion and promptly opens the windows, not minding the flies that enter. Finding herself cloistered in her claustrophobic stuffy room, Pollyanna initially feels isolated and dejected, but she glances out the window and finds solace in the view—for there are "trees," a lovely church, and "the river shining just like silver" (25). Pollyanna is most relieved when she realizes she can open the windows and have fresh air: she "was leaning far out, drinking in the fresh, sweet air" (26). Paying "no heed" to the flies that entered and "buzzed noisily about the room" (26), she nimbly climbs to an adjacent tree with plentiful branches that "looked like arms outstretched, inviting her" (26). "Clinging like a monkey," Pollyanna maneuvers her way through the branches, and lands "on all fours in the soft grass" (26). This engagement with the natural world enables her to recapture the sense of home and belonging her minister father provided for her in the Midwest wilderness. She is pleased to encounter and speak with Old Tom, Aunt Polly's lifelong servant, working in the garden, and makes her way to another idyllic spot, which she sees in the distance: "Beyond the garden, a little path through an open field led up a steep hill, at the top of which a lone pine tree stood on guard beside the huge rock. To Pollyanna, at the moment, there seemed to be just one place in the world worth being in—the top of that big rock" (26).

Pollyanna's affinity with nature brings her closer to Aunt Polly's servants, Tom and Nancy, who intuitively understand her innate love of nature. Tom's livelihood is the garden; he has worked as Aunt Polly's gardener for ages and he comforts Pollyanna with stories about her mother

as a child. Nancy, who comes from a family of farmers, can most relate
to poor Pollyanna's hankering for nature, as Nancy also feels displaced
and yearns for the countryside, where live her "own dear mother, and her
equally dear brother and sisters" (46). Out of the goodness of her heart,
Nancy promises the homesick Pollyanna a trip to see her family in the
countryside, if her aunt agrees. Aunt Polly, cooped up for many years in
her stately homestead, cannot begin to fathom Pollyanna's connection
to nature—or to a sense of community. She scolds her ward and denies
her a proper meal for having taken an excursion to that "big rock" and
arriving late for dinner (26). At breakfast the next morning, Pollyanna is
scolded for letting flies into the house. Aunt Polly first accuses Nancy of
letting the flies in, but Pollyanna quickly takes the blame and shows not
only compassion for the servant but an innate appreciation of nature: "I
reckon maybe they're my flies, Aunt Polly. . . . There were lots of them
this morning having a beautiful time upstairs" (37). Interestingly, both
Pollyanna and the servants are comrades in arms against the domineering Aunt Polly, with her rigid ways and haughty attitudes. Aunt Polly is
appalled at the suggestion that her niece has been complicit in letting in
the flies; she gives orders to Nancy to keep the windows shut until the
screens arrive and "to go through every room with the spatter" until every
fly is killed (38). She then lectures Pollyanna on "her duty" to keep the
windows shut—explaining how flies present a health hazard (39). She also
gives Pollyanna a pamphlet explaining the dangers associated with flies.
Pollyanna, in her inimitable style, sees the more beautiful side of nature's
wonders: "I never saw anything so perfectly lovely and interesting in my
life. I'm so glad you gave me that book to read! Why, I didn't suppose flies
could carry such a lot of things on their feet" (39).

This episode shows Pollyanna's affiliation with nature—and illustrates
the book's ecofeminist politics, which offers sympathy toward the downtrodden, whether they are children, animals, or social outcasts (orphans,
misfits, underclass, with whom Pollyanna identifies). As ecofeminist critics
Karen J. Warren and Jim Cheney assert, "Ecological feminism is a feminism
which attempts to unite the demands of the women's movement with those
of the ecological movement in order to bring about a world and worldview
that are not based on socioeconomic and conceptual structures of dominance" (244).[5] Pollyanna, as friend to nature, is able to teach the neighborhood to get back to a healthier sense of community and a reverence for the
environment, which comes close to a spiritual awakening for the town, an
awakening separate from the fraudulent church doctrine the imperialist
Ladies' Aiders, for example, espouse. It is telling that Pollyanna, an orphan

child, whose father often felt discouraged as a mission minister out West, comes back from the West—no longer a frontier, but definitely less "civilized" than eastern civilization—as a type of redemptive child who will teach the townspeople the meaning of "living" (43).

As Pollyanna explains early on to Aunt Polly, in what sounds like a Romantic protest against the regimented learning Aunt Polly recommends (with such typical "girlish" activities as reading to her aunt, cleaning, cooking, sewing, scheduled every day at a prescribed hour), there are more important things in life than adhering to a schedule or learning gender-prescribed duties. She explains to Aunt Polly that living should be more self-centered: "doing the things you want to do: playing outdoors, reading (to myself, of course), climbing hills, talking to Mr Tom in the garden, and Nancy, and finding out all about the houses and the people and everything everywhere" (43). Aunt Polly, in a role reversal and in exasperation, slowly learns the lesson Pollyanna has to teach her—and she finally learns appreciation for the environment and for her neighbors.

The paradigm for this book might be Swiss author Johanna Spryi's eco-conscious children's novel *Heidi* (1880), which shows the distinctions most emphatically between city-dwellers and mountain dwellers (even more emphatically than the New England and western dwellers). Heidi's life-affirming role in that novel is similar to Pollyanna's. She is able to rejuvenate the sickly and paralyzed city dwellers with her love of the mountains. In fact, she is sent to her grandfather in the alms, upon her mother's death, and learns to love the initially surly man who keeps his distance from his neighbors, as he shows deep reverence for nature and despises the false religious conventions of the neighbors and their hypocritical stance toward healthy living. For him, nature is God, in the vein of most Romantics, and he instills in Heidi a love of nature and faith in its goodness. Through his condemnation of the hypocritical villagers, Heidi learns the truths of nature. Grandfather explains the bird's croaking sounds as signs of ridicule of the gossiping villagers; to Grandfather, the bird's message amounts to good advice: "If you would separate and each go your own way and come up here and live on a height as I do, it would be better for you!" (44). Heidi becomes adept in the skills of a farm girl as she learns to milk cows, graze animals, work in the barn, cook and eat healthy food, until the citified and underhanded Aunt Dete, with her "fine feathered hat" and pretentious skirt (70), arrives. Aunt Dete recommends that Heidi work as the companion to a girl in Frankfurt, much against the wishes of the grandfather, who has finally experienced a sense of a cozy home through the girl's presence—and distrusts everything connected to

the commercial center of the city. The majesty of the Swiss Alps is juxtaposed with the spiritual bankruptcy of the German city.

Heidi is totally lost in Frankfurt: though she loves Clara Sesemann, the
girl she was sent to help, the orphaned girl misses her grandfather and the
natural landscape he represents. Clara, like Heidi and Pollyanna, has lost
her mother, and Clara's father is rather aloof and absent with his business
ventures, at least to start with. Heidi resents "the long list of rules as to
general behavior" (87) preached to her by the stern housekeeper, Fräulein Rottenmeier (the list of rules sounding very much like Aunt Polly's
protocol for good behavior). Missing her companions in nature, Heidi is
thrilled to discover a litter of kittens, which she rescues and brings home
with her, much to the consternation of the overbearing and pretentious
Fräulein Rottenmeier, who calls the kittens "'horrid little things'" (105) and
"'dreadful little animals'" (106), much in the same vein as Aunt Polly when
Pollyanna brings home Fluffy and Buffy.

But Heidi does find a friend in the more nurturing, congenial, and
down-to-earth servant Sebastian, who reminds Heidi of her goatherd
friend on the alm, Peter. She delights Sebastian with her wayward country
ways, and he, notably, is the one who opens up the window for her so she
can attempt to see far away into the valley (97; cf. the window's significance in *Pollyanna*, above); he is also the one who suggests that she should
climb to the top of the church tower to attempt to see the countryside.

Like Pollyanna, Heidi craves the solace of nature when feeling abandoned and homeless. At first, she refuses to be educated by the tutor,
who quickly gives up on the backward Heidi, to whom the lessons she
shares with Clara seem meaningless. It is only when the very maternal
and compassionate grandmother of Clara, Frau Sesemann, appears at the
Frankfurt home that Heidi can learn her letters. Frau Sesemann refuses
to believe that Heidi can't be educated; she first touches her heart by giving her picture books conveying pastoral images of the countryside, and
then engages her mind. Heidi is ultimately able to rejuvenate the sickly
and paralyzed city dwellers with her love of the mountains, so that in the
end, Clara regains her health through a sojourn with her on the alm. Even
the life-weary, good doctor of the city, who discovers that the "ghost in
the house" is none other than Heidi sleepwalking, realizes that a return to
the alm is necessary to restore her health (149). In the process, he too is
rejuvenated when he visits Heidi in the mountains. He learns to appreciate "the waving flowers, the blue sky, the bright sunshine, the happy bird"
and to feel that Heidi's words about urban distress ring true: "no one is
sad up here, only in Frankfurt" (221). And so the final pages of the book

show the urban doctor, whose spirit had been blighted in the city with the death of his daughter, now moving into the newly renovated house of Heidi and Grandfather in the country and leaving behind (once and for all) the life-destroying city of Frankfurt. As Peter O. Büttner and Hans-Heino Ewers point out, Frankfurt represents discontinuity and limitations, and the respectable house of Mr. Sesemann reflects the artificiality and lifelessness of the city, ultimately manifested in Clara's disease, which imprisons her in the wheelchair (25). Anne-Marie Gresser also shows the dichotomy between the bucolic Swiss landscape and the barren German city: the absence of domestic animals as pets in the bourgeois Sesemann household (until Heidi's arrival) is an inauspicious sign. When Heidi returns to the mountains and Clara visits, their health is restored; even the city doctor with all his medical knowledge cannot remain healthy in Frankfurt—he is sick at heart. This reliance upon nature and simple country values (and a nostalgic sense of the past) will also prove important for the health and welfare of patients and doctors in *Pollyanna*.

Both Heidi and Pollyanna show a love of nature and of animals, and both girls refuse to participate in socially sanctioned practices of shunning the working class (hence their affiliation with the servants in both novels). Ecofeminist theory promotes equality and freedom for the oppressed or injured, whether that is subjugated people, animals, or natural landscapes, and in some ways there is an overlap with the agenda of Marxist criticism and postcolonial criticism, in the ecofeminist sympathy for the working class and the exploited "other." In her introduction to *Ecofeminism: Women, Culture, Nature* (1997), editor Karen Warren asserts: "What makes ecofeminism distinct is its insistence that nonhuman nature and naturism (i.e., the unjustified domination of nature) are feminist issues. Ecofeminist philosophy extends familiar feminist critiques of social isms of domination (e.g., sexism, racism, classism . . .) to nature" (4). Ecofeminist theory thus advocates a policy of communal living—and the necessity of subverting a patriarchal, capitalist, or imperialistic system that would dominate any group within society.

Both Heidi and Pollyanna are finally able to transform the community and soften the several disgruntled, angry boys who threaten harmonious communal values through their lack of cooperation. And although both girls are averse to formal modes of discipline and pedagogy, they finally allow themselves to be educated on their own terms (which requires the notion of play time, in nature, going back to an earlier Romantic sense of education, like Froebel's or Pestalozzi's). In discussing the fragmented world of the city in the context of *Heidi*, Büttner and Ewers cite Rousseau as showing the negative effects of enclosed urban living—and his advice that children spend enough time in the fresh air to gain strength and health (25). As girls close to nature, and still not conscious of the bifurcation that mechanized or industrial society creates between "female nature" and "male civilization" (as French feminist Hélène Cixous has described the everlasting battle between the sexes), until they experience their own crisis of maturation, Heidi and Pollyanna effect change through their close ties with the natural landscape. Heidi experiences a disturbing phenomenon of sleepwalking in Frankfurt, and Pollyanna sustains a life-altering accident, in her encounter with the modern symbol of alienation, the car. In the process of growing, suffering, and finally healing, both girls challenge oppressive systems of medicine, education, commerce, and religion.

Neither of these natural girls "sell out" to the evils of consumerism, even if Pollyanna is initially disappointed that she did not have a sumptuous rug in the room Aunt Polly originally prepares for her (although her renovated room does include the desired carpet), and even though Heidi enjoys a momentary sense of joy recalling her alpine home after Clara's grandmother presents her with a lovely and expensive picture book illustrating the beauty of the countryside. In both texts, it is clear that women who have "sold out" to consumer goods or hypocritical views of charity are as insensitive and reckless as the men in that same environment. Thus, in *Heidi*, Aunt Dete (the ostentatious sister of Heidi's deceased mother) would send Heidi to the wealthy Frankfurt family in an effort to acquire more wealth for more sumptuous clothing. Similarly, in *Pollyanna*, the Ladies' Aid Society members, on the frontier or in Aunt Polly's Vermont town, are wrongheaded about priorities. The churchgoing women of Beldingsville would willingly and hypocritically support a poor child in India but not the orphan Jimmy Bean who so desperately needs a home, despite Pollyanna's pleas.

And yet, it is clear that both Heidi and Pollyanna can provide the more mechanized and robotic members of society with the wherewithal to deal with the emptiness that has deadened them. Heidi brings joy and hope to the urban child Clara, who has resigned to a life of paralysis foisted upon her by urban doctors; Pollyanna's adherence to the natural code represented by the good country doctor saves her. In both texts, organized religion is seen as a dark force that works against the goodness implicit in nature. So it is not any child who can heal the jaded neighbors, and it is not the lost boy figure, Jimmy (in *Pollyanna*) or Peter (the goatherd in *Heidi*), but it is very specifically the girl who has the innocence and the healing feminine touch needed to bring about such change. Pollyanna hears old

Mr. Pendleton's desire for a woman's touch that is needed in his bachelor home, but seems unaware that she possesses that skill. As Pollyanna likes to repeat, when she is trying to make a home for Jimmy at Pendleton's, "You said only a—a woman's hand and heart or a child's presence could make a home" (153).

The love of animals is a quality that both Heidi and Pollyanna can transfer to their love of humans, especially those who have been spiritually wounded. In fact, many children's books, from the late nineteenth century onward, attempt to "civilize" children by promoting respect toward animals, or living in harmony with nature. This theme was especially true in the United States after the establishment of the ASPCA in 1866, and literary texts for children thereafter advocated a more nurturing and respectful view of animals.[6] Pollyanna, after the fly appreciation episode, becomes obsessed with finding stray animals and making a home for them. In an effort to make a home for herself as an orphan child, Pollyanna first learns how to make helpless creatures feel safe. First she brings home a stray kitten, much to the consternation of Aunt Polly, "who abhorred cats" and has a nervous fit when she sees it (78). The series of helpless creatures grows: next comes "a dog, even dirtier and more forlorn, perhaps, than was the kitten" (78). Aunt Polly finds herself becoming, unwittingly, "a kind protector and an angel of mercy—a role that Pollyanna so unhesitatingly thrust upon her" (79). But when Pollyanna brings home "a small, ragged boy" in the shape of Jimmy Bean, Aunt Polly does resist taking him in— and so the humanization process (for both Aunt Polly and the boy) takes a bit longer.[7]

In both of these girlhood classics, the girls' gentle behavior toward animals and people is in contradistinction to the behavior of the young boys, who seem restless and dangerous, to the community, to themselves, and, at times, to nature. Part of the problem stems from their lack of education, and the other part from the lack of a mother's touch (and at times from a combination of the two, a maternal education). The orphan Pollyanna tries to teach the orphan Jimmy Bean manners, as she immediately is aware that "This was not a nice boy" (80). Heidi befriends a simple rural lad, Peter, who because of his poverty has not been educated (his grandmother is blind, his mother trying to eke out a meager existence). Ultimately, because of her emotional connection to Peter through her love of nature (the mountain landscape, his goats), Heidi can reach him. Believing in the natural ability to learn after her own success in Frankfurt, Heidi teaches Peter to read upon her return to the alm, something that the village schoolteacher was unable to do. Peter later becomes jealous of

Heidi's friendship with the crippled city girl, who comes to visit Heidi in the mountains in an effort to restore her health. Seeing Clara as a rival for Heidi's affection, Peter pushes her wheelchair off the cliff; and though this gesture finally liberates Clara from the chair, because she is forced to take a risk and be self-reliant, it is one of the darker moments of the book. Peter goes through a traumatizing period of self-hatred before he is brought back into harmony with the community. Clearly, the boy's presence is seen as threatening to the sisterhood that exists between the two girls in *Heidi*. And his symbolic paralysis runs deeper than Clara's, until he is restored to the community and accepts the education that Heidi brings to him.

Both Pollyanna and Heidi need to deal in a maternal way with the wildness and threatening qualities of the boys they would civilize. When Pollyanna meets Jimmy, he is surly—with good cause—and refuses to behave nicely for the still hard-hearted, not yet transformed Aunt Polly. Indeed, he tries to pretend that he is not looking for a home— as he coolly whittles away at a small stick (79–80). From a Freudian perspective, he tries to shut Pollyanna's kindness out with his phallic self-centeredness. When threatened by her overtures of kindness, he does not know how to react: "The boy stirred restlessly, gave her a surprised look, and began to whittle again at his stick, with the dull, broken-bladed knife in his hand" (80). Initially, he resists Pollyanna's overtures of kindness as he resorts to the mechanical whittling and as he hides behind his weapon. But Pollyanna's amiability is disarming, and finally he cannot resist admitting that he is looking for a real home, with a real mother, "I'd like a home—jest a common one, ye know, with a mother in it, instead of a Matron" (81). He frames his search for a home in terms of a masculine activity, as hunting. Since his father has died, he has resorted to "hunting" for a home: "So I'm a huntin' now. I've tried four houses, but—they didn't want me—though I said I expected ter work, 'course" (81). But Jimmy, the boy with ambitions of working, is rejected by all: by the Ladies' Aiders who prefer the image of a helpless boy in India, the object they could colonize, and even by Aunt Polly, who has not yet enjoyed the softening effect of Pollyanna's presence. Pollyanna raves about her Aunt Polly's kindness, suggesting that she will adopt him as she has adopted her: "Why, my Aunt Polly is the nicest lady in the world—now that my mama has gone to be a Heaven angel" (82). Thinking in these maternal terms, Pollyanna tries to offer the gift of motherhood to the poor orphan Jimmy. Even when he fantasizes about having a mother in Aunt Polly, he does reclaim that original swaggering pose Pollyanna detected in him upon their first encounter: "I'd work,

ye know, an' I'm real strong" (82). He has already been indoctrinated to
think that he cannot simply be a child but that he is a little man—that
he must impose his physical self upon the world of work. When Aunt
Polly describe him as a "ragged little beggar," the boy reclaims pride and
dignity by thinking in grown-up terms of masculine worth: "I ain't a
beggar, marm, an' I don't want nothin' o you. I was cal'latin' ter work, of
course, for my board an' keep" (84). When Pollyanna insists upon pleading her case to the Ladies' Aid Society to find Jimmy a home, he reminds
her to tell them, "'I'd work—don't forget ter say that'" (86).

Pollyanna later softens him by actually finding a home for him with
Mr. Pendleton, but she also learns of the hypocrisy in the community who
refuse to mother this wayward child. And the energies of the book are
focused on finding a simple, natural home. Even the reclusive Mr. Pendleton, who finally does take in Jimmy when he realizes he cannot adopt
Pollyanna, unwittingly frames the conflict of the book for so many village
dwellers as having a house, but not a home. He laments that "his great
grey pile of stone has been a house—never a home"; he then insists that
"'It takes a woman's hand and heart, or a child's presence, to make a home'"
(140). As many ecofeminists have noted, the culture of caring is reflective
of ecofeminist thinking.[8]

Pollyanna, through her ease in nature, finds herself a home and then
creates that feeling for the adults who are out of touch with their inner
child. Her success is not just with Aunt Polly, but also with those whose
hearts she touches on visits to their houses or in natural landscapes. Thus,
on her first visit to the bedridden, grumpy Mrs. Snow, Pollyanna's cheerful and disarming manner has the invalid sit upright in bed for the first
time in ages, surprising her daughter, Milly. Moreover, Mrs. Snow allows
Pollyanna to let the light in; Milly is surprised that she finds the curtain
up, for the first time in ages. Once again, Pollyanna literally is able to bring
a breath of fresh air to stuffy houses. In anticipating Mrs. Snow's eccentric
ways, Pollyanna is able to fulfill her needs by bringing to her, one day, lamb
broth, chicken, and calf's-foot jelly, all of the foods the old lady says she
craves, on one day or another. In this manner, she nurtures on both the
physical and spiritual level.

Pollyanna's alliance with nature, and her ability to cure others through
her vital connection to nature, is best exemplified in Pendleton Woods—
in two of her encounters with venerable citizens: old man Pendleton, the
bitter man who has trapped himself in his mansion, and then the frus-
trated minister, who reminds her of her father. It is telling that both men
have lost faith in humanity, and Pollyanna has the ability to restore it.

During one of the rare days on which she has no "sewing or cooking lesson" (93), Pollyanna enjoys a walk across the "green quiet of Pendleton Woods" and reflects upon her recent disappointment with the Ladies' Aiders, who have denied help to Jimmy Bean because of their preference for hosting "missionary teas" and helping children across the globe. Tellingly, it is the sight of the natural beauty that restores Pollyanna's faith in the goodness of humanity. Looking up to "the patches of vivid blue between the sunlit green of the tree-tops" (94), Pollyanna reflects upon the hypocrisy of the Ladies' Aiders and finds solace in the beauty of nature, even believing that Nature would teach the misguided ladies' society the meaning of true compassion: "if they were up here, I just reckon they'd change and take Jimmy Bean for their little boy, all right" (94). It is at that moment that she chances upon the barking dog, who ultimately leads her to Mr. Pendleton, who has taken a bad tumble in the forest. Pollyanna recognizes the dog as Pendleton's, and with her ability to communicate with animals, she is able to understand the dog's "whining and barking," which leads her to Pendleton that she may save him (95).

It is somewhat ironic that she meets the injured Mr. Pendleton, with his broken leg, at the moment she is thinking about her disappointment in securing a home for Jimmy at the Ladies' Aid Society meeting, for Pendleton also has a false sense of charity, as he uses his money to take trips to exotic global locations and to purchase a touch of the exotic with sumptuous artifacts he finds in foreign markets. (Yet, he too, will later learn, after Pollyanna's accident, the true meaning of home and charitable giving in his later adoption of Jimmy.) At this juncture, she is exhorted to return to Pendleton's mansion to call Dr. Thomas Chilton for help—and she finds a house filled with books and "dust, dust, dust" (98), this in strange contrast to the spot in the forest where Pendleton lies injured. Upon her return to the forest, Pollyanna assures him that the doctor will be there shortly. When Pendleton apologizes for his brusque manner, Pollyanna asserts that although he might be "cross outside," he is not "cross inside" (98)—taking the proof from the kind manner in which he treats his dog and explaining, "how dogs and cats know the insides of folks better than other folks do" (98). As Pollyanna cradles old man Pendleton's head and holds his hand, the dog all the while at his side, she seems blessed by nature, much in the vein of Romantic children who find solace in nature (even the implike Pearl in *The Scarlet Letter*). Not only can Pollyanna speak to animals, but they feel safe in her presence: "A bird alighted fearlessly within reach of her hand, and a squirrel whisked his busy tail on a tree-branch almost under her nose" (99).

After this episode, the injured Pendleton, through frequent visits from Pollyanna, begins the long process of healing, which brings him to a true conversion moment, one that permits him to see the follies of reckless spending for exotic baubles and the benefits of thinking about charity beginning at home. Indeed, the false connection of the Ladies' Aiders, with their displaced maternity, to the "little India boys" (154) is associated in Pollyanna's mind to Mr. Pendleton's hoarding of exotic objects. She erroneously muses, at one point, that he is hoarding his "gold pieces" to send to the "heathen" poor (155). In Pollyanna's mind, the lure of the exotic has tainted both the Ladies' Aiders and Mr. Pendleton, and the proselytizing interests of both converge. Mr. Pendleton entertains her by showing him his special curios he has collected as a tourist to distant lands, and Pollyanna almost becomes an armchair traveler in the process, feeling seduced by the collection: "The box was full of treasures—curios that John Pendleton had picked up in years of travel—and concerning each there was some entertaining story, whether it were a set of exquisitely carved chessmen from China, or a little jade idol from India" (127).

This is perhaps Pollyanna's darkest moment, as she takes on the Western prejudice about the meaning of the jade idol by concluding that it might be "better to take a little boy in India to bring up—one that didn't know any more than to think that God was in that doll-thing—than it would be to take Jimmy Bean, a little boy who knows God is up in the sky" (127). True, Pollyanna knows that the Ladies' Aiders are misguided in their desire to proselytize the "heathen" other, and she knows, too, that Pendleton filling his rooms with these foreign curios and books will not create the home he desires.[9] If Pollyanna momentarily revels in the product of imperialistic trade or plundering, it is not necessarily for her sake but for others: she fancies giving some of these souvenirs "to Aunt Polly and Mrs Snow and—lots of folks" (136). But she still remains most dazzled by natural occurrences, by the sun glinting through the thermometer at Pendleton's window and creating a rainbow on his pillow. She is even more seduced by the prisms he permits her to attach to the window, which transform his "dreary" room into a "fairyland" and illuminate her with rainbow light, a natural but magical phenomenon that clearly delights her (136).

Several chapters after Pollyanna's encounter with Mr. Pendleton in his woods, and on the same day she brings comfort to Pendleton with talk of the possibilities of his adopting the homeless Jimmy, she has another life-altering encounter with a similarly misguided town venerable who has lost his faith. "Revd Paul Ford was sick at heart" (156) because of the false priorities among those in his congregation, specifically the disruptive gossip of Ladies' Aiders, feuding between two of his deacons, bickering among a jealous choir, squabbles among the Christian Endeavor society, and the resignation of several staff members of his Sunday school. After a year of such discord, the Reverend Ford, at his wits' end, "climbed the hill and entered the Pendleton Woods, hoping that the hushed beauty of God's out-of-doors would still the tumult that His children of men had wrought" (156). Although the reverend starts practicing a sermon he'd written to reveal his congregation's shortcomings, he realizes the negative message about the Pharisees' hypocrisy would only silence his parishioners: his resounding tone simply hushes "the birds and squirrels . . . into awed silence" (158). The clergyman tearfully flings himself on the ground.

Pollyanna appears at that moment to save the day, glad that the pastor has not broken a leg like Mr. Pendleton. She intuits the secret of his sorrow: a non-compliant and less than enthusiastic congregation, a source of despair that afflicted her recently deceased missionary father. The sudden appearance of Pollyanna transforms Reverend Ford's manner of perceiving nature and people. While Pollyanna takes in the beauty of nature, the minister gazes "at a leaf on the ground a little distance away—and it was not even a pretty leaf. It was brown and dead" (159). Seeing this, Pollyanna "felt vaguely sorry for him" (159). Pollyanna, who has the natural gift of sympathy, intuits his problem and tells him the story of her father's frustration as a minister out West, recommending that he consult the biblical "rejoicing texts" her father would read—and also indulge in the glad game. Reverend Ford returns to his home, renewed in this faith in people, and embarks on writing a sermon that will make his congregation "glad" to do the right things (163). The resulting sermon, of course, is successful, but not as successful as Pollyanna's accident, which will transform all the bickering and jaded neighbors. Reverend Ford is a good type of minister, not like the proselytizing minister who initially tries to convert Heidi's grandfather by condemning him to a life of isolation if he does not repent of mistakes made in his youth. As both Heidi and Pollyanna know, pessimism does not inspire.

Curiously, Dr. Chilton, despite his disappointment in his former love for Pollyanna's aunt, is the villager who immediately appreciates the value of Pollyanna's optimism. He sees how she can easily cure the depression and isolation of the neighbors, and "prescribes" her as a cure for Mr. Pendleton. As the only man of conviction and optimism in the text, at least before Pollyanna's arrival, Dr. Chilton is the type of country doctor who readily makes friends among his patients. His open-mindedness, integrity, and homespun manner of healing bring a modicum of happiness to the town. But, like Mr. Pendleton, he too is missing "a woman's hand and heart, or a child's presence to make a home" (165), as Pollyanna intuits. Tellingly, after Pollyanna's accident, it is Dr. Chilton with his homespun ways who can finally locate a doctor, a college friend of his, who has cured someone of a similar paralysis in a neighboring village. It is clear that Aunt Polly's Dr. Warren has not been able to help Pollyanna, nor can Dr. Mead, the specialist from New York. Significantly, Dr. Warren drives a car, and immediately after Pollyanna's accident, we hear "Dr Warren was hurrying as fast as another motor car could bring him" to care for her (168). Dr. Chilton, who is closer to nature and whom Pollyanna dubs "her doctor" throughout the entire ordeal (187), still drives a horse-drawn gig, in which Pollyanna enjoys riding (113–15). And it is Dr. Chilton who finds a doctor who can cure Pollyanna.

Both *Heidi* and *Pollyanna* have underlying Gothic plots—related to the horrors of urbanization—as part of the change that brings about catastrophe. In *Heidi*, the young rural girl becomes a veritable ghost in the bourgeois Sesemann household, where the haughty servant, Fräulein Rottenmeier, wants to rename Heidi because her name is not Christian enough, calls her by her middle name, Adelaide, and so robs her of an identity. Gradually becoming paler and sick in spirit, Heidi actually becomes the ghost of the household, in chapter 12, "The Ghost in the House," as she sleepwalks many nights, startling the servants. Clara's father, Herr Sesemann, the voice of rationality, returns from a business trip and tries to make sense of the ghostly intrusion, which Fräulein Rottenmeier blames on some abominable behavior of his ancestors: "what is going on in the house points to some terrible thing that has taken place in the past and been concealed" (155). Partially to prove her wrong, Herr Sesemann calls his wise friend, the medical doctor, to help him solve the mystery. Both stay up all night, waiting and are terrified to see a specter: "The moonlight was shining in through the open door and fell on a white figure standing motionless in the doorway" (158). The specter turns out to be none other than the sleepwalking Heidi "in her little white nightgown," who, startled by the men's presence and terrified by the men's revolvers, looks at them with "wild eyes" and trembles "from head to foot, like a leaf in the wind" (159). Heidi explains to the wise doctor that she is always trying to return to the mountains of her Grandfather's house in her dreams, and the doctor rightly diagnoses the problem of the sleepwalking Heidi who is stuck in the urban landscape: "the child is consumed with homesickness to such an extent that she is nearly a skeleton already, and soon will be quite one" if she remains in Frankfurt. Sounding much like the wise doctor in

Pollyanna, the Frankfurt doctor prescribes a return to the countryside for Heidi, as she is "not one to be cured with pills and powders" (161). The good doctor ends up retreating to the countryside with Heidi and providing for her and her grandfather, in essence becoming Heidi's surrogate father in the final chapter (comparable to the conclusion in *Pollyanna*, where Dr. Chilton becomes Pollyanna's surrogate father after his marriage to Aunt Polly).

The randomness of the offstage car accident that almost paralyzes Pollyanna for life is emblematic of all that is shockingly destructive and devastating in the early twentieth century.[10] Pollyanna, returning from school, crosses the road "at an apparently safe distance in front of a swiftly approaching motor car" (167), and then the horrifying accident occurs, with the driver leaving the scene of the accident. Many contemporary newspaper articles attest to the dangers of automobiles—to horses and to people—and to the nuisance of smells and sounds associated with such vehicles. One editorial in 1904 states the problem succinctly: "it is not surprising that a very general hostility to automobiles is found in the country districts and suburbs of cities; and this is aggravated by the attempts, often successful, of automobilists to escape from the officers of the law by putting on greater speed." The short editorial goes on to lament the sad situation where a car struck and killed an old man, but "the automobile driver rushed away and is unknown to this day,"[11] a situation which actually befalls Pollyanna. Another author, a college professor attempting to show the positive side of driving an automobile, does agree that common courtesy and respect for life is needed: "No one who is not keenly appreciative of the strength, and power for evil, of an uncontrolled auto, and no one who is not sure of his own self-control, should ever own or drive an automobile."[12] Sounding like a modern defense of owning weaponry, this critic points to common sense, self-control, and respect for others as his guiding principles as a driver. In some ways, the message of *Pollyanna* says the same.

Pollyanna's Gothic episode revolves around the automobile accident. The strikingly short title of chapter 23, "An Accident," is in keeping with the discord of the chapter. We hear abruptly that it was "the last day of October that the accident occurred" in the narrative of *Pollyanna* (167). We don't need a rural Gothic Halloween during this time period to set a horrifying mood, but it is interesting that Porter makes that the day of the accident. More ghoulish than a spirit who would whisk Pollyanna away is the anonymous and "swiftly approaching motor car" (recalling the newspaper editorial, above) which strikes her down without stopping. Like the Modernist malady in *The Great Gatsby* (1925) embodied in the tragic car accident, the level of disconnectedness in the crash that injures Pollyanna is startling: "Just what happened, no one could seem to tell afterwards. Neither was there anyone found who could tell why it happened or who was to blame that it did happen" (167). Perhaps the most poignant moment of the accident scene occurs with the servant Nancy and the gardener Tom grieving in the garden outside Pollyanna's window. A sobbing Nancy laments the existence of automobiles: "'I always hated the evil-smellin' things, anyhow—I did, I did!'" (168); and she describes Pollyanna's paralysis, somberly, "And now she—she can't—drat that automobile" (194). Tom seconds her curse by associating the automobile with the devil and with disease: "She's hurt infernally, all right—plague take that automobile" (169). The last chapter has Pollyanna in rehabilitation eagerly looking forward to returning home to her Aunt Polly and new uncle (Dr. Chilton, amply rewarded for his goodness) and swearing off automobiles: "I don't think I shall ever want to ride anywhere any more. It will be so good just to walk" (227). Of course, the physical paralysis is merely a sign of the town's erstwhile emotional paralysis, and this book, like Johanna Spyri's *Heidi*, offers a cautionary tale to readers who would neglect their natural abilities for the artificial contrivances of modern civilization and, with that, a humanistic connection to all that is vital to the wellbeing of a community.

Notes

1. Case in point: Joe Sutliff Sanders's exhaustive recent (and otherwise compelling) study of orphan girls, *Disciplining Girls*, makes no mention of *Heidi*. Alice Mills compares Pollyanna to *Anne of Green Gables* and *Rebecca of Sunnybrook* Farm but leaves out the orphan aspect! She describes the plot as "a poor girl transforming the lives of all the unhappy people among whom she comes to live, winning hearts with her unspoiled innocence" (88). It is ironic that contemporary literary critics leave out the Heidi equation. During the early twentieth century, many booklists compiled in U.S. magazines, especially children's magazines, saw *Heidi* as a great favorite, and then shortly after, *Pollyanna* as well. They often followed *Little Women*, as, for example, in an April 7, 1927, compilation of favorite American girls' books, where *Little Women* placed first, followed by (in order) *Heidi* and *Black Beauty*.

2. Heidi actually has two grandmother figures—the goatherd Peter's blind grandmother, who evokes Heidi's sympathy, and Clara's good and righteous grandmother, who teaches her how to read in the Sesemann household. This will fulfill Heidi's promise to the good old grandmother on the alm, where she will eventually help educate Peter.

3. Several critics have discussed the sentimentality of the individual texts. (I have not found studies that connect both texts.) Phyllis Bixler Koppes feels that Spyri's "Heidi is

unmistakably flawed by sentimentality and didacticism" (71). Oddly enough, Koppes feels that Heidi is "exemplary rather than typical" (170) and claims she is unable to understand why Clara and Peter cannot attain the sentimental apotheosis or redemption associated with Heidi; but she neglects the entire orphan dimension (270). Though she does not present an ecofeminist approach, she does assert that Heidi "combines the best qualities of Art and Nature" (170), inadvertently merging the binaries that ecofeminists also try to combine. Alice Mills, writing about Pollyanna, distrusts the sentimentality: "Pollyanna is both victim and expert manipulator, under the guise of the innocently loving child" (103). Joe Sutliff Sanders is cynical about sentimental portrayals of orphan girls in the Progressive era, suggesting that such girl protagonists no longer have to sacrifice as completely as they did at the height of sentimental writing in the mid-nineteenth century. Although the girls still have to help improve the lives of adults around them, "a duty that was their chief responsibility in sentimental novels," the "performance of these duties in the Progressive era provides . . . material and social comfort for the girls themselves" ("Spinning Sympathy" 42). I do not support Sanders's suggestion that Pollyanna's goodness stems from the desire for monetary rewards; she is not mercenary.

4. Motherhood becomes problematic from an ecofeminist perspective, as earlier studies essentialized the natural and maternal. Previously, feminists might have associated motherhood with nature, and certainly Romantics might have done that, but as Gretchen T. Legler writes, "Ecofeminists . . . argue that constructions of nature as female (as mother/virgin) are essential . . . to the maintenance of hierarchical ways of thinking that justify the oppression of various 'others' in patriarchal culture by ranking them 'closer to nature'" (228). Though I am not equating maternal with natural, I am suggesting that the culture of compassion promoted by ecofeminists might promote the image of sentimental and sympathetic motherhood, which extended the notion of home to the dispossessed. Naomi Wood reminds readers that Romantic writers such as Rousseau and Wordsworth depicted Nature "as the child mother or nurse, an influence that works for the good and well-being of the child" (198). However, she then proceeds to look at a more baneful mother image in nature in such fantasy writers as Hans Christian Andersen and Charles Kingsley. Maude Hines and John Stephens write about the Romantic tendency to equate nature with children. Stephens suggests that the recent paradigm in children's literature is not domination over nature, but "an attitude of caring, wonder and understanding of the natural world" (41). Though he applies his idea to recent children's literature, it can also be applied to Pollyanna. Most ecopedagogical approaches to children's literature focus on contemporary literature.

5. Although early feminist critics, using binary constructions, maintained that nature was allied with the feminine or the maternal, recent ecofeminist critics refute the notion that caring for the universe is gender-specific and explain that binary patriarchal constructs that show antagonism between us/them and uphold a nature/civilization paradigm wreak havoc not simply on the environment but inevitably on oppressed groups of people (women, working class, impoverished, racial minorities, etc.). Ecofeminist criticism, then, has become more political, and most ecofeminists refer to Karen Warren's pioneering work in ecofeminist theory—and most now focus on a culture of caring as part of the equation. Warren maintains that "an ecofeminist ethic is an inclusivist ethic

that grows out of and reflects the diversity of perspectives of women and other Others. It emerges from the voices of those who experience disproportionately the harmful destruction of nonhuman nature" (Ecofeminist Philosophy 99). Greta Gaard asserts that "ecofeminists tend to believe hierarchy takes place as a result of the self/other opposition" ("Living Interconnections" 3). In a more fleshed out definition, Gaard explains that "the position and treatment of women, animals, and nature are not separable" and she maintains that "ecofeminists make connections among not just sexism, speciesism, the oppression of nature but also other forms of social injustice—racism, classism, heterosexism, ageism, ableism, and colonialism—as part of western culture's assault on nature" ("Children's Environmental Literature" 323). The ensuing "logic of domination" involves alienation, hierarchy, and domination (323). Janis Birkeland asserts that "the very essence of ecofeminism is its challenge to the presumed necessity of power relationships. It is about changing from a morality based on 'power over' to one based on reciprocity and responsibility" (19). Christopher Cohoon suggests that French feminist Luce Irigaray's critique of the patriarchal nature/culture dichotomy leads inevitably to a call to dismantle the system—to eliminate the traditional binary opposition that subordinates nature to culture—but also to reflect upon the positive aspects of nature in relationship to women (208).

6. Many recent critics of children's literature note how, from the late nineteenth century onward, children are increasingly encouraged to be kind and respectful toward their pets or to animals in general (see Menefee; Grier; Mason). Lori Gruen makes a case that women and animals have often been categorized together as inferior/submissive, and thus denied certain rights.

7. Significantly, later, after the accident, it is from the animals (and from natural objects) that Pollyanna draws some strength when she is left in seclusion: "Pollyanna petted the dog, smoothed the cat's sleek head, admired the flowers and ate the fruits and jellies that were sent to her" (185).

8. The ethic of care is a central tenet of ecofeminist thinking. Barbara Cook, analyzing the work of nature writer and philosopher Kathleen Dean Moore, asserts that an "environmental ethic of care" involves "a natural sense of caring for ourselves, our families, and our natural world" (39). Bryan Moore actually uses the term "ecocentrism" to sound more inclusive: "Ecocentrism suggests an egalitarian agenda. For this reason, it is inextricably connected to feminism, in context often called ecofeminism, because both women and land communities have been exploited by a destructive, patriarchal tradition. An ecocentric view will seek to redress the exploitation of minorities" (8). He also maintains that we will reevaluate our concept of religion and view the land and animals with increasing dignity. See also studies by Bloodhart and Swim and by Harvester and Blankinsop on how ecofeminism involves inclusionary practices.

9. Recently, post-colonial theory has called for "ecojustice." From the perspective of "environmental post-colonial criticism," the cultural imperialism of the West has oppressed minorities and destroyed natural landscapes. See Clark (129), and for a discussion of how women and non-Western people are oppressed, see the seminal study by Vandan Shiva.

10. The other Modernist image of discord and alienation in the text is the telephone, which is not used for real communication but to announce horrible events, like Mr. Pendleton's fall and Pollyanna's accident. Also, in chapter 10, Pollyanna is called away from Mrs. Snow's bedside, summoned by a telephone call from Aunt Polly whose message is that Pollyanna "hurry" for she had "some practising to make up before dark" (71). The telephone is seen as a real obstacle to communication throughout, as when an alienated Aunt Polly calls the Ladies' Aid Society that she cannot make the meeting on account of a headache—a meeting that is vital to little Jimmy's adoption. The automobile episode is especially sinister, as the discord and disconnectedness that Pollyanna originally saw in the community and then cured seems to require Pollyanna as a scapegoat figure that actually merges all classes and disparate groups. Many town pariahs and eccentrics appear at Aunt Polly's doorstep upon hearing of Pollyanna's accident. The Widow Benton, now wearing a cheery blue instead of her customary black, to express the newfound gladness Pollyanna brought her, speaks "of her grief and horror at the accident" (201). Likewise, the woman from the "wrong side of town," Mrs. Tom Payson, tells Aunt Polly how dear Pollyanna was to her and her children and how the accident has caused her and her husband to reevaluate the marriage—and to stay together for the sake of the family. So even as she is lying immobile, Pollyanna is able to bring up positive change for the community by making the voices of the downtrodden more inclusive.

11. "The Automobile Problem." *Watchman* 8.86 (September 1904): 36. American Periodical Series. Web. 20 August 2013.

12. A. J. Cook, "The Automobile Universal." *Outlook* 29 August 1909, 89:18, American Periodical Series, p. 988. 20 August 2013.

Works Cited

Birkleland, Janis. "Ecofeminism: Linking Theory and Practice." *Ecofeminism: Women, Animals, Nature.* Ed. Greta Gaard. Philadelphia: Temple UP, 1993. 13–59. Print.

Bloodhart, Brittany, and Janet K. Swim. "Equality, Harmony, and the Environment: An Ecofeminist Approach to Understanding the Role of Cultural Values on the Treatment of Women and Nature." *Ecopsychology* 2.3 (September 2010): 187–94. Web. 2 March 2012.

Büttner, Peter O., and Hans-Heino Ewers. "Arkadien in bedrohlicher Landschaft: Die Mehrfachcodierung der Schweizer Berge in Johanna Spyris *Heidi*-Romanen" (1880/81). *"Über alle Gipfeln": Bergmotive in der deutschsprachigen Literatur des 18. bis 21. Jahrhunderts.* Eds. Edward Bialek and Jan Pacholski. Dresden: Neisse, 2008. 12–28. Print.

Clark, Timothy. *The Cambridge Companion to Literature and the Environment.* New York: Cambridge UP, 2011. Print.

Cohoon, Christopher. "The Ecological Irigaray?" *Ecocritical Theory: New European Approaches.* Eds. Axel Goodbody and Kate Rigby. Charlottesville: U of Virginia P, 2011. 206–16. Print.

Cook, Barbara J. "Multifaceted Dialogues: Toward an Environmental Ethic of Care." *Women Writing Nature: A Feminist View.* Ed. Barbara J. Cook. New York: Lexington, 2008. 33–40. Print.

Gaard, Greta. "Children's Environmental Literature: From Ecocriticism to Ecopedagogy." *Neohelicon* 36.2 (2009): 321–34. *ProQuest.* Web. 2 March 2012.

——. "Living Interconnections with Animals and Nature." *Ecofeminism: Women, Animals, Nature.* Ed. Greta Gaard. Philadelphia: Temple UP, 1993. 1–12. Print.

Gresser, Anne-Marie. "De l'Alpe suisse au bestiaire fantastique: les animaux chez Johanna Spyri et Adelheid Duvanel." *L'Amour des Animaux dans le Monde Germanique.* Eds. Marc Cluet and Jean-Michel Pouget. Rennes: Presses Universitaires de Rennes, 2006. 191–200. Print.

Grier, Katherine C. *Pets in America: A History.* Chapel Hill: U of North Carolina P, 2006. Print.

Gruen, Lori. "Dismantling Oppression: An Analysis of the Connection between Women and Animals." *Ecofeminism: Women, Animals, Nature.* Ed. Greta Gaard. Philadelphia: Temple UP, 1993. 60–90. Print.

Harvester, Lara, and Sean Blenkinsop. "Environmental Education and Ecofeminist Pedagogy: Bridging the Environmental and the Social." *Canadian Journal of Environmental Education* 15 (2010): 120–34. Web. 18 March 2012.

Hines, Maude. "'He Made *Us* Very Much like the Flowers'": Human/Nature in Nineteenth-Century Anglo-American Children's Literature." *Wild Things: Children's Culture and Ecocriticism.* Eds. Sidney I. Dobrin and Kenneth B. Kidd. Detroit: Wayne State UP, 2004. 16–30. Print.

Koppes, Phyllis Bixler. "Spyri's Mountain Miracles: Exemplum and Romance in *Heidi.*" *Lion and the Unicorn: A Critical Journal of Children's Literature* 3.1 (1979): 62–73. Print.

Legler, Gretchen T. "Ecofeminist Literary Criticism." *Ecofeminism: Women, Culture, Nature.* Ed. Karen J. Warren. Bloomington: Indiana UP, 1997. 227–38. Print.

Mason, Jennifer. *Civilized Creatures: Urban Animals, Sentimental Culture, and American Literature, 1850–1900.* Baltimore: Johns Hopkins UP, 2005. Print.

Menefee, Joan. "Good Masters: Child-Animal Relationships in the Writings of Mark Twain and G. Stanley Hall." *Enterprising Youth: Social Values and Acculturation in Nineteenth-Century American Children's Literature.* Ed. Monika Elbert. New York: Routledge, 2008. 227–44. Print.

Mills, Alice. "*Pollyanna* and the Not So Glad Game." *Children's Literature* 27 (1999): 87–104. *ProQuest.* Web. 2 March 2012.

Moore, Bryan L. *Ecology and Literature: Ecocentric Personification from Antiquity to the Twenty-first Century.* New York: Palgrave Macmillan, 2008. Print.

Porter, Eleanor H. *Pollyanna.* 1913. New York: Oxford UP, 2011. Print.

Sanders, Joe Sutliff. "Spinning Sympathy: Orphan Girl Novels and the Sentimental Tradition." *Children's Literature Association Quarterly* 33.1 (2008): 41–61. *Project Muse.* Web. 12 March 2012.

——. *Disciplining Girls: Understanding the Origins of the Classic Orphan Girl Story.* Baltimore: Johns Hopkins UP, 2011. Print.

Shiva, Vandan. *Staying Alive: Women, Ecology, and Development.* 1988. New York: South End, 2010. Print.

Spyri, Johanna. *Heidi.* 1880. New York: Oxford UP, 2010. Print.

Stephens, John. "From Eden to Suburbia: Perspectives on the Natural World in Children's Literature." *Papers: Explorations into Children's Literature* 16.2 (2006): 40–45. Print.

Warren, Karen J. *Ecofeminist Philosophy: A Western Perspective on What It Is and Why It Matters.* New York: Rowman and Littlefield, 2000. Print.

———, ed. *Ecofeminism: Women, Culture, Nature.* Bloomington: Indiana UP, 1997. Print.

Part 2

IDEOLOGICAL *POLLYANNA*

6

The "veritable bugle-call": An Examination of *Pollyanna* through the Lens of Twentieth-Century Protestantism

ASHLEY N. REESE

> Paul Ford's sermon the next Sunday was a veritable bugle-call to the best that was in every man and woman and child that heard it. (196)

A Sentimental Reflection

Eleanor H. Porter's *Pollyanna* is a text that reflects the United States at a crossroads: the conservative 1800s had ended and the secularizing influence of the world wars was yet to come. The so-called Golden Age of Anglophone children's literature with its abundance of "quality" texts, written in the latter half of the nineteenth and the beginning of the twentieth centuries, was creating a rich foundation upon which children's novels could build. Children's books were no longer constricted to specific genres or certain religious or moral expectations, or at least not to the same extent as their predecessors, for example the March sisters' efforts to mimic the pilgrim's journey in an attempt to overcome their flaws in *Little Women*, first published in 1868. That said, literary texts frequently build upon their heritage, and *Pollyanna* is no exception.

The sentimental domestic genre, generally written with female readers in mind, was one that English author James Janeway's 1671 text *A Token for Children* had "[i]nadvertently [. . .] begotten" (Avery 34). Janeway's writings about thirteen children who lived godly, exemplary lives, and then died godly, inspiring deaths was widely available in America from the 1680s until the late nineteenth century. The text had profound impact on domestic fictions of the nineteenth century. His text was more overtly Christian than any following this tradition, as his protagonists are generally depicted either fervently discussing God or speaking to Him in prayer. The message to child readers is clear: in order to avoid burning in hell, one must actively try to live in a way that pleases God.

This tradition resurrected itself in the American domestic fiction of which *Pollyanna* is part. Nineteenth-century novels are "filled with cohorts of pious little girls" (34), from Beth March who is "too good" for this world, to Katy Carr in *What Katy Did*, who is foolhardy and tomboyish and, when an accident leaves her crippled, must then learn to be the patient "angel of the house" (Foster and Simons 94, 112). These domestic novels generally promote Christianity without implementing the threat of hellfire, or forcing the child protagonists to die in order to keep them in a state of childhood innocence. While Janeway's Puritan Christianity focuses on the sinful nature of people, in particular children, these domestic novels often feature a protagonist who is either already angelic, following the Romantic tradition, or who achieves such godliness through the course of the novel. Similarly to these domestic novels' heroines, the eponymous Pollyanna Whittier leads a holy life. Like the protagonists of Janeway's heritage, Pollyanna inspires those around her with her insistence on seeing the bright side of any situation. In contrast to heroines such as Katy whose illnesses affect themselves alone, and much more like the protagonists in *A Token*, Pollyanna's accident which leaves her crippled is not so much for her own sake, but, instead, inspires those around her to convert to a different lifestyle. Despite this resemblance to Janeway's text, she remains a more modern heroine than Beth or Katy and, arguably, represents the end of this traditional children's genre of godly girls' stories (Sanders 52).

Peter Hunt observes that the "great difference in *Pollyanna* from its predecessors in the nineteenth century is that it is taking on the religiously self-righteous . . . rather than colluding with them" (207). Though she may be considered saccharine, Pollyanna's gladness profoundly sets her apart from the religious heroines before her; for example, the language of the glad game, the crux of the novel, excludes any biblical references. Hunt, however, goes on to state that "[t]his is a secular innocence, not simply a general critique of adult pessimism" (207).

Seizing on this notion of Pollyanna as a departure from the heroines before her, I read Pollyanna as a socially engaged heroine but one who, contrary to Hunt's proposition, is a decidedly religious figure. While *Pollyanna* is more covertly Christian than other heroines of this sentimental genre, deviating from the typical protagonist's explicit engagement with prayer and biblical teachings in an effort to become a better woman, the text not only reflects the next step in the evolution of the domestic genre, but also mirrors the religious attitudes and debates of its time, emerging as a piece of social and religious commentary in a time of extreme transformation in America, from Puritanical religious judgments to that of a more socially aware faith. Similarly, the 1960 Disney film provides a point of comparison and departure from Porter's novel, with the film continuing to promote a glad game that influences church and community while promoting a strong Americanism that almost overpowers the Christianity of Porter's novel.

Protestantism at the "Turn of the Century": The Social Gospel

At the beginning of the twentieth century, explicit reference to Christianity in children's books was sinking into the assumed background culture constructed within the texts, thereby reflecting the society in which the books were written. As Robert Handy frames it, there was a simultaneous growth of secularism despite the "pervasive assumption that America was still a Christian nation" (118). The revelation of Charles Darwin's theory of evolution had shaken the world, and various strands within the Protestant denominations coped with it in different ways: some took offense to it and insisted that the Bible was the ultimate authority, others let it exist separately in a *laissez-faire* approach, and others incorporated it into their faith, considering both to be valid (Mead 174). As the theory of evolution shook many people's faith in principles they had once thought unquestionable, industrialization was becoming more prominent, bringing with it poor and unsanitary housing conditions for the working class. There was a heightened awareness of their plight due to the change in industry that brought the poor into the city where they lived closer to members of the upper class (Rodgers 24). Between these crises of faith and an awareness of the poor's plight, it was a natural progression that the "social gospel" should arise in the 1890s (Linder 13).

More than a theological or a specific institution's movement, the social gospel was a response by "the denominations looking for theological roots" (Mead 178). This movement went back to the basics of Christ's practical teachings: "feeding the hungry, clothing the naked, visiting the sick and imprisoned, and giving the cup of cold water for Christ's sake" (180). As Sidney Mead points out, "Perhaps it was never formulated in just this fashion, but one profound appeal of the social-gospel movement was that it made possible for many idealistic Americans' continued belief in Christianity if only 'for the work's sake'" (180). These ideas can be seen within *Pollyanna*. Pollyanna does good, spending her days visiting the sick and poor and bitter, very rarely engaging directly with actual theology. She is glad, most likely because of the "rejoicing texts," but the narrator does not attribute her optimism to time spent reading these passages from the Bible or praying (192). Pollyanna pleads to her aunt to be allowed "just to—to live" during her summer vacation, and she spends that free time performing what contemporary readers would have recognized as "Christian acts" (51). The leaders of the social gospel were quick to criticize the prevalent evangelical bent of Christianity, insisting that it was too individualistic, too focused on an individual's purity, as well as too "otherworldly" in its emphasis on converting people so that they might go to heaven rather than taking care of their well-being while on Earth (Marsden 312). *Pollyanna* does not fall into this trap, with only a brief mention of heaven in the context of where Pollyanna's parents now "live" and almost no mention of an individual's salvation, leading to the conclusion that it is indeed a social gospel text.

This form of Christianity was also in some ways a response to what commentators have called the Gilded Age of the latter half of the nineteenth century. During the Gilded Age, wealth was viewed as a blessing from God, and its pursuit was a top priority. Business owners were less concerned with how their workers were treated and more concerned with how much money their enterprises were making (Marsden 280). The social gospel focused its efforts on what these businessmen chose to overlook: the impoverished workers living in the slums. Porter's criticism of the negative attitudes held by some of the upper class toward helping those less fortunate is taken a step further in her sequel *Pollyanna Grows Up*, in which Pollyanna frequently expresses frustration at the wealthy's lack of engagement or assistance to the poor living in Boston, where she spends the first part of the text. Within *Pollyanna*, the parallel is drawn using Aunt Polly, who is wealthy, not a businesswoman but certainly an embodiment of the upper class. Pollyanna, the prime example of the social gospel, is juxtaposed with her aunt. Polly declares to her inquiring niece that she is not "sinfully proud" of the gifts "that the Lord has seen fit to bestow upon me, . . . certainly not of *riches!*" (25). Thus, Aunt Polly, like the businessmen of the Gilded Age, attributes her wealth to God. She generally does what is morally right, but always out of a sense of duty or obligation, begrudgingly, in stark contrast to her niece, who does right simply because she wants to. Aunt Polly does give to charity, through the Ladies' Aid Society and by providing meals weekly to Mrs. Snow, an invalid. All of her efforts to help the poor are done without a sense of joy, leading Pollyanna to proclaim, "Aunt Polly, please, . . . isn't there any way you can be glad about all that—duty business?" (52).

Ultimately, it is only through Pollyanna that her aunt becomes aware of and even introduced to some of the castoffs of society, for example Mrs. Payson, an impoverished woman of ill repute who comes to see Polly regarding Pollyanna's health at the end of the novel. Mrs. Payson resembles the woman who washes Christ's feet with her tears and perfume in the Gospel of Luke. Like Mrs. Payson, she is woman with a bad reputation, and the Pharisee Simon looks down on Christ for allowing her to touch him. The appearance of Mrs. Payson alludes to Pollyanna's Christ-like acceptance of all people regardless of their reputations or social status. By listening to Mrs. Payson's praise of Pollyanna, unlike Simon who is hostile to the woman, the beginning of a transformation is signaled, as Polly moves away from a Pharisee position. It is directly after this encounter that Polly learns of the glad game from Nancy. Whether or not Simon heeds Christ's teachings is not made clear in the Bible, but Polly is capable of being changed by Pollyanna's influence. Mead identifies indifference as a defining feature of the Gilded Age (of which Aunt Polly is a product), the overarching theme being that if all is well with the individual then all is well in general (154). This detachment characterizes Polly for most of the novel. In contrast, Pollyanna is actively bent on doing good as she ushers the social gospel into her town of Beldingsville, and eventually into the life of her aunt.

Doing God's Work at Home and Abroad:
The Missionary Motif

Along with the efforts to help the working poor through the social gospel, missionary work was also a growing part of turn-of-the-century American Christianity. The presence of missions is embedded throughout *Pollyanna*, and is central to the origins of Pollyanna's glad game. It is because her family relies on the donations of strangers through missionary barrels that Pollyanna does not receive the doll she requested, but rather crutches, and this inspires her father to teach her how to be glad in disheartening circumstances. The American missionary effort began in the early 1800s, birthed alongside the revival movement, but was interrupted mid-century by the Civil War. As the nation began to recuperate during the Reconstruction Era, from 1865–77, there was a resurgence in missionary work, both at home and abroad, that lasted well into the twentieth century. In fact, George Marsden refers to 1890–1920 as the "golden age of Protestant missions" (296). There were, at its height, 7,219 American Protestant missionaries abroad, and approximately $13 million voluntarily given by parishioners each year (Conn 750). This focus was a uniting force across the different Protestant denominations.

Additionally, as Christianity's effectiveness as a religion was reevaluated, Protestantism's claims to validity lay with its strong ties to nationalism. Many felt that to be Protestant was to be American, and vice versa; as Mead notes, "If a culture is the tangible form of a religion, in the United States that religion was Protestantism" (134). This perceived relationship was demonstrated in the American church's approach to foreign missions. Where previously missionaries had sought to win converts, now they also served as unofficial intermediaries for the United States' advancements in medicine, technology, and education (Mead 119). Missionaries were ushering in the spirit of the church and democracy, acting as ambassadors for what Horace Bushnell called "the brightest hope of the ages": America (qtd. in Conn 752). William Clebsch notes the unique position of the nation, as well as that of the church, as "new concern for the liberty and welfare of mankind arose out of America's new role, accepted soon after Reconstruction, as a muscular member of the family of nations," catapulting the American experiment to a place of "universal significance" (200). Simultaneously, the success of foreign missions led religious leaders to promote Christianity as a universalism (200). In the words of Clebsch, "If the perspective was half profane and half religious, the vision was none the less truly ecumenical" (200). And it was with this belief in the universalism of the American and Protestant dream that missionaries were sent to convert the "heathen."

There were domestic missionaries as well as foreign ones, of which Pollyanna's father represents the former. These ordinary ministers left their homes along with "civilization" and stable living conditions in the East, and traveled west to America's frontier. The original influx of these missionaries was at the beginning of the nineteenth century, but as more people moved west, more ministers were needed. Domestic missions, though recognized by the church, were not as glorified as those on foreign fronts, possibly because the poverty of uncivilized America was more familiar than an exotic land that those left behind could scarcely imagine. Presented in the novel as the Reverend Ford's reflection, these missions took place "in a little Western town with a missionary minister who was poor, sick, worried, and almost alone in the world" (194). Aunt Polly's dislike of Pollyanna's father is clear, as she goes so far as to forbid Pollyanna from referring to him in her presence. At the beginning of the novel we are told that Mr. Whittier, with his "young head full of youth's ideals and enthusiasm, and a heart full of love," had been chosen over the older man of wealth preferred by the Harrington family (5). Pollyanna's mother was then disowned, leaving a rift between the two families. This scenario, while providing a convenient storyline for an orphan girl to return east to her wealthy maiden aunt, also reflects the then widespread opinion of domestic missions. And it is this attitude toward helping those locally that is criticized and transformed in the process of the novel.

The most compelling engagement with mission work in the novel occurs in the storyline of Jimmy Bean, an orphan Pollyanna befriends. He desires a home, complete with "folks" who care about him (98). Pollyanna is certain that her aunt will take him in just as she took in Pollyanna; however, much to Pollyanna and Jimmy's disappointment, Aunt Polly refuses to adopt any "ragged little beggars from the street" (101). Pollyanna then decides to bring his plight before the local Ladies' Aid Society, the same organization that helped her prior to her move east. Each member refuses, much as Aunt Polly had, to take the boy into her home. One woman suggests that the society offer their charity donation to help raise the boy, but it is soon concluded that their efforts to assist a local child would not be recognized: it "sounded almost as if they did not care at all what the money did, so long as the sum opposite the name of their society in a certain 'report' 'headed the list'" (111). It would appear that, for these women, giving to foreign missions had greater appeal, more glamour, but most importantly, received higher recognition.

That these women do not care for the child in need right before them, but only for those they will never see, is ironic and reflects the hypocrisy of the Pharisees of Christ's time—referenced by the minister of Beldingsville in his sermon text—who were criticized for doing good only when others were around to witness it and praise them (Spurgeon 350). This is not a direct criticism of foreign missions, nor does it relay the message that wanting to help the less fortunate abroad is a bad thing—as Pollyanna asserts, "'[n]ot that but it's good, of course to send money to the heathen, and I shouldn't want 'em not to send some there'" (101). Rather, its message becomes that those nearby are just as important as those overseas. Pollyanna notes that the Ladies' Aid "acted as if little boys *here* weren't any account—only little boys 'way off. I should *think*, though, they'd rather see Jimmy Bean grow—than just a report!" (101).

In a strong contrast to the desire to do global good for the sake of praise, all of Pollyanna's transformative actions lead people to focus their attention on their neighbors and the citizens of their hometown. For example, Pollyanna smoothens the relationships the embittered Mrs. Snow has with those who help her, and even convinces the invalid woman to contribute to the cause of doing good for others—Mrs. Snow begins to use her time to knit "baby blankets for fairs and hospitals" (239). This transformation simultaneously reflects the spirit of the social gospel movement and serves as a pointed reminder that foreign countries are not the only places containing people in need. If missionary work at its core is more than the spreading of democracy and American values, then it should occur in America's own backyard, in contemporary readers' own backyards.

Pollyanna's domestic missionary work is more evident in her search for a home for Jimmy Bean. She broaches the topic to her friend, Mr. Pendleton, whom she initially assumed was a missionary himself, because Nancy tells her that:

> "Some years [Mr. Pendleton] jest travels, week in and week out, and it's always in heathen countries—Egypt and Asia and the desert of Sarah you know."
> "Oh, a missionary," nodded Pollyanna. (79)

That Pollyanna assumes Mr. Pendleton to be a missionary demonstrates more than an innocent, childish view of the world. It reveals the prominence of this movement as a motif within the novel. Mr. Pendleton is none other than the suitor her mother rejected for Pollyanna's missionary father. Since that rejection, he has become a recluse, separating himself from the outside world. When he meets Pollyanna, he asks her to live with him as his little girl. She also refuses, mimicking her mother's decision. Pollyanna's rejection, however, forces Mr. Pendleton out of his bitter cycle. Rather than retreating from the world once more, Pollyanna's influence and injury transform Mr. Pendleton's outlook on life, and he chooses to do what he can for another child: he adopts Jimmy Bean. By opening his home and heart to a boy in need, Mr. Pendleton comes to resemble the domestic missionary with whom Pollyanna's mother fell in love, while also becoming the man Pollyanna originally assumed him to be.

"[I]f 'twasn't for the rejoicing texts": The Biblical Passages

Although the whole text of *Pollyanna* is filled with religious undertones, the only biblical quotes in the novel occur in the chapter describing the encounter between Pollyanna and Reverend Ford, the local minister. When Pollyanna comes across him in a field, he is "sick at heart," troubled by his congregation's tendencies of "wrangling, backbiting, scandal, and jealousy" (187). After trying numerous approaches to change, he has decided to deliver a "hellfire and brimstone" sermon, using Matthew 23:14: "But woe unto you, scribes and Pharisees, hypocrites! for ye devour widows' houses, and for a pretence make long prayer; therefore ye shall receive the greater damnation" (*King James Version*). This passage is from a larger sermon Christ gives to the Pharisees in the last week of his life. In it he directs his wrath toward those religious leaders, or "false teachers," who guide astray their followers, the people Christ has come to save (Spurgeon 349).

There is a clear resemblance between this chastisement and the hypocrisy of the Ladies' Aid in wanting to give where their efforts would receive the most acclaim. Charles Spurgeon, in his commentary on Matthew, published twenty years before *Pollyanna*, states that the Pharisees in this particular text care more about how people rather than God view them. Verse 13 even chastises the "hypocrites" because "ye shut up the kingdom of heaven against men; for ye neither go in yourselves, neither suffer ye them that are entering to go in" (Matthew 23:13). Although the Ladies' Aid members' decision to refrain from helping Jimmy Bean does not doom the young boy to lead a life apart from the church, the social gospel does interweave the two ways of being good Christians. By helping the poor, those in need might be converted to Christianity. Finally, the last verse in this passage warns the Pharisees who have followed the scruples of the law by paying the tithe, 10 percent of their earnings, to the temple, for even the spices they purchase, but who then have "omitted the weightier matters of the law, judgment, mercy and faith; these ought ye to have done, and not to leave the other undone" (Matthew 23:23). In many ways, Aunt Polly's acts of "duty" mirror those of the Pharisees, doing only what is expected of her and neglecting any sort of mercy toward those whom she is helping.

John Kilgallen notes that Christ's major complaint against the religious leaders "is their absolute misjudgment of what is pleasing to God" (186). Whether the Ladies' Aid Society and Aunt Polly attempt to please God with their actions is unclear, and it is similarly never stated that this is Pollyanna's motivation per se. Reverend Ford's choice of this text, however, stems from his observations of the congregation, through various other occurrences that are recounted—strife within the choir and the resignation of several leaders of the Sunday school, among others—which have failed to actually please God, or at the very least to comply with biblical teachings. This sermon text is presented as the last resort, as "the Reverend

Paul Ford understood very well that he (God's minister), the church, the town, and even Christianity itself was suffering" (188). Reverend Ford recognizes that these verses are a "bitter" and "fearful denunciation," but worries that this is the only step left to take (189).

Reverend Ford does not follow through with his plan to chastise the congregation because Pollyanna interrupts him while he is planning his sermon. Pollyanna arrives just when he begins to pray for guidance, making it seem that Pollyanna is indeed sent from God. In the course of their conversation, Pollyanna begins to tell him about the "rejoicing texts" to which her father clung when things in his congregation became challenging (192). Unwittingly, the little girl—who is the embodiment of the social gospel movement, along with the positivity brought by the Christian-like glad game—begins to transform the minister's way of thinking. Lois Keith posits that Pollyanna's "own faith in God and in human nature is unquestioning," and, in the same spirit, their conversation leaves the minister filled with hope and charitable thoughts (144).

The passage around which the Reverend ultimately decides to center his sermon is not one of woe and accusation but one of Pollyanna's "rejoicing texts": "'Be glad in the Lord and rejoice, ye righteous, and shout for joy all ye that are upright in heart'" (Psalms 32:11). Not only does this verse assume that the listeners are in fact righteous and striving to do good, but it is a part of one of the few psalms with the theme of penitence. Generally, a psalm is a "prayer, hymn, meditation on history, or exhortation," which reflects on God or on the gift and power of Scripture (Grogan 10); there are but a few that center on actively seeking forgiveness (85). The beginning of this psalm is pessimistic: "When I kept silent, / my bones wasted away / through my groaning all day long" (*New International Version*, Psalms 32:3).[1] The psalmist, traditionally believed to be the biblical King David, is weighed down by the guilt of sin, and it is only when he repents and begs God for forgiveness that he is able to rejoice. But more than rejoice, the author wants to teach others how to be righteous. There is a natural progression presented here: one recognizes that God is merciful, one feels guilt for sin, one asks God for forgiveness, after receiving it one teaches others of God's mercy, and then one can fully "shout for joy" (Psalms 32:11). All these layers of meaning are contained within Reverend Ford's new sermon text. Instead of preaching woe to those who lead others astray, he celebrates the joy that can be theirs if they are willing to spread the word. Repentance and sorrow, even instructing and teaching others, are all necessary steps to that joy. The difference is only a slight shift in emphasis, but the result is to make the daily practice of Christianity more approachable.

In addition to Pollyanna's story of her missionary father, there is another story that Reverend Ford comes across that cements his decision to change his attitude in the sermon to his congregation. In it a boy, Tom, refuses to "'fill his mother's woodbox'" (194). Tom's father knows that should he scold the boy and believe the worst of him, chances are the task would remain undone. So, instead, he says to Tom, "'I'm sure you'll be glad to go and bring in some wood for your mother,'" expecting him to do the "right thing," because "[w]hat men and women need is encouragement" (195). The insertion of this story not only makes concrete the transformation in Christianity, a shift toward more kindness and grace in faith, it also illustrates the difference that Pollyanna's Christianity brings to the town. She does not convert people to faith because she cries over their sins or preaches of their damnation to hell, but rather she loves them; she brings them food, visits them, and expects them to want to behave in a similar manner. As Keith posits, Pollyanna's "God . . . seems cheerful, loving and kind—like Pollyanna herself" (144). Reverend Ford's sermon is transformed from the Puritanical "woe is you, sinner" to the "veritable bugle-call to the best that was in every man and woman and child that heard it," Christianity's positive counterpart (196). *Pollyanna* demonstrates the effective and positive power that results in this shift from a more Puritanical religion to a new model of Christianity. The story of *Pollyanna* appears to have this representative role not only in Porter's novel, but also in one of the film adaptations.

Coda: The Film's Patriotic Christianity

Similar to the change that occurs between Janeway's *A Token for Children* and *Pollyanna*, so another reinterpretation of Christianity in America occurred in the 1950s, which the 1960 film *Pollyanna* by Walt Disney reflects. There are various ways a film might be adapted, which Geoffrey Wagner delineates as "transposition," or an attempted word-for-word adaptation (222); "commentary," where the film is changed purposely to make a particular statement; and "analogy," where the "originary" text is but a point of departure for the completely reworked cinematic version (223). Disney's film, which restructures the narrative around a town bazaar for which the citizens must band together to overcome Aunt Polly's control over the town's businesses and people, resembles Wagner's concept of "commentary." The basic themes—Pollyanna's glad game and the transformations of the individuals around her—remain true to the novel. George

Bluestone correlates "faithful" with "successful," noting that lucrative films are rarely critiqued for being unfaithful in their interpretations (114).

In the spirit of Bluestone, but without the cynicism, my analysis of the 1960 *Pollyanna* is driven less by its faithfulness to the originating text—though, as K. Brenna Wardell notes in her chapter in this collection, it was not a financial success, it is still considered by many to be Disney's "best live-action film ever" (Griswold 217)—and more by how the differences between the two showcase 1913 and 1960 American Christianities. Dudley Andrew notes that the social theorist perspective, including Marxism, posits that people create through inevitable ideological filters, thereby causing even films to be a product of the ideals and beliefs of their time, which justifies viewing Disney's *Pollyanna* in light of the contemporary Christian atmosphere (28–29).

The 1950s saw resurgent religious, though not necessarily Christian, behavior in the lives of Americans; Clebsch states, "It would be difficult to find a decade in all American history when religion wore a face more appealing to American culture than it did during the 1950's" (8). There was a renewed need to be grounded in faith as the outlook on humanity grew increasingly pessimistic after the conflicts of the first half of the twentieth century. Additionally, the impact of the failure of modern science to "provide all of the answers once expected from it, especially concerning the nonmaterial aspects of life" promoted this need (Linder 16). Despite this apparent dependency on faith, many religious leaders feared that organized religion would not survive in the modern world (Clebsch 8). Perhaps that is why there existed a nostalgia for the "religious certainties from the nation's past" (Linder 16), which could have been part of the impetus for the Disney adaptation of *Pollyanna*, as the then almost fifty-year-old novel, as noted by Wardell, provided a mirror with which to reflect back on a simpler era. The film contains religious elements, though, in keeping to the spirit of the book, there is no mention of Christ or specific Christian doctrine. Its setting is a predominantly Christian society—the characters attend church on Sunday and the minister's two sermons are depicted in their entirety over the course of the film. Throughout two world wars, Christianity had retained strong ties to patriotism, and America both adopted the motto "In God We Trust" and added "under God" to the Pledge of Allegiance during the 1950s (Wells and Woodbridge 431). Being religious, though not necessarily Christian, was synonymous with being an American. As President Eisenhower declared, "'Our form of government has no sense unless it is grounded in a deeply felt religious faith, and I don't care what it is'" (qtd. in Linder 16).

Disney's adaptation reflects this union between religion and patriotism. Pollyanna's parents are changed from being domestic missionaries to being stationed in the British West Indies (*Pollyanna*). Apart from allowing the actress Hayley Mills to maintain a hint of her English accent, this also makes a statement about the perceived condition of the United States. The desire to convert Americans to Christianity was no longer overwhelming. America, in its highly patriotic state, was celebrating both what it had become and the roots from which it had grown, seen in the nostalgia and patriotism of the film. At the beginning of the film, it is established that the town of Harrington, named for Aunt Polly's father, is now controlled by his heir Polly Harrington, in a sort of monarchy. When the citizens of Harrington, however, decide to reclaim control over the orphanage in order to replace it, a bazaar is organized to raise the necessary funds. Very few plan to actually attend the bazaar though, as it would be a direct defiance of Aunt Polly's wishes. With the bazaar on the brink of failure, it is Pollyanna, ironically a major supporter of the fundraiser, who mentions that "no one owns a church," leading those in charge to ask Reverend Ford to mention the bazaar from the pulpit (*Pollyanna*). The church, however, along with other local businesses, is under the influence of Polly, and, despite their earnest request, Reverend Ford refuses to speak for the bazaar organizers. Pollyanna unknowingly intervenes again, and, as in the novel, comes across him in a field and shares what the film calls the "glad passages" (*Pollyanna*). But rather than beginning with the biblical texts, she tells Reverend Ford that her father "read something somewhere that helped him," a quote attributed to Abraham Lincoln: "When you look for the bad in mankind expecting to find it, you surely will" (*Pollyanna*). It was this rather secular idea from an American leader that had spurred Reverend Whittier on to seek the good in people, and then to locate the biblical glad passages. The made-up quote supports the theory that the Disney film attempts to cement the connection between Americanism and Pollyanna's glad gospel. Reverend Ford is later heard boldly declaring, "No one owns a church—no one," which mirrors the American separation of church and state (*Pollyanna*).

The next scene is that of the Reverend Ford delivering his sermon, which is juxtaposed to the hellfire-and-brimstone sermon played out earlier in the film. After sharing one of the glad passages, he paraphrases Lincoln's supposed words, declaring to his congregation, "'I should have been looking for the good in you'" (*Pollyanna*). His transformation, which appears attributed in equal parts to Lincoln and God, leads to the request that the town support the bazaar. The entire town, apart from Aunt Polly, does come; they band together and reclaim ownership of their town. Pollyanna's glad, albeit godly, presence has inspired the town's people to change—to make an effort to care for each other and the welfare of the town's orphans. They have become better citizens and better Christians, interweaving the two concepts that appeared inseparable in the decade preceding the film. And the town, once known by its "ruling" family, is amended on the train station sign to read: "Harrington: The Glad Town" (*Pollyanna*).

Conclusion

Pollyanna, as both the 1960 film and the novel, reflects each era's view of Christianity, with the film adaptation representing the complex connection between American patriotism and being religious, generally Protestant, and the novel engaging with prevalent Christian movements, the social gospel and mission work. Porter's novel, however, goes so far as to make a critical statement about contemporary Christianity. *Pollyanna* is more than a didactic text about making the most of every situation; rather it promotes a new type of Christianity, one that includes more glad texts than "woe, sinners" chastisements. The Christian faith was at a crossroads when *Pollyanna* was first published, and this domestic fiction novel places Christianity on a new path, one with an emphasis on charity both at home and abroad. *Pollyanna*'s Christianity is far removed from the strict Puritanical rules and warnings of damnation, and is less focused on foreign missions than contemporary religious leaders advocated, but is a new embodiment—a Christianity that remembers Christ's teachings to help *all* of those less fortunate and to "rejoice in the Lord." Porter uses the domestic fiction genre as a vehicle to bring girls' fiction into the modern era. With the glad game's advocate at the fore, Christianity proffered a clear path forward, and this legacy was furthered by the Disney adaptation. Just as *Pollyanna* the novel was but a "modern shadow" of the traditions begun by *A Token for Children*, so the 1960 film updated Porter's story, making it a Christian vehicle for a new generation, a "veritable bugle-call" (196) for Christianity in the modern age.

Note

1. The New International Version of the Bible was used in this instance for a clearer understanding of the verse than the King James Version provides.

Works Cited

Alcott, Louisa May. *Little Women*. New York: Bantam Dell, 2007. Print.

Andrew, Dudley. "Adaptation." *Film Adaptation*. Ed. James Naremore. New Brunswick: Rutgers UP, 2000. 28–37. Print.

Bluestone, George. *Novels into Film*. Berkeley: U of California P, 1957. Print.

Clebsch, William A. *From Sacred to Profane America: The Role of Religion in American History*. New York: Harper & Row, 1968. Print.

Coolidge, Susan. *What Katy Did*. 1872. London: Puffin, 2009. Print.

Conn, H. M. "Missions, Evangelical Foreign." *Dictionary of Christianity in America*. Ed. Daniel G. Reid. Downers Grove: InterVarsity, 1990. 749–53. Print.

Foster, Shirley, and Judy Simons. *What Katy Read: Feminist Re-Readings of "Classic" Stories for Girls*. Iowa City: U of Iowa P, 1995. Print.

Griswold, Jerry. *Audacious Kids: Coming of Age in America's Classic Children's Books*. Oxford: Oxford UP, 1992. Print.

Grogan, Geoffrey W. *Psalms*. Cambridge: William B. Eerdmans, 2008. Print.

Handy, Robert T. *A Christian America: Protestant Hopes and Historical Realities*. Oxford: Oxford UP, 1971. Print.

The Holy Bible: New International Version. Colorado Springs: International Bible Society, 1984. Print.

Hunt, Peter. *Children's Literature*. Oxford: Blackwell, 2001. Print.

Janeway, James. *A Token for Children; Being an Account of the Conversion, Holy and Exemplary Lives, and Joyful Deaths, of Several Young Children*. London: Thomas Ward, n.d. Print.

Keith, Lois. *Take Up Thy Bed and Walk: Death, Disability and Cure in Classic Fiction for Girls*. London: Women's Press, 2001. Print.

Kilgallen, John J. *A Brief Commentary on the Gospel of Matthew*. Lewiston, NY: Edwin Mellen, 1992. Print.

King James Version Bible. London: Collins, 2011. Print.

Linder, R. D. "Introduction: Division and Unity: The Paradox of Christianity in America." *Dictionary of Christianity in America*. Ed. Daniel G. Reid. Downers Grove: InterVarsity Press, 1990. 1–22. Print.

Marsden, George M. "The Era of Crisis: From Christendom to Pluralism." *Christianity in America: A Handbook*. Eds. Mark A. Noll, Nathan O. Hatch, George M. Marsden, David F. Wells, and John D. Woodbridge. Grand Rapids: William B. Eerdmans, 1983. 277–391. Print.

Mead, Sidney E. *The Lively Experiment: The Shaping of Christianity in America*. New York: Harper & Row, 1963. Print.

Naremore, James, ed. *Film Adaptation*. New Brunswick: Rutgers UP, 2000. Print.

Noll, Mark A., Nathan O. Hatch, George M. Marsden, David F. Wells, and John D. Woodbridge, eds. *Christianity in America: A Handbook*. Grand Rapids: William B. Eerdmans, 1983. Print.

Pollyanna. Dir. David Swift. Perf. Jane Wyman, Hayley Mills, Richard Egan. Walt Disney Productions, 1960. Film.

Porter, Eleanor H. *Pollyanna*. 1913. London: Puffin, 1994. Print.

———. *Pollyanna Grows Up*. 1915. London: Puffin, 1996. Print.

Reid, Daniel G., ed. *Dictionary of Christianity in America*. Downers Grove: InterVarsity Press, 1990. Print.

Rodgers, Daniel T. *The Work Ethic in Industrial America, 1850–1920*. Chicago: U of Chicago P, 1979. Print.

Ruether, Rosemary Radford, and Rosemary Skinner Keller, eds. *Women and Religion in America. Vol. I: The Nineteenth Century*. New York: Harper & Row, 1982. Print.

———. "Introduction." *Women and Religion in America. Vol. I: The Nineteenth Century*. Eds. Rosemary Radford Ruether and Rosemary Skinner Keller. New York: Harper & Row, 1982. viii–xiv. Print.

Sanders, Joe Sutliff. "Spinning Sympathy: Orphan Girl Novels and the Sentimental Tradition." *Children's Literature Association Quarterly* 33.1 (2008): 41–61. Web. 11 April 2012.

Smith, Gary Scott. *The Search for Social Salvation: Social Christianity and America, 1880–1925*. Lanham: Lexington, 2000. Print.

Spurgeon, Charles H. *Commentary on Matthew: The Gospel of the Kingdom*. 1893. Edinburgh: Banner of Truth Trust, 2010. Print.

Wagner, Geoffrey. *The Novel and the Cinema*. Cranbury, NJ: Associated UP, 1975. Print.

Wells, David F., and John D. Woodbridge. "Christianity in a Secular Age: From the Depression to the Present." *Christianity in America: A Handbook*. Eds. Mark A. Noll, Nathan O. Hatch, George M. Marsden, David F. Wells, and John D. Woodbridge. Grand Rapids: William B. Eerdmans, 1983. 392–491. Print.

7

Pollyanna, the Power of Gladness, and the Philosophy of Pragmatism

JANET WESSELIUS

What struck me upon reading *Pollyanna* again as an adult is how the glad game resonates with the philosophy of American pragmatism. Pragmatism is widely considered to be the only philosophy indigenous to America, and it continues as a significant philosophical school beyond those national boundaries. As such, it would not be surprising if there are a number of themes in this classic American novel that resonate with an American philosophy. However, such an exploration has not been done to date, possibly because, despite a small number of recent studies, we rarely expect or look for philosophical insights in a children's story.[1] Nevertheless, a careful reading of *Pollyanna* reveals remarkable and noteworthy similarities to pragmatism.

Pollyanna is well known through the eponymous novel and films, and the significant number of sequels and adaptations. What is perhaps less well known is the context in which *Pollyanna* was created. Pragmatism was part of the intellectual milieu of late-nineteenth- and early-twentieth-century America, particularly the pragmatism developed by William James (1842–1910), who is widely considered to be the most original and influential of the pragmatists.[2] Moreover, pragmatism was understood— or was being constructed as—a particularly American philosophy, and James was eulogized as its father.[3] As the influential philosopher Josiah Royce argued the year after James died and the year before *Pollyanna* was published, "the pragmatic doctrine, that both the meaning and truth of ideas shall be tested by the empirical consequences of these ideas and by the practical results of acting them out in life . . . is . . . a characteristic Americanism in philosophy" (588). Furthermore, James "has given utterance to ideas which are characteristic of a stage and of an aspect of the spiritual life of this [American] people. . . . [I]n him certain characteristic aspects of our national civilization have found their voice" (582–83).[4] Known as the most influential philosopher in the United States in his life-time, James was also influential and well known outside of his country; he was the first American invited to give the Gifford Lectures on Natural Religion in Edinburgh in 1901–02.

James was born into a privileged family in New York, the eldest of four siblings among whom were the novelist Henry James and the essayist Alice James. Although James spent much of his childhood in Europe— and hence his education was as much European as it was American— James was very much part of the elite of American society; for example, his godfather was Ralph Waldo Emerson. James earned a degree in medi-cine from Harvard University in 1869, and was appointed to the faculty at Harvard in 1872. James was both a philosopher and a psychologist; he was not only a founding member of pragmatism (with Charles Sander Peirce and John Dewey), but is also known as the father of modern psy-chology. His first publication, *The Principles of Psychology* (1890), is one of the cornerstones of modern psychology. Other significant publications include *The Will to Believe* (1896), *The Varieties of Religious Experience* (1902) (a text based on his Gifford Lectures), *Pragmatism: A New Name for Some Old Ways of Thinking* (1907), and *The Meaning of Truth* (1909). As a professor, James was influential in American scholarly and cultural circles: his students included Oliver Wendell Holmes, Teddy Roosevelt, Gertrude Stein, W. E. B. Du Bois, and George Santayana, among others. It is reasonable to suppose that Eleanor H. Porter would have been famil-iar with James's pragmatism, if not his actual work in philosophy and psychology.

The first part of this chapter explores how the pragmatist principle of the will to believe resonates with the glad game. The second section focuses on the themes of power and knowing in *Pollyanna* that seem to be shared with pragmatism. The chapter concludes with an exploration of the dark side of the glad game and a discussion of "pollyannaism" in particular.

James's Will to Believe and Porter's Glad Game

The path by which James came to develop pragmatism is interesting in the context of the pragmatic themes in *Pollyanna*. James's philosophy originated with his suffering throughout his youth from melancholia and thoughts of suicide. In addition to being diagnosed with neurasthenia,

James suffered from a variety of physical ailments. As James later tells it, he decided that he would rather believe in free will than in determinism, that the position of determinism was pessimistic and depressing.[5] He would, in short, will himself to believe in those things that were uplifting. Here, I have given a caricature of James's pragmatism; it is, of course, far more complex and sophisticated. However, this sketch serves for my purposes in introducing some of the most unique and controversial themes in pragmatism: namely, the will to believe and how beliefs shape, and sometimes create, reality. Pragmatism, as developed by James, insists that thought is a form of action; moreover, thought can create reality and as such is a form of power. Thinking pessimistically is behaving pessimistically, and the person who does so will make reality brute and uncaring; optimistic thinking leads to optimistic behavior and creates a reality that is vivid and joyful. James himself was able to overcome the extreme melancholia of his youth and live a happy and productive life. In terms of his own philosophy, his contented and productive life was evidence for the truth of his philosophy.

These pragmatic themes—albeit simplified—can be seen in the central scene in *Pollyanna* where Pollyanna explains the glad game to Nancy. It should be noted that Pollyanna repeatedly describes this game throughout the novel, thereby demonstrating its centrality to the novel. When Nancy tells Pollyanna that she is to have only bread and milk for supper eaten in the kitchen, Pollyanna says that she is glad because she likes bread and milk and, moreover, likes to eat her supper with Nancy. Nancy demurs, and in response Pollyanna shares the story of the crutches, explaining that after receiving the disappointing package from the Ladies' Aiders, her father introduced her to the game of "'just [finding] something about everything to be glad about—no matter what 'twas" (36–37). The glad game is at the heart of *Pollyanna* (and deeply familiar to its readers); the novel is about how Pollyanna and those around her are affected by the game. Moreover, the glad game is what makes Pollyanna a unique character in literature. A version of the glad game is familiar even to those who have not read the book. In many ways, we can see the glad game as an exploration of the powers of the human mind, the power to shape reality. Similarly, James's pragmatism developed out of his study of human psychology.[6]

But is Pollyanna genuinely glad that she does not have to use crutches? Or is the game merely a sentimental refusal to deal with the reality that she is a disappointed and doll-less little girl? A few paragraphs later, Pollyanna herself admits that it is not always easy to play the glad game but "'when you're hunting for the glad things, you sort of forget the other kind—like the doll you wanted, you know" (30). The point here, as generations of readers have realized, is that even if gladness is not the first (and as James would say, involuntary) response, *choosing* to select one aspect of the situation (for example, receiving, but not needing, crutches) and actively *focusing* on "the glad things" creates a different reality, that of, for example, a happy little girl who finds the game "lovely" and "fun" and rejoices in her strong legs.

Compare this passage in *Pollyanna* (published in 1912) to a passage from James's *The Varieties of Religious Experience* (1902):

> If, then, we give the name of healthy-mindedness to the tendency which looks on all things and sees that they are good, we find that we must distinguish between a more involuntary and a more voluntary or systematic way of being healthy-minded. In its involuntary variety, healthy-mindedness is a way of feeling happy about things immediately. In its systematical variety, it is an abstract way of conceiving things as good. Every abstract way of conceiving things selects some one aspect of them as their essence for the time being, and disregards other aspects. . . . When happiness is actually in possession, the thought of evil can no more acquire the feeling of reality than the thought of good can gain reality when melancholy rules. To the man *actively* happy, from whatever cause, evil simply cannot then and there be believed in. . . . Much of what we call evil is due entirely to the way men take the phenomenon. It can so often be converted into a bracing and tonic good by a simple change of the sufferer's inner attitude . . . ; its sting so often departs and turns into one of relish when, after vainly seeking to shun it, we agree to face about and bear it *cheerfully*, that a man is simply bound in honor, with reference to many of the facts that seem at first to disconcert his peace, to adopt this way of escape. Refuse to admit their badness; despise their power; ignore their presence; turn your attention the other way; and so far as you yourself are concerned at any rate, though the facts may still exist, their evil character exists no longer. Since you make the evil or good by your own thoughts about them, it is the ruling of your thoughts which proves to be your principle concern. The deliberate adoption of an optimistic turn of mind thus makes its entrance into philosophy. (James, "Religious Experience" 101–2; emphasis added)

So reading the glad game through James's pragmatic eyes, we can see that it is a "voluntary or systematic way of being healthy-minded," a "way of conceiving things as good" by "select[ing] some one aspect of them as their essence for the time being, and disregard[ing] other aspects" (101–2). Playing the glad game (or adopting a pragmatist attitude) is to be *actively* happy in the sense that it requires an act of will on the part of the player (or the pragmatist). The game has rules and one must *choose* to play, as is made clear to every character in *Pollyanna*. For example, Mr. Pendleton (at first) refuses both to take Jimmy Bean into his home and to be glad: "'Well, I won't,' ejaculated the man decisively. 'Pollyanna, this is sheer nonsense! . . . I think I prefer lonesomeness'" (151). Similarly, James clarifies that one must choose to be healthy-minded by his use of active verbs: "face," "refuse," "despise," "ignore" evil, and "turn" your attention away; one must "deliberately adopt an optimistic turn of mind" (101–2).

However, James's pragmatism goes beyond simply choosing to look on the bright side of things. According to James, we make "the evil or good by our own thoughts about them" and so it is by actively "ruling" of our thoughts that we create a reality (101–2). To paraphrase James's words in the passage above, "though the facts may still exist, their evil character exists no longer"; and indeed, bad facts "can so often be converted into a bracing and tonic good by a simple change of the sufferer's inner attitude." This is the will to believe. Consider the following passage from an address given by James to the Philosophical Club of Yale and Brown Universities entitled *The Will to Believe* (and published in 1896):

> Turn now . . . to a certain class of questions of fact, questions concerning personal relations, states of mind between one man and another. *Do you like me or not?*—for example. Whether you do or not depends, in countless instances, on whether I meet you half-way, am willing to assume that you must like me, and show you trust and expectation. The previous faith on my part in your liking's existence is in such cases what makes your liking come. But if I stand aloof and refuse to budge an inch until I have objective evidence, until you shall have done something apt [to prove that you like me] . . . ten to one your liking never comes. . . . The desire for a certain kind of truth here brings about that special truth's existence; and so it is in innumerable cases of other sorts. (James, "Will to Believe" 23–24)

It certainly seems to be the case that Aunt Polly's love for Pollyanna is one of those "innumerable cases." When Pollyanna first comes to live with her aunt, Aunt Polly wants nothing to do with the little girl but takes her in out of a sense of duty. However, Pollyanna acts from the very beginning as if Aunt Polly not only wants to take her into her home, but actually loves her and, slowly but surely, Aunt Polly does come to love her niece. Originally, James developed his theory of the will to believe in support of the rationality of believing or having faith, particularly religious faith. To use his own autobiographical example, science taught him that free will was false and that determinism was true; and this scientific "fact" that everything, including the reality of his own life, was determined and that he could do nothing to change it led him to despair. As a last resort, he chose to believe and act as though he did have free will, that he could be responsible for his own life, and this active choice to believe (which includes a change in behavior) "saved" his life. In fact, this is the thinking that led James to conclude that "life is worth living."

In "Is Life Worth Living?" published in 1895, James writes of the "soul sickness" that often accompanies the "metaphysical *tedium vitae* which is peculiar to reflecting men" (38) He was, of course, one of those reflecting men. He says to his audience:

> many of you are students of philosophy, and have already felt in your persons
> the skepticism and unreality that too much grubbing in the abstract roots
> of things will breed. This is, indeed, one of the regular fruits of the over-
> studious career. Too much questioning and too little active responsibility
> lead, almost as often as too much sensualism does, to the edge of the slope, at
> the bottom of which lie pessimism and the nightmare or suicidal view of life.
> But to the diseases which reflection breeds, still further reflection can oppose
> effective remedies. (James, "Worth Living" 38–39)

What follows in this talk is James's "further reflection" in which his "final appeal is to nothing more recondite than religious faith" ("Worth Living" 39).

Religion certainly plays an important role in *Pollyanna*, and a form of it did so in James's own life. However, we would miss his point if we equated religion or religious faith with Christianity or any other religious institution, for James has in mind a far more pluralistic (to use his own word) spiritual reality. By religious faith, James means a "faith in the existence of an unseen order of some kind" ("Worth Living" 51). In what follows I quote parts of his "further reflection" ("Worth Living" 39) that I argue are relevant to understanding the pragmatic themes in *Pollyanna*:

> I wish to make you feel . . . that we have a right to believe the physical order
> to be only a partial order, that we have a right to supplement it by an unseen
> spiritual order which we assume on trust, if only thereby life may seem to
> us better worth living again. . . . [B]elief and doubt are living attitudes, and
> involve conduct on our part. . . . Our faculties of belief [which are classed
> with Darwin's "accidental variations"] . . . were given us to live by. And to
> trust our religious demands [i.e., our "inner need of believing that this world

is a sign of something more spiritual and eternal than itself"] means first of all to live in the light of them, and to act as if the invisible world which they suggest were real. It is a fact of human nature, that men can live and die by the help of a sort of faith that goes without a single dogma or definition. . . . Often enough our faith beforehand in an uncertified result *is the only thing that makes the result come true.* ("Worth Living" 52, 54, 56, 59)

Pollyanna's more conventionally religious beliefs, such as her belief that "father's gone to heaven to be with mother and the rest of us, you know" (14), are paralleled by her belief that Aunt Polly loves her (which James would also consider a religious belief). Surely, believing that Aunt Polly— her only remaining family—loves her is a belief that makes Pollyanna's life "better worth living again" in spite of being an orphan, and so, on James's terms, she has a right to believe it. Moreover, Pollyanna lives in light of this belief and acts as though this belief were real. Her belief in the love of Aunt Polly is an act of faith and as such "involves conduct" on her part, as we see time and time again in the novel. From the very beginning, Pollyanna behaves toward her aunt as though she were loved: when she first meets Aunt Polly she hugs her—"Pollyanna had fairly flown across the room and flung herself into her aunt's scandalized, unyielding lap" (18)—and even after being punished for being late for her first supper, Pollyanna hugs her aunt good night—"*quite as a matter of course* Pollyanna came straight to her aunt's side and gave her an affectionate hug" (32, emphasis added). She is not acting as though her aunt loves her as a strategy for making her aunt love her but rather because she sincerely believes that such is the case. Her belief in the love of Aunt Polly is a will to believe.

The power of Pollyanna's thought-in-action is powerful even though it is not realistic in the usual sense. We readers know, as do characters like Nancy, that Aunt Polly does not care for Pollyanna. However, Pollyanna knows no such thing; she knows that Aunt Polly loves her, of course. To reiterate, Pollyanna's thought-in-action is not a strategy; it is an integral part of her knowing.[7] For James, knowing is believing, and in *Pollyanna* the power of ("unrealistic") knowing is made concrete.

Beyond the Glad Game: The Power of Pollyanna's Knowing

The will to believe has to do with (what we now recognize as) psychology, but it is also an epistemic position. James's will to believe is more than "putting a good face on things." According to him, our thoughts can often shape, and even create, reality. Thought is powerful; it is action or deed (hence, the name "pragmatism" from the Greek word for "deed"). James often uses the phrase "the right to believe" interchangeably with "the will to believe" (in, for example, *The Will to Believe*). The will to believe is part of his argument that it is rationally permissible to believe in some cases without any evidence of truth prior to adopting (and acting on) it. According to James, in some instances the only way to get evidence for the truth of a belief is to embrace the belief before there is any evidence. Once again, we can see how this philosophy resonates with the behavior and belief of Pollyanna with regard to Aunt Polly: she believes that her aunt loves her, and by the end of the novel Pollyanna has abundant evidence that her aunt does, indeed, love her.

Recall the above passage from *The Will to Believe*, which ends with "the desire for a certain kind of truth here brings about that special truth's existence" (24). As I noted above, James's pragmatism is much more than the psychology of positive thinking. According to James, our beliefs—which are themselves a form of action—and consequent behavior sometimes create reality. To put it baldly, sometimes thinking it does make it so. As James says "there are, then, cases where a fact cannot come at all unless a preliminary faith exists in its coming. *And where faith in a fact can help create the fact*," it is reasonable to choose to will that belief (James, *The Will to Believe* 225).

We can see that such is often the case with Pollyanna. According to James, the activity of thinking is enormously powerful. Pollyanna's insistent optimism and inveterate gladness give her a kind of power. Her power is in sharp contrast to the adults around her who, we read, are often struck speechless by Pollyanna. However, this power is not derived from her positive attitude. The effect of Pollyanna and her glad game is far more complex: Pollyanna acts on her beliefs (as James would say) and her actions bring about the reality. For example, she believes that Aunt Polly loves her and wants Pollyanna to live with her; through her sincere actions based on this belief, it indeed becomes the case that Aunt Polly does love Pollyanna. In the character of Pollyanna, we see that acting as though something is so can make it so. Paradoxically, the realism of the adults renders them powerless, whereas Pollyanna's active beliefs empower her to transform her life and the lives of those around her.

Aunt Polly's love for Pollyanna is not the only example of the power of thought in action. Pollyanna believes that her aunt is good and kind, and by the end of the novel, Aunt Polly is indeed good and kind. Moreover, after Pollyanna's accident, we (and Aunt Polly) learn of all the changes brought into people's lives—such as Mr. Pendleton, Mrs. Snow and Milly, the Widow Benton, Mrs. Tarbell, and Mrs. Payson—by Pollyanna and her glad game. One of the most striking examples of the power of the will to believe is the change in Reverend Paul Ford's congregation. After meeting Pollyanna and being told about the glad game, Reverend Ford stumbles upon a story in a magazine article that concludes with this paragraph (which exemplifies some of James's pragmatism):

> What men and women need is encouragement. Their natural resisting powers should be strengthened, not weakened. . . . Instead of always harping on a man's faults, tell him of his virtues. Try to pull him out of his rut of bad habits. Hold up to him his better self, his *real* self that can dare and do and win out! . . . The influence of a beautiful, helpful, hopeful character is contagious and may revolutionize a whole town. . . . People radiate what is in their minds and in their hearts. If a man feels kindly and obliging, his neighbors will feel that way, too, before long. But if he scolds and scowls and criticizes—his neighbors will return scowl for scowl and add interest! . . . when you look for the bad, expecting it, you will get it. When you *know* you will find the good—you get that. (160)

Instead of administering the scolding in a sermon he was planning, Rev. Ford realizes that there is a connection between this article and Pollyanna's father's focus on the "shining eight hundred" rejoicing texts in the Bible (161). Those "rejoicing texts" (157) inspired the glad game and the sermon that Rev. Ford preached that "was a veritable bugle-call to the best that was in every man and woman and child that heard it" (161). After Pollyanna's accident, Aunt Polly tells her:

> Why, Pollyanna, I think all the town is playing that game now with you—even to the minister! I haven't had a chance to tell you, yet, but this morning I met Mr Ford when I was down to the village, and he told me to say to you that just as soon as you could see him he was coming to tell you that he hadn't stop being glad over those eight hundred rejoicing texts that you told him about. So you see, dear, it's just you that have done it. The whole town is playing the game, and the whole town is wonderfully happier—and all because of one little girl who taught the people a new game, and how to play it. (206)

It is, of course, in this scene that Aunt Polly both allows Pollyanna to speak again of her father and tells her that she knows the glad game and will play it with her. I would suggest, however, that it is not Pollyanna who "ha[d] done it"—or at least, not Pollyanna alone. The change in the reality of people's lives comes because they *choose* to play the game, because their "desires for a certain kind of truth [. . .] brings about that special truth's existence" (James, "Will to Believe" 24). Certainly, Pollyanna's cheerfulness inspired the townsfolk to look on the bright side of things, but the circumstances of their lives change as a direct result of their changed attitudes.

However, the truly controversial part of pragmatism has less to do with the changes a positive attitude can bring than with its view of knowing and truth, as I alluded earlier. I think a similar view of knowing and truth is implicit in *Pollyanna* as well. In the novel, we see that Pollyanna is often mistaken: she certainly misunderstands many of the adults with whom she comes into contact, and her most glaring mistake is her (wrong) understanding of the relationships between Mr. Pendleton, Dr. Chilton, and Aunt Polly. She eventually realizes that Mr. Pendleton loved her mother, Jennie (and not Aunt Polly, as she thought at one point), but she does not realize until the last scene of the penultimate chapter that Dr. Chilton was Aunt Polly's lover many years before. We readers, of course, come to know these relations much earlier than she does. However, this lack of knowledge in no way diminishes Pollyanna's power. In fact, I argue later on that the knowledge of the adults in the novel renders them powerless in many respects. According to James, our usual view of knowledge as a mirror image or copy of the world (literally, a re-presentation) is misguided.[8] Pragmatism is in large part a criticism of—and alternative to—a representationalist theory of knowledge and its associated theory of truth as correspondence to reality. For James, the question for any philosophy was not "is it true?" but "what are its consequences?"; the question was not so much "do I understand reality correctly?" but rather "how am I to live?" For James, if a philosophy could give a satisfactory answer to the latter question, it would be able to answer the former question in the affirmative. Truly empirical knowledge was not knowledge that re-presented the world as a photograph re-presents a scene; rather, genuinely empirical knowledge has positive and practical effects for the knower.

A common criticism made of pragmatism is that it is "not realistic," that "the truth has nothing to do with knowing."[9] Similar criticisms are made of *Pollyanna*; indeed, we now have a word, *pollyannaism*, that means an unreasonable, unrealistic, or illogical optimism. Both pragmatism and *Pollyanna* are accused of wishful thinking. However, let us take James at his own word and examine the consequences of the knowledge of the adults in *Pollyanna*. Certainly, the adults in the novel are all, for the most part, quite realistic. They face reality and it makes them unhappy. Nancy knows that Aunt Polly is a bitter, middle-aged woman, but this knowledge in no way empowers her; rather, it makes her timid and afraid of Aunt Polly. Mrs. Snow fully faces the fact that she is bedridden, and, consequently, she is miserable and makes those around her miserable. Mr. Pendleton is thwarted in love and "prefers the lonesomeness" (151). Dr. Chilton and Aunt Polly are both lonely and disappointed, but do not know how to settle their quarrel.

The adults in the novel are powerless in the face of Pollyanna's determined optimism because they have surrendered all their power to the reality they think they know. Their knowledge renders them powerless. In some ways, they are an example of what James sees as wrong and misguided in a representationalist epistemology: it promotes impotence, helplessness, quietism, and resignation. In fact, by the standards of pragmatism, the adults in the novel are not realistic at all. The realism of the adults blinds them so they cannot see that reality is constructed in tandem with human interactions, and that it consists of independently existing states of affairs and objects, but also of human responses to those independent "things." Instead, the adults mistakenly believe that things are the way they are and need to be accepted as such; they are blind to their own agency in shaping reality. We see this impotence most starkly in the response of Aunt Polly to Pollyanna's different reality. Aunt Polly chastises Pollyanna for sleeping on the tin roof of her sun parlor and tells her "For the rest of the night, Pollyanna, you are to sleep in my bed with me. The screens will be here tomorrow, but until then I consider it my duty to keep you where I know where you are." Pollyanna is glad, which leaves "Miss Polly . . . feeling curiously helpless. For the third time since Pollyanna's arrival, Miss Polly was punishing Pollyanna—and for the third time she was being confronted with the amazing fact that her punishment was being taken as a special reward of merit. No wonder Miss Polly was feeling curiously helpless" (48). No wonder, indeed. Later on, when Pollyanna brings home a forlorn and dirty kitten to the cat-hating Aunt Polly, she finds herself "powerless to remonstrate": "Miss Polly opened her lips and tried to speak; but in vain. The curious helpless feeling that had been hers so often since Pollyanna's arrival, had her now fast in its grip," and

> The next day it was a dog, even dirtier and more forlorn, perhaps, than was the kitten. And again Miss Polly, to her dumbfounded amazement, found herself figuring as a kind protector and an angel of mercy—a role that Pollyanna so unhesitantly thrust upon her as a matter of course, that the woman—who

abhorred dogs even more than she did cats, if possible—found herself as before, powerless to remonstrate. (75–76)

Can we reasonably say that Aunt Polly is the realistic person and Pollyanna unrealistic? Aunt Polly's realism and superior position as the adult do not help her at all in the face of Pollyanna's lack of realism. In fact, she is "bested" by a little girl she does not even like.

The relationship between Aunt Polly and Dr. Chilton is a good example of how the adults in the novel surrender power over their own lives in the face of "unalterable reality." Aunt Polly and Dr. Chilton quarreled in their youth, and that such a quarrel happened is indeed reality and unalterable. However, they allow this reality to determine the next twenty years of their life. The fact that the quarrel happened cannot be changed, but what happens next is open to the decisions of Aunt Polly and the doctor, as is made evident by their eventual marriage. Mr. Pendleton's unrequited love for Pollyanna's mother Jennie is another example of the surrender of power. Mr. Pendleton acts as though his disappointment in love must result in a bitterness that touches every area of his life; Pollyanna shows him that although he cannot force someone to love him—Pollyanna herself refuses to live with him—he can choose how he responds to such disappointment. After all, he continues to love Pollyanna despite her refusal (in direct contrast to how he responds to her mother's refusal of him), and eventually finds a surrogate son in Jimmy.

Having knowledge and being realistic do not have positive results for the adults of *Pollyanna*. Despite her lack of knowledge or realism, Pollyanna is both happier and more powerful than the adults around her, until they too find the truth in the glad game. What sense does it make to say that Pollyanna is not realistic, does not understand the truth of the reality around her? James says "the truth of an idea is not a stagnant property inherent in it. Truth *happens* to an idea. It *becomes* true, is *made* true by events. Its verity *is* in fact an event, a process: the process namely of its verifying itself, its very-*fication*. Its validity is the process of its valid-*ation*" ("Pragmatism's Conception of Truth" 217). Surely, on this understanding, Pollyanna's knowing is truer—that is, more in touch with reality—than any other character's knowledge. True ideas put us into a satisfactory relation to the world ("What Pragmatism Means" 203–4). Truth happens to our ideas when our ideas align with reality, such as Aunt Polly learning to love Pollyanna or when Mr. Pendleton warms up to Jimmy (and adopts him as a son). By the end of the novel, truth has happened—sometimes in unexpected ways—to all of Pollyanna's most cherished ideas.

However, Pollyanna's paralysis as a consequence of her accident pushes the glad game to its very limits. Such accidents happen in our world (and not just in novels), and the fact that bad things happen to good people challenges the power of the will to believe. Indeed, in the next section, I argue that this accident and the resulting paralysis gives rise to the realization on the part of many readers that there is a problem with this determined optimism, despite its capacity to empower the believer.

The Dark Side of the Glad Game

The fact that *pollyannaism* is a word in our language indicates at least two things: it is evidence of the widespread influence of *Pollyanna* in English-speaking cultures, and it is also evidence of a significant negative reaction to *Pollyanna* as a novel and to the glad game in particular, since pollyannaism is an unrealistic, unreasonable, or illogical optimism. These two facts together also indicate, I think, that *Pollyanna* taps into some very deep concerns and experiences in our societies. *Pollyanna* has deep roots in our social imaginaries, and those deep roots also explain the presence of pragmatic themes in the novel; both the novel and the philosophy are imbued with their origins and contexts.[10]

But what of pollyannaism? Is that a fair charge to level at the novel? In discussing this question, one could speak of the novel's historical and cultural context and the optimism of the age. However, I prefer to pursue a philosophical line of reasoning. As noted earlier, I have given a deliberately simplified version of pragmatism (and only that of James) because my focus is on *Pollyanna.* Nevertheless, despite the common criticism of pragmatism—that it is unrealistic and has an insufficient respect for the truth—it is not accused of pollyannaism. Perhaps this is one place where the comparison between *Pollyanna* and pragmatism breaks down. At the same time, perhaps pragmatism can still help us understand *Pollyanna,* even in its susceptibility to pollyannaism.

There is a dark side to the glad game; namely, the glad game is predicated on the actuality of grief; that is, the glad game only comes into existence and takes its deepest inspiration from grief. For example, the glad game arises out of Pollyanna's deeply felt disappointment at receiving crutches; obviously, both the other characters and we readers recognize and share that deep grief—even though it is hardly described in the novel—given the strength of the response to this scene. Moreover, just as the scene gives short shrift to Pollyanna's grief—and certainly does not even begin to explore its depth—the role of her father in inventing the glad game appears to be one of denying the validity of a little girl's grief. This is indeed a dark side.

Despite how we now understand pollyannaism and *Pollyanna*, the heroine herself is full of grief; Pollyanna is grieving her mother, her father, and her home out west. Roxanne Harde's chapter in this collection offers a more in-depth analysis of grief and trauma in *Pollyanna*, and suggests that by giving Pollyanna's father a voice and presence in his daughter's life, the glad game functions as a means for Pollyanna to work through her grief. It is surely significant that the only other child in *Pollyanna* is not just lonely like many of the adults; Jimmy is an orphan, an unwanted child who is explicitly rejected—by Aunt Polly, two Ladies' Aid Societies, and Mr. Pendleton, who eventually relents. Only Pollyanna accepts him. And yet, very little is made of what must be this little boy's soul-destroying grief at having no one to care for him, not to mention his repeated experiences of rejection. If there is something irritating about this novel as the charge of pollyannaism suggests, it is not the gladness; it is the invisibility, and perhaps repression, of actually experiencing and living with grief. The glad game can deteriorate into a denial of grief (or any other negative emotion or experience). For a pragmatist, the emphasis is on choosing to see reality differently, whereas Pollyanna, as a disappointed, doll-less young child, is told by her father to be glad that she does not need crutches and that she should in essence get over her disappointment. Anyone who has been told to eat their Brussels sprouts because there are starving children elsewhere knows that this sort of admonition is cold comfort. One wonders how much choice Pollyanna—and Jimmy for that matter—has in beginning to play the game.

There are some hints in *Pollyanna* that there are limits to the glad game. For example, Pollyanna tells Dr. Chilton that "being a doctor would be the very gladdest kind of business there was" because he is glad to help people (110); when Nancy suggests instead that perhaps the doctor can be glad because he is not the one who is sick, Pollyanna says "'of course that *is* one way [to play the game], but it isn't the way I said. And—somehow—I don't seem to like the sound of it. It isn't exactly as if he said he was glad they *were* sick, but—You do play the game so funny sometimes, Nancy'" (112). However, Pollyanna never gets beyond the acknowledgment that there is something wrong here. Later on, Pollyanna herself says to Nancy (when Nancy is glad that Aunt Polly has been called away to a funeral) that "it must be that there are some things that 'tisn't right to play the game on—and I'm sure funerals is one of them. There's nothing in a funeral to be glad about" (98). Pollyanna here seems to be dimly aware that grief cannot simply be willed away. Still, the complexity of the relation between deeply felt grief and willing happiness in spite of that grief is not dealt with in depth in the novel.[11]

Maybe *Pollyanna* is criticized not because of its unreasonable optimism, but because the glad game too easily ignores or represses a negative state by positing an overly simple positive state. For example, the bright side of paralysis is *not* that one at least *had* legs and thereby accomplished many glad things (even though that is what Pollyanna says: "I can be glad I've *had* my legs, anyway—else I couldn't have done that!" [206]). We might say that a sudden disability gives one a new or unique perspective on life (to simply gesture at how one might attempt to think positively about paralysis). In other words, in this particular example—which is the ultimate playing of the game in the novel—we can see that there is not enough of a legitimate connection between the negative state—paralysis—and the positive state—being grateful that one had been able to walk at an earlier time in one's life. The connection just is not there—it is what philosophers call a *category mistake* (and, of course, category mistakes are irritating). A category mistake is made when things of one sort are treated or understood as things of another sort; usually, this mistake can only be seen when the meanings of things in question are unpacked and one realizes that they could not properly be understood as belonging to another category. So, for example, Pollyanna's paralysis has nothing to do with—is not in the same category as—her previous mobility, while the state of receiving crutches but not needing them is very much germane to her mobility. In other words, paralysis in the present is not necessary for one to enjoy one's past mobility; if it were, we should all wish for future paralysis so as to be "truly glad" in our current mobility today. This situation is unlike the original situation where Pollyanna receives unnecessary crutches: there is a definite connection between receiving crutches and not needing them. The connection is one of superfluousness and it is a superfluousness that most would be glad of, whereas I doubt many who have experienced or observed the sheer joy of a child running or dancing would claim that that joy requires or is enhanced by the expectation or certainty of eventual paralysis, quite the contrary. I cannot see how the glad game would work backwards, as it were; if it did work so, perhaps Pollyanna should be glad that she did not receive a doll in the missionary barrel because she might have lost it in the future. Pollyanna herself does not trivialize or deny her own depression during her temporary paralysis nor do the other characters; but neither does she explicitly acknowledge that her paralysis might be one of those things that "'tisn't right to play the game on" (98).

If there is something like a category mistake in the novel, it might be because, quite simply, there are indeed some things one should not play the glad game on. There is, for example, nothing in the paralysis of a child to be glad about; something that is so irredeemably bad is in another category altogether. Of course, the thorough badness of paralysis does not mean that the child (and her family) can never be glad again. As James argued, some facts cannot be changed, but how we live our life is a matter of our will to believe: "there is an element of real wrongness in the world, which is *neither to be ignored nor evaded*, but which must be squarely met and overcome by the soul's heroic resources" ("Religious Experience" 396, emphasis added). Pollyanna does, I think, meet her paralysis squarely head on in the end; however, it is too much a "real wrongness" to be overcome by the glad game. A game does not seem to take the reality of the hurt seriously; it is a matter for—in the category of—a "soul's heroic resources."

But, then, how are we to understand Pollyanna's paralysis in the novel? How are we to read this critical scene? If Pollyanna's paralysis is redemptive at all—if there is something in it that one can reasonably find to be glad about—it is that it brings together Aunt Polly and Dr. Chilton, who says, "Little girl, I'm thinking that one of the very gladdest jobs you ever did has been done today'" (218); at least, this repaired relationship is the most significant positive result. But it is obvious, given their love for Pollyanna, that neither character would wish paralysis on Pollyanna so that they could live happily ever after. And so, Pollyanna's paralysis, despite its glad results, remains troubling for the reader. It is—like a category mistake—an incongruity that we have a hard time making fit.

However, this incongruity highlights the prevalence of immobility as a theme in the novel: not only does the gladness game originate in Pollyanna receiving crutches, but Mrs. Snow is bedridden, Mr. Pendleton is incapacitated by a broken leg, and Pollyanna is paralyzed and eventually has to use crutches herself.[12] I note that paralysis (and immobility) are apt metaphors for the kind of quietism to which accepting the facts of reality leads. Some facts are beyond changing—James would agree—but accepting the intransigence of those facts results remarkably often in a completely passive resignation, such that some facts are accepted that need not be accepted at all, as turns out to be the case with Pollyanna's paralysis. More complicatedly, such an acceptance often blinds us to the power that we do have. For example, the reader can imagine Aunt Polly and Dr. Chilton saying that their quarrel inevitably causes their separation (or "forces" them to part); however, a quarrel does no such thing. As we all likely know from our own experience, we choose how to respond to a quarrel (just as we have a great deal to do with a quarrel happening in the first place or the form it takes); it is not that a quarrel is not damaging— sometimes immensely so, as it was for Aunt Polly and Dr. Chilton—but even a great deal of damage does not ineluctably lead to a complete break in the same way that dropping a brick will inevitably lead to the brick hitting the ground.

Perhaps this is how we should understand Pollyanna's paralysis: it is an example—and perhaps caution of—the extremity that we often require to make us realize our own power. As Mr. Pendleton says about "the skeleton in his closet": "In fact, I *know* that a 'nice little boy' would be far better than—my skeleton in the closet. Only—we aren't always willing to make the exchange. We are apt to still cling to—our skeletons, Pollyanna" (152). James's point is that we have a choice—even not making a choice, or resignation, is itself a choice. Moreover, he argues that "the part of wisdom as well as of courage is to *believe what is in the line of your needs*, for only by such belief is the need fulfilled. . . . You make one or the other of two possible universes true by your trust or mistrust,—both universes having been only *maybes*, in this particular, before you contributed your act" (James "Will to Believe" 59). The glad game shows us that we have a choice about how to live our lives: we can choose to cling to our skeletons or we can choose to adopt a child. In similar fashion, James's pragmatism presents us with a choice about how we are to live our lives.

Finally, both the glad game and pragmatism tell us that in large part, we shape our reality. Pragmatism is a philosophy and *Pollyanna* is a children's novel, so there are both similarities and differences. But the similarities I have picked out show that this children's novel itself contributes to the making of our shared reality. The enduring significance of pragmatism in the scholarly world is paralleled by its influence in a beloved children's novel. *Pollyanna* shapes our imaginaries—the place where we make sense of our lives, where we fashion and tell our stories—so the very novel itself and its cultural influence are a "will to believe."

Notes

1. For example, in Peter R. Costello's *Philosophy in Children's Literature*, Claire M. Brown explores issues of "moral sainthood" in *Pollyanna*.

2. Indeed, Royce also claims that James is one of only three representative American philosophers, the other two being Jonathan Edwards and Ralph Waldo Emerson (3).

3. The United States was not the only country in which pragmatism was developed (as James was more than once at pains to point out), but it is certainly the case that the country embraced it as a quintessentially American philosophy.

4. Although Royce's summation of pragmatism here is accurate, he goes on to caution that this one-sentence summary alone is a "crude interpretation" (588).

5. See "The Dilemma of Determinism" (1884).

6. John R. Shook argues that "James's pragmatism developed from his investigations into the mind's capacities" (8).

7. I use the word *knowing* here deliberately to draw attention to the position in pragmatism that knowing is always an action, a relation between the knower and the known, and not a static object as is suggested by the word *knowledge*.

8. One of the most well-known contemporary pragmatists' works is *Philosophy and the Mirror of Nature* by Richard Rorty, in which representationalism is challenged.

9. See James's responses to some of these criticisms in "The Pragmatist Account of Truth and Its Misunderstanders" (1909). The same criticisms are made of contemporary pragmatists such as Richard Rorty.

10. My understanding of social imaginaries has been shaped by Jacques Lacan, *Four Fundamental Concepts of Psycho-Analysis* (1994); Cornelius Castoriadis, *The Imaginary Institution of Society* (1987); and Charles Taylor, *Modern Social Imaginaries* (2004).

11. James deals with the criticism that the will to believe is simply a denial of evil in several places; he says, repeatedly, that "a little reflection shows that the situation is too complex to lie open to so simple a criticism" ("Will to Believe" 101) and argues that one must understand the role that free will plays. There is, of course, no such argument in *Pollyanna*; it depends on how one reads the novel (and, of course, on how the novel has been read, which is my focus).

12. Strangely, immobility played a large role in James's own life. His sister, Alice James, to whom he was very close, was bedridden for a significant portion of her adult life.

Works Cited

Castoriadis, Cornelius. *The Imaginary Institution of Society*. London: Polity, 1987. Print.

Costello, Peter R. *Philosophy in Children's Literature*. Plymouth: Lexington, 2012. Print.

James, William. "The Dilemma of Determinism." 1884. *The Will to Believe and Other Essays in Popular Philosophy*. New York: Dover, 1956. Print.

———. *The Principles of Psychology*. 1890. New York: Henry Holt. Print.

———. "Is Life Worth Living?" *The Will to Believe and Other Essays in Popular Philosophy*. 1895. New York: Dover, 1956. Print.

———. *The Will to Believe and Other Essays in Popular Philosophy.* 1896. New York: Dover, 1956. Print.

———. *The Varieties of Religious Experience: A Study in Human Nature.* 1902. New York: Random House, 2002. Print.

———. "What Pragmatism Means." *The Essential William James.* 1907. Ed. John R. Shook. Amherst, NY: Prometheus, 2011. Print.

———. "Pragmatism's Conception of Truth." *The Essential William James.* 1907. Ed. John R. Shook. Amherst, NY: Prometheus, 2011. Print.

———. *Pragmatism: A New Way for Some Old Ways of Thinking.* New York: Longmans, Green, 1907. Print.

———. "The Pragmatist Account of Truth and Its Misunderstanders." *The Essential William James.* 1909. Ed. John R. Shook. Amherst, NY: Prometheus, 2011. Print.

———. *The Meaning of Truth: A Sequel to "Pragmatism."* New York: Longmans, Green, 1909. Print.

Lacan, Jacques. *Four Fundamental Concepts of Psycho-Analysis.* London: Penguin, 1977. Print.

Porter, Eleanor H. *Pollyanna.* 1913. Mahwah: Watermill, 1989. Print.

Rorty, Richard. *Philosophy and the Mirror of Nature.* Princeton: Princeton UP, 1977. Print.

Royce, Josiah. 1911. "William James and the Philosophy of Life." *The Varieties of Religious Experience: A Study in Human Nature.* New York: Modern Library, 2002. Print.

———. *William James and Other Essays on the Philosophy of Life.* New York: Macmillan, 1911. Print.

Shook, John R. "Introduction." *The Essential William James.* Ed. John R. Shook. Amherst, NY: Prometheus, 2011. Print.

Taylor, Charles. *Modern Social Imaginaries.* Durham: Duke UP, 2004. Print.

8

When Pollyanna Did Not Grow Up:
Girlhood and the Innocent Nation

DOROTHY KARLIN

When Eleanor Hodgman Porter published *Pollyanna* in 1913, the United States was attempting to alter its international role and, in order to do so, its image. In political rhetoric and in literature, the nation had long been portrayed as the offspring of European countries, Britain's rebellious son. With the 1904 Roosevelt Corollary to the Monroe Doctrine, the United States government shifted its role to that of a kindly brother by sanctioning a policy of international interventionism; it labeled the nation closer to if not quite like imperial England but also above "heathen" India or "savage" Latin America. With the 1898 Spanish-American War, the United States had, in fact, become an imperial power, annexing Guam, Puerto Rico, and, briefly, the Philippine Islands, and the nation had to articulate how it intended to use its power both at home and abroad. This changing national identity affected writing other than explicit political rhetoric, even resolutely apolitical novels written for children. To justify imperialist practices, the nation presented itself as a beacon of morality and social consciousness, and *Pollyanna* fits within a corpus of domestic fiction that served to inculcate and promote images of America's childlike goodness. Part of a tradition of sentimental novels, Porter's novel constructs the innocent child to inhabit and represent the faultless nation, thereby modeling citizenship for child readers.

Early-twentieth-century literature frequently served as a vehicle for sociopolitical engagement, and reform-minded writers tried to make the country a more principled brother for other nations. In the midst of the Progressive Era—the social response to the conditions created by rapid industrialization—writers did not often portray domestic bliss when they turned their pens to national affairs. Early investigative journalists, muckrakers including Upton Sinclair, Theodore Dreiser, and Ida Tarbell, "took it upon themselves to enlighten the public about the details of the underside of American life" (Sage) through articles for magazines with ever-increasing circulation and novels read by the growing middle class. Hoping to spark reform, writers depicted urban maladies, corrupt business practices, and political dishonesty.

In addition to this politically purposeful literature, *Pollyanna* has similar goals without the open agenda. It draws on its child audience to soften its criticism, and it avoids discussing uncomfortable social realities. It does not depict societal problems with the same detail or verisimilitude; instead of inciting specific legal actions, the novel calls for a philosophy of gladness that can heal the community. With her sunshiny nature, Pollyanna inspires other characters and young readers with her relentless optimism and inexorable naïveté. Building on historic depictions of women as "angels in the house," domestic literature has frequently invoked belief in women's higher nature and inherent morality to model harmony at home. In the early twentieth century, these female counterparts balanced male representations of the nation as a rebellious son and a domineering brother with sweet daughter and virtuous mother. Together, these male and female representations worked within the national imagination to justify benevolent interventions domestically and internationally. As a novel for girls, *Pollyanna* uses conceptions of both gender and age to enable its portrayal of American values.

The construction of childhood has long served an important symbolic function in creating a national image for the United States. Literary representations resonate with and add to pervasive images of the youthful country. This essay will explore how *Pollyanna* purveys an idea of America based in rural New England and grounded in its construction of girlhood as a state of innocence. The novel mitigates conflicting notions of American identity—child/adult, boy/girl—in order to aid in the acculturation of its child audience, shaping its lessons through its setting and plot and the circumscription of its narrative to supposed childhood concerns. Despite excluding political affairs, *Pollyanna* nonetheless functions as a national allegory, calling for the preservation of existing social hierarchies. Moving back from the West, Pollyanna brings youth to New England, reinvigorating the region without shifting socioeconomic power structures or acknowledging other power structures. Through her, the novel unites girlhood with idealized American values; it calls for a nation based on a preservation of a youthful optimism that requires both a willful ignorance and the protection of that ignorance.

Domestic Novels as Political Allegories

On first encounter, *Pollyanna* comes across as distinctly apolitical and possibly timeless. Recently orphaned, a young girl moves from poverty in a generic West to live with her rich aunt in a generic town in New England. The disavowal of the broader context, however, does not separate the narrative from history. Instead, it situates the novel within a tradition of domestic novels that focus on social maneuvering within smaller communities and the family. The novel deploys a gentle national allegory to create an ideal domestic space (referring both to the individual home and the political sphere). By focalizing through its girl character, the 11-year-old Pollyanna, Porter deploys a particular homemaking narrative that centers on the child/caretaker bond. Pollyanna's philosophy of gladness makes her a model daughter and a model citizen.

I have appropriated the term *national allegory* from Doris Sommer in order to understand the process by which novels participate in the creation of nation (41). Referring to Benedict Anderson's imagined communities, Sommer plumbs the connection between the emotional and the political, which, she argues, fiction deploys differently from newspapers and other writings. Sommer looks at nineteenth-century Latin American domestic novels to demonstrate how the works helped foster a notion of national identity by allegorically bonding the political and the erotic, the nation and heterosexual love. She focuses on the novel's manipulation of libidinal desire, writing: "every obstacle that the lovers encounter heightens more than their mutual desire to (be a) couple, more than our voyeuristic but keenly felt passion; it also heightens their/our love for the possible nation in which the affair could be consummated" (48).

Sex, however, is not the only desire that fiction can exploit. I propose that *Pollyanna* accesses a different kind of erotic that is perhaps less titillating, but no less compelling. Pollyanna seeks familial, not conjugal bonds, and her story makes the reader want to create a space in which she can safely, and permanently, exist. The novel uses childhood innocence to fuel its nation-building project, tapping into its readers' desire to protect the vacuous purity it ascribes to its central child character.

Innocence and Home Spaces: Pollyanna as Allegory

As *Pollyanna* creates an image of unmarred innocence, it constructs the girl as the most innocent member of the home. Through this depiction of girlhood virtue, the novel purifies the home and in turn strengthens the established social order in its New England setting. It remedies internal discontent through two entwined national allegories: a child's homecoming and a rekindled relationship. Mr. Pendleton, the town's rich, cantankerous miser and former suitor to Pollyanna's mother, connects the two narratives when he tells Pollyanna, "It takes a woman's hand and heart, or a child's presence, to make a home, Pollyanna, and I have not had either" (Porter 181). Dr. Chilton expresses similar sentiments when he calls his habitation "a pretty poor apology for a home.... They're just rooms, that's all—not a home" (213). Both men invoke the emotional properties of home spaces, and they emphasize their inability to achieve emotional fulfillment alone. By delineating what they lack (wives and offspring), they promote the need for familial bonds and direct the novel's allegory. As with novels that rely on romance, *Pollyanna* pushes for the creation of the family in order to create a home, but family does not need to develop organically through coupling and childbirth.

By using a static version of childhood, the novel prevents its plot from permanently altering social structures. It proposes adoption instead of childbirth as a means to create the home and the family, and in Porter's novel marriage is not the necessary foundation for the nuclear family. *Pollyanna* may create slightly unconventional ties, bringing together different classes (Aunt Polly and Dr. Chilton as well as Mr. Pendleton and Jimmy Bean) along with the offspring of wayward relatives (Pollyanna), but it does not call for the propagation of those bonds. Tellingly, the novel's romance belongs to an older generation. Aunt Polly and Dr. Chilton resurrect their youthful courtship, but their middle-aged romance is not a fertile space. Similarly, Pollyanna proposes 11-year-old foundling Jimmy Bean as the solution to Mr. Pendleton's woes. The novel brings together two (seemingly) different classes, but the bachelor and boy do not form a fruitful union. In Porter's world, disparate classes can and should come together, but only those of the same class should reproduce. Before marrying Pollyanna in *Pollyanna Grows Up*, Jimmy discovers that he descends from Boston Brahmins. Whereas Sommer points to marriage and the promise of childbirth as key components in national romances, *Pollyanna*, without its sequel, does not provide a means for a literal reproduction of nation. Instead, characters can construct homes from available ingredients because their construction will not reproduce itself.

Within this framework of retrograde romance and adoption, the novel seeks to bring together different factions. Even as it addresses class differences, it allows minimal disruptions to the established social structure, which it maintains by locating the central difference within the family. While Pollyanna attempts to help all citizens of Beldingsville, Vermont, she focuses most energy on repairing the rift within the Harringtons, fortifying the upper strata of New England society. She becomes the antidote to the rupture her mother, Jennie, caused. Instead of marrying the rich New Englander John Pendleton, Jennie chose a life of penury in first the South and then the West as "a home missionary's wife" (Porter 6). Through this choice, she alienated herself from her family of origin, thereby weakening it and seemingly leading toward its extinction. Neither of her sisters, the featured Polly and the deceased Anna, have children. In the initial exposition, Porter writes, "time had not stood still for the occupants of the great house on the hill":

> [Miss Polly] was forty now, and quite alone in the world. Father, mother, sisters—all were dead. For years now she had been sole mistress of the house, and of the thousands left her by her father. There were people who had openly pitied her lonely life, and who had urged her to have some friend or companion to live with her. But she had not welcomed either their sympathy or their advice. She was not lonely, she said. She liked being by herself. (7)

Dwelling in the upper echelon of New England society, Aunt Polly, on the one hand, has become estranged from all other classes and from other members of her own class, which is dwindling in numbers. On the other hand, Jennie did not have marked success in a lower social class. All her children but Pollyanna died, and she and her husband eventually died as well. Rather than permanently linking the Harrington and Whittier names and binding different classes, Jennie manages to create only Pollyanna. Once her parents have died, Pollyanna is no longer tethered to her immediate birth family, especially her much-loved but socially questionable father; instead she becomes the means to preserve, if not truly repopulate, the Harrington estate.

Replacing Marital Bliss with Childhood Innocence

Porter targets a young audience through her character Pollyanna, distilling broader issues into family concerns. She uses childhood instead of marriage to bring factions together, and that shift, typical in American self-construction, affects and stultifies the story's trajectory. Porter borrows popular tropes from children's books written in the preceding half century, but focuses entirely on the protagonist's childhood. With limited drama and romance, she creates an appealing but static narrative. Comparing *Pollyanna* with *Anne of Green Gables* and *Rebecca of Sunnybrook Farm*, Perry Nodelman writes, "The Utopia these novels progress towards is actually a regressive world of perfect childlike innocence" (153). Despite arising from the Progressive Era, *Pollyanna* is not a vessel for change.

Porter appoints children as the appropriate recipients for Pollyanna's lessons in gladness and uses her intended audience to justify the narrow focus. In the early twentieth century, constructions of childhood evolved, affecting the scope of *Pollyanna* and explaining its relegation of heterosexual romance to an adult domain. The United States in the nineteenth century saw its fair share of domestic novels/national romances, but it also saw the rise of children's literature. Rather than avoiding romance, however, early novels written for children and/or read by them fit narratives of sexual desire into their didactic projects. Some of the first examples, such as Susan Warner's *The Wide, Wide World* (1850), Maria Cummins's *The Lamplighter* (1854), and Louisa May Alcott's *Little Women* (1868) and its sequel *Good Wives* (1869), use the marriage plot, and each can be read as allegorically uniting domestic desire and national unity. With marriage comes an idealized notion of nation, and these novels use satisfied desire to promote national unity, providing lessons in heteronormativity and patriotism to their young audience. Although the authors have different ideologies and respond to different historic moments, their texts deploy marriage to further their projects, and they use the discourse of desire to imagine the nation.

Unlike *Pollyanna*, these earlier narratives not only follow the characters through their childhood but also show them reach adulthood, connecting personal growth and fulfillment with the reward of marriage. Alcott's Beth March recognizes the inherent inertia caused by her lack of plans. Resigned to her death, in *Good Wives* she tells Jo: "I have a feeling that it never was meant that I should live long. I'm not like the rest of you; I never made any plans about what I'd do when I grew up; I never thought of being married, as you all did" (435). As a national allegory, Alcott's novel relies on the other sisters for symbolically laden marriages. Their romances touch upon issues of class and national origin in ways that Beth's permanent innocence cannot.

Written several decades later, *Pollyanna* (1913) comes closer to following Beth's trajectory than her sister's narratives, but sidesteps Beth's tragic ending. By relegating the marriage plot to a tangential role, Porter's novel finds a way to employ a Beth-like goodness. Like Beth, Pollyanna acts on other characters through her ingenuousness, which the novel maintains by ending before Pollyanna can mature. Looking at the development of sentimental literature, Robin Bernstein explains the nineteenth-century shift in the construction of childhood from sinful to innocent. Porter's text limits its focus to its protagonist's preadolescence, and in her youth Polly-anna embodies the idealized purity and emptiness that Bernstein explores in *Racial Innocence: Performing American Childhood from Slavery to Civil Rights*. Pollyanna is, as Bernstein suggests of children in eighteenth- and nineteenth-century children's literature generally, "sinless, absent of sex-ual feelings, and oblivious to worldly concerns" (6). Through most of the novel, she is 11 years old. Any romantic ambitions she may develop do not occur until the sequel, *Pollyanna Grows Up*, which was published two years later and, rather abruptly, adds eight years to the protagonist's life. In fact, Pollyanna has no future ambitions in the first novel, romantic or oth-erwise. The narrow scope shifts the focus from the dynamic possibilities of libidinal desire to the nostalgic desire for the fixed state of innocence.

The Nostalgic Nation of Children's Literature

Through this preservation of purity, *Pollyanna* becomes the vehicle for adult nostalgia. The erotic aspects of desire do not affect the protagonist because the novel is invested in limiting her knowledge and the knowl-edge of its readers. Looking at British works from the early twentieth cen-tury, Daphne Kutzer investigates how the combination of nostalgia and protection preserved the glorification of empire longer in children's nov-els than in those for adults:

> The presentation of childhood as an ideal, innocent kingdom of its own is
> linked to a . . . crucial difference between children's texts and adult texts:
> adults may be aware that a long-accepted cultural code is crumbling, that the
> world is shifting in unnerving and poorly understood ways, but they want
> both to shield children from these changes and encourage them to continue
> believing in and practicing cultural beliefs and codes that are no longer
> unquestioned in the adult world, perhaps in an unconscious desire to main-
> tain those earlier cultural codes. (xvi)

Regardless of whether adults want to maintain earlier cultural codes, in children's literature they rarely attempt to convey how poorly understood the world is. Kutzer writes that "the role of children's texts, both fictional and nonfictional, is to help acculturate children into society and to teach them to behave and believe in acceptable ways" (xv). Writing to a past version of self and speaking from an assumed position of cultural authority, children's book authors often create texts that celebrate an idealized, simplified past in order to protect an intended child audience from uncomfortable social realities.

As an example of national rhetoric and a work designed for children, *Pollyanna* plays on the desire inherent in nostalgia rather than erotic desire. It functions in a manner similar to Latin American national romances, but it deploys emotions connected with childhood in place of those connected with romance. Frequent depictions of the United States as a child nation make this focus on the child character both easy and effective in a nation-building project. In *Audacious Kids: Coming of Age in America's Classic Children's Books*, Jerry Griswold writes: "from the Revolution through the mid-nineteenth century, America's political writers and thinkers consistently understood their country's history in terms of the story of a child engaged in oedipal rebellion against the tyranny and despotism of its macrocosmic father, the king" (94). In the decades following the Civil War, the national imagination required a revised myth: "one that pictured America as having achieved a more advanced state of childhood. Instead of constant filial rebellion and secession, politicians spoke of the need for the restoration of domestic harmony" (*sic*, 94). With the rift evidenced by and augmented by the Civil War, subsequent nation-building projects required a more amicable rhetoric, shifting from rebellion against an external authority (i.e., England) to agreement within the nation.

By arriving at domestic harmony through the child instead of the adult, *Pollyanna* constructs the home and the family without disrupting innocence. The novel takes advantage of the intersection of national romances and children's literature to control the domestic space. Rather than anticipating a union through marriage, the novel shows how to create an ideal home through the adopted child, an allegory Claudia Nelson explores in *Little Strangers: Portrayals of Adoption and Foster Care in America, 1850–1929*, in which she writes, "it is the problems of the private sphere, not the public, that the fictional orphan solves" (136), fulfilling the role frequently assigned to fictional mothers. Looking at the 1909 White House Conference on the Care of Dependent Children, Nelson demonstrates how "private mothercraft . . . was yoked with the power of public organization" (137). *Pollyanna* may alleviate problems in the domestic space, but the family is the nation's strength: private is public. Another aspect of Progressive politics, the discussion about childcare nonetheless relies on idealizing a past state. While the child is constructed as a site of hope, the child can only age out of her purity and innocence, so her rhetorical strength is always already nostalgic. She is the sign of the future but strong only in her perpetual youth.

Childhood and Nation Formation: Foreign Affairs

Pollyanna creates the ideal home through the female child. Writing about the allegorical functions of *Little Lord Fauntleroy* (1885) and *Adventures of Huckleberry Finn* (1885), Griswold does not address the different constructions of girlhood and boyhood as microcosmic representations of the political macrocosm. The two, however, work in tandem. The brash, adventurous oedipal boy may represent the nation asserting itself in business or on the international stage, but the sweet, innocent girl belongs at home to preserve American values and morals, the foundation of the social-mindedness and political reform of Progressive Era America.

In "Jane Austen and Empire," post-colonialist Edward Said lambasts the British author for her complicity in colonialism. Although later critics have complicated Said's reading, domestic novels provide a necessary counterpart to imperialist texts. In imperialist rhetoric, women live in an insular space, ignorant of the horrors of the barbaric lands and peoples found in the far reaches of the globe. They have no understanding of the source of their comfort. While men struggle in the darkness, their women maintain a pure space at home. Ignoring international affairs, the nation preserves its virtue through a happy myth. Women, with their necessarily uninformed morality, represent the nation. According to this gender binary, women must preserve their virtue to protect civilization. While at home, within the feminine space, the men must not speak of their experiences beyond its boundaries, and the women should not admit to knowledge of them.

Adhering to this dichotomy, *Pollyanna* betrays little knowledge of international relations beyond mentions of the "heathens" in India and Mr. Pendleton's trips to foreign shores. In 1913 the United States increasingly had a role in global politics. Until the early twentieth century, the Monroe Doctrine had governed U.S. foreign policy; introduced in 1823, it was designed to protect the Western hemisphere from continued colonial incursions. Based on this policy, the United States government would consider European interference in the newly formed North and South

American nations acts of aggression and would respond accordingly. Around the time *Pollyanna* was published, the United States shifted from this defensive policy to more aggressive, if supposedly friendly, international involvement. In December 1904, in his annual message to Congress, Theodore Roosevelt delivered his corollary to the Monroe Doctrine. He proclaimed that the United States, as a "civilized nation," had the right to stop "chronic wrongdoing" throughout the Western Hemisphere as well as in the Far East, Armenia, and the Philippines (Roosevelt). Based on this policy, the United States justified intervention with "international police power." Roosevelt's successor, William Taft, believed in economic expansion, and he built on Roosevelt's policy with his own "dollar diplomacy," which aimed to advance and protect American businesses in other countries. Roosevelt coupled international intervention with improved domestic conduct, however, writing: "We have plenty of sins of our own to war against, and under ordinary circumstances we can do more for the general uplifting of humanity by striving with heart and soul to put a stop to civic corruption, to brutal lawlessness and violent race prejudices here at home than by passing resolutions about wrongdoing elsewhere" (Roosevelt). Roosevelt articulates the national sentiments that inspired the social reform of the Progressive Era. In this historical context, *Pollyanna* cleanses the domestic space. Mirroring political rhetoric, the novel works to uplift humanity by ensuring good behavior at home. It creates this inward focus by ignoring external events.

Childhood and Nation Formation: The National Sphere

While *Pollyanna* includes discontented individuals and bickering groups, it does not in any way indicate corruption, lawlessness, or race prejudice—the troubles Roosevelt ascribes to home and that "muckrakers" sought to redress with their writings. On the contrary, Porter's novel creates a space with few evident social hierarchies beyond socioeconomic class, and no evidence of multiple races beyond Nancy's Irish presence. It draws on its rural Vermont setting to render race a non-issue; according to the 2010 U.S. Census, Vermont remains one of the whitest states in the union (United States). Pollyanna may meet members of lower classes, such as Mrs. Payson, a woman with an unsavory reputation who lives at the edges of Beldingsville, but she only ever encounters a non-Caucasian in the sanatorium "many miles from here" (246). In a letter home, she mentions

"Black Tilly, who washes the floor" (247). This African American presence in the final passage calls attention to the lack of race in the rest of the novel. In *Discovering Black Vermont: African American Farmers in Hinesburgh, 1790–1890*, Elise Guyette writes:

> The historical myth of a white, slave-free Vermont grew out of the desire to save white, Anglo-Saxon, Protestant culture and identity in the face of large migrations to the North before and after the Civil War. The myth . . . hardened into absolute truth as new Canadian and European immigrants flowed into the area in larger numbers than any Yankee could remember. (5)

Guyette refers to the myth of an all-white Vermont, populated entirely by Yankees, in order to dispel it. Porter, on the other hand, accesses that myth in order to exploit it. Her novel avoids racial and ethnic divides.

As ever, the nation was not free from racial issues at the time. In fact, the eugenics movement was in full swing. Describing the *de jure* white supremacy in ascendancy at the turn of the century, Nancy Ordover writes: "Early eugenics proponents, drawn from the ranks of scientists, politicians, doctors, sexologists, policy makers, reactionaries, and reformers, held that through selective breeding humans could and should direct their own evolution" (xii). Relying heavily on Etienne Balibar's work, Ordover shows how eugenics served racialist and nativist agendas, proposing a means to purify the nation through artificial selection. Guyette proves that Vermont was not immune to racism—in the 1920s the state implemented its own eugenics project—but she identifies the popular, enduring perception of Vermont as both homogeneous and tolerant. *Pollyanna* deploys the setting as the site of nation, home to American ideals of open-mindedness safe from visible marks of difference.

The novel distills the whiteness of the setting in the character of Pollyanna. She embodies the racial innocence of Robin Bernstein's theorizing: "innocence was not a literal state of being unraced but was, rather, the performance of not-noticing, a performed claim of slipping beyond social categories" (6). The novel focuses on Pollyanna not noticing social categories, particularly class, but race is not a category that she need not notice. Blond and blue-eyed, Pollyanna is as white as Little Eva of *Uncle Tom's Cabin*, but she has no African American lap on which to perch. She may not notice race if confronted by difference, but she and her home are safely nestled in the white-washed construction of Vermont, which is as pure and wholesome as maple syrup.

Cleansing the Home with Gladness:
Pollyanna's Unconscious Evangelism

As "the child's presence" (Porter 181), Pollyanna enables the creation of a stronger domestic unit, but her particular charm derives from her sunshiny purveyance of goodness as a Christian presence. Pollyanna arrives in Vermont as an insular home missionary, and the limited scope of her religious work further constricts the home to shelter women and children. She becomes the means to purify the home. With unconscious innocence but deliberate, decidedly conscious optimism, she enlivens and improves the disgruntled and discordant community. Whereas her father and mother traveled to different regions within the United States to spread gladness, Pollyanna circumscribes that work to her aunt's home and inhabitants of the town. The novel frequently mentions the attention paid to the "heathen" in foreign countries in order to demonstrate the hypocrisy of overseas charity that ignores nearby need. When Pollyanna tries to convince the Beldingsville Ladies' Aid to help Jimmie Bean, she finds that "they would rather send all their money to bring up the little India boys than to save out enough to bring up one little boy in their own town" (117). With her innocent reflections, she becomes the vehicle for criticism of this focus on evangelism overseas. Instead of sending money abroad, she advocates a healing of local conflicts through local aid. Significantly, the novel suggests that women, in this case the Ladies' Aid, should not be involved in imperialist pursuits. They should practice virtue within the home, and focus their energies on helping children.

Pollyanna has a positive influence on the community; her use of the glad game affects everyone from Aunt Polly to Mrs. Snow, a chronic invalid, and Mrs. Payson, a woman of ill repute. Spreading her father's optimistic gospel, she teaches everyone to change their outlooks and rethink their dissatisfactions. With her infectious cheerfulness, she seems to be an agent of change, albeit not necessarily revolutionary. Despite her ability to change the community and even her "criticism of convention" (qtd. in Griswold 221), the narrative limits the changes she can make. Jerry Griswold praises Pollyanna for her cunning: "she gets her way by being glad—and such innocent gratitude seems not only above reproach, but invulnerable to suspicion" (219). He speaks of her radical innocence, writing: "What is conspicuous about the conclusions of many of America's children's classics . . . is not an inevitable surrender to 'things as they are,' a sensible surrender to level-headed realism and maturity" (235). Rather than marking the conclusion of the work, however, that radical innocence marks Pollyanna's entrance in the novel. To maintain innocence, the novel inhibits what she can know about her manipulation; she does not realize what she can accomplish with it.

Imagining the Nation through the Good Girl

Pollyanna's power, then, relies on her race, youth, and gender. Griswold compares Pollyanna to Tom Sawyer, labeling both tricksters. Unlike Tom, however, Pollyanna cannot know what she does. Griswold wants her to be the same artful character, but the preservation of childhood innocence has a strongly gendered component. Clearly *Pollyanna*, as it showcases childhood, relates to the Bad Boy books of the postbellum era, which Kenneth Kidd explores in *Making American Boys: Boyology and the Feral Tale*. The male characters are also vehicles of adult nostalgia for childhood innocence, but the boys do not need to display the same level of virtue that Pollyanna does in order to remain blameless. Books of the Bad Boy genre provide a space for boys to have a delinquency that "is both 'innocent' and promises future success" (Kidd 54). According to Kidd, Bad Boy books present boyhood in Spencerian evolutionary terms: "boyhood becomes the synecdoche for evolution and the law of progress" (17). Boys' childhood innocence belongs to their savage phase; they are aware of what they do, but they are not held accountable because they will outgrow their natural wickedness. In contrast, as a girl Pollyanna's only acts of disobedience arise from her inability to anticipate her aunt's rules and from speaking with embarrassing candor. She is never bad, certainly never wicked, and she does not intentionally try to get her way. When proposing Jimmy Bean as Ladies' Aid beneficiary, she wonders if she "was Aunt Polly's little girl from India?" (131), but that query only highlights her naïveté. She believes in morality and devotion to missionary work in a literal way that cannot comprehend the complexities of imperialism and Orientalism. She speaks of "heathens" but does not know what this means. In contrast, Jimmy reminds her to tell the Ladies' Aid that he will work, musing "biz'ness is biz'ness, even with Ladies' Aiders" (131). Pollyanna recognizes virtue as a motivating force, whereas Jimmy has a more work-oriented idea of the world. With her industrious optimism, she and the bad boy may fulfill similar functions, but she does so by being the good girl.

The novel highlights Pollyanna's manipulation, but she is only effective if she does not know. Her innocence, the ingenuousness of the young girl, depends upon ignorance. She recognizes that she has to choose to play the glad game—she does not naturally appreciate every hardship and frustration—but she does not know how well she uses it to make other characters, particularly her aunt, meet her expectations of their virtue. The novel deploys this lack of awareness without explicitly defining it. In the sequel, Aunt Polly articulates it, telling her husband, "It's her unconsciousness that saves the whole thing" (19). As Aunt Polly, now Mrs. Chilton, explains: "She knows, of course, that you and I, and half the town are playing the game with her, and that we—we are wonderfully happier because we are playing it. . . . But if, consciously, she should begin to be anything but her own natural, sunny, happy little self, playing the game that her father taught her, she would be—just what that nurse said she sounded like—'impossible'" (19).

Pollyanna recognizes the power of the game, but she remains unaware of the power of her nature. She is effective because she expects others to live up to what the text constructs as her childish assumptions. Other characters do not want to betray her trust, so she unintentionally plays on their knowledge of their own lack of virtue. In the first book, Aunt Polly frequently feels helpless and powerless in the face of Pollyanna's expectations. When she refuses to take in Jimmy Bean, she feels "a curious sense of desolation—as of something lost" (111). In this scene she recognizes that she does not deserve Pollyanna's absolute trust in her goodness; and on a broader scale, that sense of loss is adult nostalgia for girlhood virtue.

Home Again: Restoring Hope, Prolonging Childhood, and Protecting the Innocence

The plot creates a false forward momentum; it solves Pollyanna's need for love and belonging in a happy domestic space. Drama enters the plot when Pollyanna gets hit by a car and can no longer walk or be glad. Many critics have read the novel as a book about disability, notably Lois Keith in *Take Up Thy Bed and Walk: Death, Disability and Cure in Classic Fiction for Girls*. Keith pinpoints the narrative purpose of this accident: Pollyanna's "*gladness* is put to the ultimate test" (150). Devastated by the thought of an unhappy Pollyanna, the community visits her to explain how they have learned to appreciate their current situations. They do everything in their power to return the little girl to her former state. Pollyanna's disabled self embodies nostalgia's yearning for the past; she has lost her perfect childhood self. Her loss mimics adulthood's loss without incurring its permanence. Adults may not be able to return to innocence, but Polly-anna can (and does!) regain the ability to walk and the ability to play the glad game.

While Porter was unlikely to be deliberately conveying United States policies of the early twentieth century, her didactic engagement both reflects the ideology of the time and has ideological ramifications. With her portrayal of the good girl, she advocates a particular style of citizen-ship. Rather than create a "muckraker," Porter promotes nonpolitical civic engagement through innocence that refuses to notice social differences and negativity. Her criticisms of narrow-mindedness and class inequities do not necessarily condone imperialist practices, but her novel fits within a broader literature. As part of this system, her good girl functions as the necessary counterpart to male representations of the nation. With good-ness achieved at home and innocence preserved, the nation can assert itself as a model of morality.

As Pollyanna learns to walk again at the sanatorium, she returns to her initial optimism, and her final letter to her happily married aunt and uncle promises her return home. The novel creates the need for her capacity for hope and for belonging by removing both. Pollyanna's temporary separa-tion from home, much like the promise of matrimony in the initial pub-lications of *The Wide, Wide World* and *Little Women*, provokes the desire for fulfillment. Once she goes back to Vermont, Pollyanna can restore the ideal family in the ideal space. Through this veneration of girlhood inno-cence, the novel purifies the home. It prohibits discontent and praises igno-rance. As a nation-building project, *Pollyanna* induces domestic harmony by uniting a community through everyone's work to protect the child's, specifically the female child's, perceived or desired innocence. Like novels that end in marriage, *Pollyanna* works to bolster unity, but the shift in focus from romance to family and home is significant. The novel deploys a young girl to heal community differences and assert appropriate values for the nation as a whole, but creates a different version of domestic har-mony and happiness from those found in national romances. In contrast with entrepreneurial boys and adventurous lads, Pollyanna is a happy, de-eroticized homemaker, providing a wholesome, cheerful counterpart to business and politics. She upholds the virtuousness of the nation. How can America be a good neighbor if no one is at home learning how to bake the apple pie?

Works Cited

Bernstein, Robin. *Racial Innocence: Performing American Childhood and Race from Slavery to Civil Rights*. New York: NYU Press, 2011. Print.

Cummins, Maria S. *The Lamplighter*. New Brunswick: Rutgers UP, 1988. Print.

Griswold, Jerry. *Audacious Kids: Coming of Age in America's Classic Children's Books*. Oxford: Oxford UP, 1992. Print.

Guyette, Elise A. *Discovering Black Vermont: African American Farmers in Hinesburgh, 1790–1890*. Burlington: U of Vermont P, 2010. Print.

Keith, Lois. *Take Up Thy Bed and Walk: Death, Disability and Cure in Classic Fiction for Girls*. New York: Routledge, 2001. Print.

Kidd, Kenneth B. *Making American Boys: Boyology and the Feral Tale*. Minneapolis: U of Minnesota P, 2004. Print.

Kutzer, Daphne. *Empire's Children: Empire and Imperialism in Classic British Children's Books*. New York: Psychology Press, 2000. Print.

Nelson, Claudia. *Little Strangers: Portrayals of Adoption and Foster Care in America, 1850–1929*. Bloomington: Indiana UP, 2003. Print.

Nodelman, Perry. "Progressive Utopia: Or, How to Grow Up Without Growing Up." *Children's Literature Association Quarterly* (1979): 146–54. *Project MUSE*. Web. 14 May 2012.

Ordover, Nancy. *American Eugenics: Race, Queer Anatomy, and the Science of Nationalism*. Minneapolis: U of Minnesota P, 2003. Print.

Porter, Eleanor Hodgman. *Pollyanna*. 1913. New York: Aladdin Classics, 2002. Print.

———. *Pollyanna Grows Up*. 1915. Champaign: Book Jungle, 2009. Print.

Roosevelt, Theodore. "Roosevelt's Corollary to the Monroe Doctrine." *Our Documents*. Web. 14 May 2012.

Sage, Henry J. "The Progressive Era: The Great Age of Reform." *Academic American*. Web. 14 May 2012.

Sommer, Doris. *Foundational Fictions: The National Romances of Latin America*. Berkeley: U of California P, 1993. Print.

United States. Census Bureau. "Overview of Race and Hispanic Origin: 2010." *2010 Census Briefs*. Washington: U.S. Census Bureau, March 2011. Web. 8 September 2013.

Warner, Susan. *The Wide, Wide World*. 1850. New York: Feminist Press, 1987. Print.

9

Pollyanna: Intersectionalities of the Child, the Region, and the Nation

PATRICIA OMAN

When the orphaned Pollyanna Whittier first sees her ugly attic bedroom in the beautiful Beldingsville, Vermont, mansion where she has come to live, she somehow overcomes her initial disappointment by being "glad" (15). Even though the room is unadorned and unbearably hot, she is enchanted by "the beautiful view from the window," which "she mentally designated" a "picture" (15). This brief scene from Eleanor H. Porter's 1913 novel *Pollyanna* demonstrates not only the unsinkable optimism that has come to be associated with the novel and with the word "Pollyanna," but also the novel's melding of two distinct genres: children's literature and regional literature. As Jerry Griswold argues, *Pollyanna* is one example of the orphan "ur-story" so common in American children's literature of the Golden Age, a story marked by the child protagonist's journey to a new life after being orphaned or abandoned. Unlike most examples of this ur-story, however, *Pollyanna* is also characterized by the conventions of regional literature. Thus, when Pollyanna sees her new bedroom, she is not only starting what Griswold calls her "Second Life" (224) but also practicing the aesthetic distance of a tourist by envisioning the landscape of Beldingsville as a painting. Porter's second Pollyanna novel, *Pollyanna Grows Up* (1914), similarly melds the conventions of American children's literature and regional literature, except this time Pollyanna plays the role of a hotel proprietor who invites another young orphan just beginning his Second Life to vacation at her aunt's Beldingsville mansion.

The association of the small Vermont town with this classic American orphan story suggests more than just the combination of two distinct genres; it also suggests a discursive compatibility between constructions of childhood and region in early twentieth-century America, especially in assumptions of the essential child and the essential region. Recent scholarship that reveals the constructed nature of "the child" and "the region" should make us question the novels' assumptions of essential categories, however. As children's literature scholars such as David Rudd have argued, for instance, biological determinism is inadequate to explain the complexity of "the child" in relation to children's literature. In other words, childhood is not the innocent and essential opposite of adulthood.

Similarly, in the area of regional literature, scholars such as Marjorie Pryse, Judith Fetterley, and Richard H. Brodhead have demonstrated that region is an ideological construct rather than a geographically determined place. Thus, while regional literature, especially local color of the nineteenth and early twentieth centuries, is often assumed to represent an essential and uncomplicated retreat from the problems of modern urban life, recent scholarship demonstrates that region is actually a representational mode that arises alongside and in response to modernity and the nation.

This chapter thus uses these recent scholarly re-evaluations of children's literature and regional literature to explore the intersection of these often ignored genres in *Pollyanna* and *Pollyanna Grows Up*. More specifically, it argues that Porter's Pollyanna novels demonstrate the intersectional alignment of several hegemonic discourses of early-twentieth-century America, including nationalism and urbanism. While these discourses may seem to adopt the marginalized perspectives of women, children, and the rural regions through the discourse of essentialism, for the most part they actually reflect ideological assumptions held by the educated, urban elite of early-twentieth-century America.

I approach this argument synchronically in increasing layers of complexity. The first section demonstrates the nationalizing impulse of the Pollyanna novels by situating them within the context of other American orphan stories, particularly L. Frank Baum's *The Wonderful Wizard of Oz*. Through a comparison with Sarah Orne Jewett's classic regional story "A White Heron," the second section explains how the intersectional alignment of the child and the nation makes it possible for the Pollyanna novels to affirm the hegemonic discourse of nation. I conclude by considering how the related discourses of gender, economic class, and ethnicity reinforce the intersectionality of childhood, regionalism, and nationalism.

Nation and Region in the American Orphan Story

The respective plots of *Pollyanna* and *Pollyanna Grows Up* would have been very familiar to readers in the early twentieth century. The tradition of the plucky orphan—what Griswold calls an ur-story—had already been established in works such as Frances Hodgson Burnett's *Little Lord Fauntleroy* (1885–86) and *The Secret Garden* (1911), L. Frank Baum's *The Wonderful Wizard of Oz* (1900), Kate Douglas Wiggin's *Rebecca of Stonybrook Farm* (1903), and Mark Twain's *The Adventures of Tom Sawyer*, to name just a few. In *Pollyanna* the title character is adopted by a wealthy aunt when her father dies. In *Pollyanna Grows Up*, Pollyanna is too old and too successfully settled with her aunt to relive the same story, so the orphan ur-story is played out through the characters of Jamie Murphy (later Carew) and Jimmy Bean (later Pendleton).

The intertextual indebtedness of Porter's Pollyanna novels to the orphan ur-story of the Golden Age has influenced the way that scholars approach them. Griswold, for instance, interprets *Pollyanna* as the defining example of the American version of the orphan ur-story, which is characterized by its "forcible shifts in perspective, techniques for seeing things differently" (235). More specifically he argues: "Although this story can be found in other national literatures, the 'spin' that Americans, particularly, give to it is a dramatic emphasis on the power of thinking. . . . Here, too, is an explanation of the particularly 'interior' nature of American children's books, with their visions of struggle in the Theater of feelings and their accounts of intramental transformation" (235). *Pollyanna* is certainly the defining example of "the power of thinking" in American children's literature. The whole point of the glad game, after all, is to change the way that people think, to make them appreciate what they have rather than to complain about what they do not have. The novel has had such a powerful cultural effect that psychologists have labeled positive cognitive reorientation "the Pollyanna effect."

While psychology is a good interpretive lens through which to analyze the "forcible shifts in perspective" in *Pollyanna*, however, it is not so useful for analyzing other American examples of the orphan ur-story. For instance, Griswold cites the green spectacles in Baum's *The Wonderful Wizard of Oz* as an example of these "forcible shifts in perspective":

> Much of *Pollyanna*, it should be clear, is also about forcible shifts in perspective, techniques for seeing things differently. And this is true of many other American childhood classics. They are full of scenes like the one in *The Wizard of Oz* in which Dorothy and her companions put on green glasses before entering Emerald City, and then marvel at how green everything looks. In *Pollyanna*, however, the equivalent image is, significantly, not

rose-colored glasses, but the prism. . . . We see how she has changed
[Mr. Pendleton] . . . reminding him of his freedom to choose. (235)

Pollyanna's prism may indeed be a symbol for her ability to change
the psychological orientation of other characters, but the green glasses
of *The Wonderful Wizard of Oz* are not analogous with Pollyanna's prism.
As Griswold points out, the prism represents the psychological reorientation of the grouchy Mr. Pendleton, but while it is true that Dorothy and
her companions see the Emerald City differently when they are wearing
the green glasses, this shift in perspective does not lead to a psychological
reorientation of any of the characters. In the 1939 MGM film *The Wizard of
Oz*, Dorothy learns to appreciate her Kansas home, but in the novel Dorothy does not suffer any crisis of appreciation. In fact, when The Scarecrow
says that he does not understand why anyone would want to go back to
"the dry, gray place you call Kansas," Dorothy replies somewhat rudely,
"'That is because you have no brains . . . no matter how dreary and gray
our homes are, we people of flesh and blood would rather live there than
in any other country, be it ever so beautiful. There is no place like home'"
(19). To be clear, Dorothy does not claim to have an emotional attachment to Kansas, just a necessary one. In an article titled "Home to Aunt
Em: Sentimental Adoption in L. Frank Baum's *The Wonderful Wizard of
Oz*," Kristin N. Taylor argues that the novel places Dorothy within debates
about child psychology in the late nineteenth century. She points out that
Dorothy brings emotional rather than economic benefits to her adoptive
parents (385) and that Dorothy's journey could be interpreted as the individual's psychological journey toward self-integration (387–90). Despite
these convincing arguments, however, the fact remains that Dorothy is a
flat character who never expresses emotion or psychological motivation.
While Dorothy completes a physical journey in the novel, she does not
complete a psychic one.

The green glasses in *The Wonderful Wizard of Oz* actually refer to the
color-coding of regions in Oz—Munchkinland as blue, Winkieland as
yellow, the Emerald City as green, and Quadlingland as red. While many
scholars, such as Henry Littlefield, have interpreted the novel as an allegory for American politics, it is important to note the more obvious like-
ness of the geography of Oz to that of the United States. Dorothy's journey
from the beautiful, settled region of the Munchkins in the East to the wild,
uncivilized region of the Winkies in the West suggests that the novel is
actually an allegory for the settling of the American frontier. Dorothy's
defeat of the Wicked Witch of the West plays out the clash of civilization

and wilderness at the heart of Frederick Jackson Turner's influential Frontier Thesis, which claims that American identity is characterized by "perennial rebirth" brought about by "expansion westward with its new opportunities" and by "its continuous touch with the simplicity of primitive society" (2–3). Dorothy's defeat of the witch and the color-coding of the regions situate the Emerald City as the central administrative region of Oz. Not only is the color green the combination of the colors blue and yellow, but Oz is unified under the rule of the Wizard when Dorothy defeats the Wicked Witch through ritual cleansing (i.e., rebirth) by throwing a bucket of water on her and sweeping "the mess" out the door (Baum 86). The changes in perspective implied by the green glasses thus symbolize the relationship between the regions of the United States and the nation as a whole. When Dorothy and her companions visit the Emerald City for the first time, they accept the assumption that the city and surrounding countryside is green, that is, a region. When they return to the city after defeating the witch and unifying Oz, they discover that the city is actually not colored at all. In other words, after unifying Oz they are able to see it as a unified country ruled over by the Wizard.

Thus, while *The Wonderful Wizard of Oz* indicates "forcible shifts in perspective," these shifts do not suggest psychological reorientation (Griswold 235). The struggle in this novel happens not in the "Theater of feelings," as Griswold suggests, but in the cultural arena of regional and national discourses (235). The American version of the orphan ur-story, therefore, may be more American than Griswold realizes. Given the emphasis on local New England identity in *Pollyanna*, it is worthwhile to effect a critical reorientation, if not a psychological one, to identify how the "forcible shifts in perspective" of this novel might relate to those of *The Wonderful Wizard of Oz*. Pollyanna is an outsider to Beldingsville, for instance. She arrives there from some "far away Western town" (Porter, *Pollyanna* 6) and then leaves at the end of the novel for a sanatorium in some unnamed city. Pollyanna therefore belongs to the vaguely identified spaces outside of Beldingsville, not to the town itself, and yet she has a profound effect on the town. By the end of the novel, most of the town's residents are playing the glad game and are much happier for it. While we might interpret this change as a psychological reorientation of the entire town, Pollyanna essentially has the same effect on Beldingsville that Dorothy has on Oz. The reorientation of Beldingsville is as much cultural as psychological since Pollyanna convinces the residents to abandon the dour traits that mark them specifically as New Englanders. Like Dorothy, Pollyanna thus exerts a constructive, even nationalizing, force on the town and its residents.

Intersectionality of the Child, the Region, and the Nation

The relationship between children's literature and regional literature should not be surprising. Not only are both genres subject to critical disdain because of their presumed subject matter, but both are also concerned with the hierarchical relationship between marginalized and hegemonic discourses. For instance, in "Theorising and Theories: How Does Children's Literature Exist?" David Rudd argues that "children's literature occurs in the space between the constructed and the constructive—and … this must be so, given the nature of language and our positioning within a variety of discourses" (23). The construct*ed* child is a sociological construct created by adult writers of children's books to reflect their beliefs about what the ideal child should be, whereas the construct*ive* child is the child who either has not been initiated into its culture's concept of childhood or consciously rejects attempts at initiation. Marjorie Pryse makes a similar argument for the constructed and constructive nature of regional literature when she distinguishes between "'local color,' which represents regional life and regional characters as objects to be viewed from the perspective of the nonregional, often urban Eastern reader" and "literary regionalism, which features an empathic approach to regional characters that enfranchises their stories and cultural perceptions" (48). As Rudd and Pryse both make clear, the clash between the constructed child or region and the constructive child or region is a matter of ideological hierarchy.

Most regional scholars today disregard assumptions about the essential nature of regional literature that dominated American literary scholarship in the twentieth century: the idea that regional literature is an authentic representation of a provincial place or bygone era. However, scholars do not agree on the manner in which regional literature is constructed. In his 1993 book *The Culture of Letters*, for instance, Brodhead argues that nineteenth-century regional literature is an attempt by the urban, educated elite simultaneously to contain and to neutralize the threat posed to national identity by increasing immigrant populations. By relegating markers of ethnic difference, such as dialect, to the peripheral regions and marking these regions as pastoral, out of time, innocent, etc., he argues, national identity is made safe and homogenous. In other words, regional literature manifests hegemonic control through the intersectional alignment of various categorical Others. In contrast, Fetterley and Pryse approach regional literature from the perspective of feminist discourse, attempting to restore nineteenth-century regional writing, which is dominated by women writers, to a legitimate place in the canon of American literature. They acknowledge that some regional literature might reflect hegemonic discourses, but because of its marginal status regional literature holds inherent possibilities for resistance to those hegemonic discourses. In fact, their 2003 book *Writing Out of Place* explores the intersectionality of women, region, and even race as markers of subversive difference in regional literature. Because the engagement of the Pollyanna novels with regional discourse is clear, we might add the child to this list of marginalized voices. The question, however, is how exactly Pollyanna relates to the region—does she represent a nationalizing force, as the previous comparison with *The Wonderful Wizard of Oz* suggests, or does she represent a regional challenge to nationalism?

Given the cultural and critical marginalization of both regional literature and children's literature, one might think that the central character of the Pollyanna novels—a female child—would be aligned discursively with the local community of Beldingsville, but that is not what happens. Even though the novel suggests that the town is better off for Pollyanna's glad game, she is never more than a tourist. As already noted, she is an outsider in the first novel and eventually leaves the town. In the second novel Pollyanna is again a tourist, because she is sent to Boston to live with Mrs. Carew for a year at the beginning of the story, and then departs for Germany soon after her return to Beldingsville. By the time Pollyanna and Aunt Polly come back from Europe, Pollyanna has matured into a young woman. Although she spends almost a year there, she ends the novel outside of Beldingsville.

Pollyanna's continuous distance from Beldingsville can be explained somewhat by the conventions of regional literature established in the nineteenth century. As Brodhead argues, starting in the 1860s regional literature appeared commonly in the "three American 'high quality' journals": the *Atlantic Monthly*, the *Century Magazine*, and *Harper's Monthly* (124). While it might seem counterintuitive that journals marketed toward the refined tastes of the urban middle class would include fiction that focused on the quaint customs of small rural communities, they almost always included "the short piece of touristic or vacationistic prose, the piece that undertakes to locate some little-known place far away and make it visitable in print" (125). The common convention of the protagonist outsider who helps readers understand the unknown, exotic subject of regional literature helped maintain the illusion that readers were actually visiting these places. Despite the novel's assertions that Pollyanna belongs in Beldingsville because her mother was a member of the prestigious Harrington family, Pollyanna functions as the protagonist outsider who helps readers understand the town. Pollyanna's sophisticated travels—to the West with her parents, to Boston on many occasions, and abroad for many years—identifies her as a proxy for a presumably educated and wealthy audience.

The discursive construction of Beldingsville as a vacation destination is made explicit in *Pollyanna Grows Up* when Pollyanna decides to turn the Harrington homestead into a boarding house for wealthy tourists. The fact that Mrs. Carew and her wards Jamie and Sadie Dean are tourists is reinforced by their willingness to pay to stay there, despite their established friendship with Pollyanna. Even though Pollyanna is technically the proprietor, however, she does not actually do much work. The guests often pitch in to let Pollyanna spend time with them as a fellow vacationer. When all the vacationing characters—with the exception of Aunt Polly—return to Boston at the end of the novel, it is clear that they represent the novel's assumed wealthy, urban audience.

The urban orientation of the novel is further evident in the group's romantic and rapturous appreciation for the natural world during their two-week camping trip. When Jamie remarks, "we seem to know each other so much better up here in the woods—better in a week than we would in a year in town" (101), Pollyanna catalogues the natural scene around them, referencing "the air," "the sky," "the woods," and "the lake" (101) as sources for this new intimacy. The rural countryside's discursive construction as a place of escape for urban tourists is made explicit by Sadie Dean, who argues, "Up here everything is so real and true that we, too, can be our real true selves—not what the world SAYS we are because we are rich, or poor, or great, or humble; but what we really are, OURSELVES" (101–2). This naive and unironic literary representation of the countryside as the only "true" state of being thus supports Brodhead's assertion that "In nineteenth-century America regional writing was not produced for the cultures it was written about. . . . It was projected toward those groups of American society that made a considerable investment in literary reading" (122). The vacationing tourists seem to believe that they are participating in an authentic rural experience, but as Brodhead's argument suggests this authenticity is an illusion that they construct for themselves.

Pollyanna's touristic distance from Beldingsville becomes even more obvious when she is compared with the young female protagonist of Sarah Orne Jewett's (1886) classic regional story "A White Heron," which is also set in New England. Sylvia is a young girl from a "crowded manufacturing town" (3) who lives with her grandmother at a small, remote farm. Even though she is not from a rural area, she nevertheless has an intimate relationship with the natural landscape, as evidenced by her grandmother's remark to a passing stranger: "There ain't a foot o' ground [Sylvia] don't know her way over, and the wild creatures counts her one o' themselves. Squer'ls she'll tame to come an' feed right out o' her hands, and all sorts o' birds" (9). The central crisis of the story is whether Sylvia will give up the location of the elusive white heron to the vacationing stranger who offers her $10 for her help. The stranger, a young man interested in ornithology, is described by the narrator as an "enemy" whose whistle is "determined and somewhat aggressive," a description that is supported by his killing and collection of birds (5). The fact that this stranger is a tourist is emphasized by his assertion that he is on "vacation" (11) and that he is willing to pay for the privilege of hunting the white heron. Although Sylvia is quite taken with the young man, she ultimately decides not to tell him where to find the white heron, thus proving her allegiance to the New England wilderness and repelling the invading, male hunter. While Sylvia and Polly-anna have many similarities—including their naiveté and their love of the natural landscape—Pollyanna is not a protective champion of the region like Sylvia. She is more like the aggressive hunter who wants to capture the white heron to construct his own aesthetic representation of the region by stuffing and displaying the bird's body. In other words, his desire to kill the white heron and therefore preserve its presumed aesthetic qualities is similar to Pollyanna's vision of the New England landscape out her window as a "picture" (Porter, *Pollyanna* 15).

Even the differences in narrative voice, particularly character focalization, between the Pollyanna novels and "A White Heron" suggest that Sylvia is more aligned with the New England countryside than is Pollyanna. In the Pollyanna novels, character focalization occurs in a few places where the emotional turmoil of a character colors the otherwise omniscient third-person narrative, for example, in the scene from the first novel where Aunt Polly is thinking about the unexpected arrival of her orphaned niece: "Miss Polly rose with frowning face and closely-shut lips. She was glad, of course, that she was a good woman, and that she not only knew her duty, but had sufficient strength of character to perform it. But—*Pollyanna!*—what a ridiculous name!" (7). The phrase "of course" and the comment on Pollyanna's name come from Aunt Polly's thoughts, even though the text does not identify them as such. A similar example occurs when the minor character Rev. Paul Ford is sitting in the woods contemplating how to approach the spiritual crisis of his congregation: "His people!—they *were* his people. Could he do it? Dare he do it? Dare he not do it?" (75). Significantly, however, character focalization does not happen with Pollyanna. The text sometimes tells readers what Pollyanna is thinking but mostly just records her actions and dialogue. Because Aunt Polly and Rev. Ford are intrinsic members of the Beldingsville community—"they *were* his people"—focalization seems to be a privilege of community belonging.

In contrast, character focalization occurs several times in "A White Heron," most notably in relation to Sylvia. The young hunter becomes the focalizer for one brief paragraph that begins, "It was a surprise to find so clean and comfortable a little dwelling in this New England wilderness" (7)—surprise would belong only to an outsider, a perspective that is made apparent in this example—but the hunter's thoughts no longer seep into the third-person narrative after he rudely ignores the grandmother's story about the family's troubles and presses Sylvia about the white heron. In other words, when he shows himself to be unsympathetic to the family and then to the birds he shoots, he is not allowed to be the focalizer anymore. Sylvia's power in this natural landscape is reflected both through the narrator's approval of Sylvia as a focalizer and the narrator's direct address to her. When Sylvia seeks out the "great pine tree," which is "the last of its generation" (14) and therefore the oldest object in the forest, the narrative transitions from third-person description of the tree, to third-person description of Sylvia's thoughts about the tree, to Sylvia's focalized thoughts: "What a spirit of adventure, what wild ambition! What fancied triumph and delight and glory for the later morning when she could make known the secret!" (15). When Sylvia has managed to climb to the top of this old tree, the narrator signals approval of Sylvia's mastery of the landscape by addressing her directly: "Now look down again, Sylvia, where the green marsh is set among the shining birches and dark hemlocks; there where you saw the white heron once you will see him again; look, look! a white spot of him like a single floating feather comes up from the dead hemlock and grows larger" (19). The narrator's directions for Sylvia to "look, look!" suggest not only approval but also help in her quest to find the white heron.

Like the characters of Aunt Polly and Rev. Ford in the Pollyanna novels, Sylvia is thus shown to be aligned with the regional community by the narrator's willingness to allow focalization. Her defiant relationship to the hunter further indicates that she is a constructive child who can resist the expectations that the adult world has for her. The region and the child are thus intersectionally aligned in "A White Heron," just as the nation and the adult are aligned. Pollyanna is not aligned with the region, however. Her inability to provide focalization for the Pollyanna novels links her to the hunter of "A White Heron" as a touristic outsider. Pollyanna and Sylvia are thus both constructive characters, but they differ in their discursive orientation. Pollyanna constructs the region from an outsider's perspective, thus reinforcing hegemonic assumptions of what the region should be, whereas Sylvia resists those hegemonic discourses. In other words, Pollyanna exemplifies Brodhead's argument that regional literature is a nationalizing discourse, whereas Sylvia exemplifies Fetterley and Pryse's argument that regional literature has the potential to resist hegemonic discourses such as nationalism.

The comparison of the Pollyanna novels and "A White Heron" demonstrates that discourses of the child and discourses of the region are indeed compatible, but there is no "natural" or essential affinity between the child and the region as constructed discursive orientations. Thus, while it is important to acknowledge the hierarchic ideological constructions of the child and the region, it is just as important to acknowledge the complex ways in which these discourses can be aligned. This complexity of hierarchic ideological discourses is probably what makes Pollyanna such a contentious character among critics. The critical debate about her incessant optimism actually seems to be a debate about whether she is a constructed or constructive child. For instance, in *You're a Brick, Angela!* Mary Cadogan and Patricia Craig focus on Pollyanna as a highly constructed child, arguing that "*Pollyanna*, the most puerile of the little rays of moonshine, is also the most intellectually debilitating. . . . its author simply has pandered to the lowest level of her readers' emotions. *Pollyanna* makes no demands on the reader's ability to think; response to its images is nothing if not automatic. Out of this sentimental rag-bag has come every cliché in the business" (xx). With their critique of sentimentality, cliché, and banality, Cadogan and Craig clearly recognize Pollyanna's lack of agency as a child, more specifically as a female child. Griswold, however, sees more design in Pollyanna's optimism, arguing that she is a "genius at 'reverse psychology'" (220). He argues specifically that "Pollyanna is only playing the fool. . . . She gets her way by being glad—and such innocent gratitude seems not only above reproach, but invulnerable to suspicion" (219). In other words, Pollyanna's manipulation of other characters is a sign of her constructive abilities. Perhaps the solution to this critical impasse, the identification of Pollyanna as either a simpleton or a subversive genius, is to acknowledge that Pollyanna is actually the discursive site for complex ideological struggles. As a highly recognizable character type within the genre of American children's literature, Pollyanna is the epitome of a constructed child. The town of Beldingsville also seems to be constructed from a nationalist perspective. Just because the region is constructed and the child is constructed does not mean that they are discursively aligned, however. Pollyanna may be a constructed child, but *she* is the one who is constructing the region for the benefit of the urban audience.

Reinforcing Nationalism through an Intersectional Matrix

So far this chapter has argued not only that American children's literature is deeply invested in discourses of region and nation and that children's literature and regional literature share assumptions of ideological hierarchy, but also that constructions of the child and the region cannot be conflated through assumptions about the essential nature of either. As categories of identity, region and child function within a matrix of other markers such as gender, economic class, and ethnicity, and it is not possible to discuss the relationship between the child and the region without addressing these discourses as well. Porter's Pollyanna novels may affirm the hegemonic discourse of nationalism, but that does not mean that the novel accepts all hegemonic discourses uncritically.

The irony of arguing that Pollyanna is both a constructed child and a constructive author of regional discourse is that she fails as a writer in *Pollyanna Grows Up.* When the Harrington fortune takes an unexpected turn and Pollyanna and Aunt Polly are faced with severely restricted resources, Pollyanna concocts a plan to earn first prize in a writing contest, despite the fact that she has never written fiction before. This contest invokes the specific scene of literature production in the nineteenth and early twentieth centuries that gave women the unprecedented chance to enter the literary world in certain genres such as children's literature and regional literature. In fact, the magazine advertisement encourages readers who have never even thought of writing to give it a try: "'This is for you—who can read this,' it ran. 'What if you never have written a story before! That is no sign you cannot write one. Try it. That's all'" (113). Pollyanna is thus trying to take advantage of the very cultural situation that allowed Porter to become a successful writer. One might expect Pollyanna to win the contest and start a career that will support herself and Aunt Polly, but that is not what happens. Not only does Pollyanna fail even to place in the contest, the winner is her wealthy, male friend Jamie Carew, who lives in Boston. Thus, the novel enters two literary genres in which women writers are allowed a measure of agency—children's literature and regional literature—and then denies the female protagonist that agency.

Pollyanna's failed attempt at becoming a professional writer is significant because it not only denigrates women writers in general it is also one of the few moments that Porter allows Pollyanna to seem genuinely foolish. Pollyanna's assertion that writing "isn't like singing" because "[y]ou don't have to have a voice for it" and "it isn't like an instrument that you have to learn how to play" (104) is uncharacteristically foolish, even ungenerous, because she makes this comment to the writer Jamie. The novel thus seems to suggest that Porter is accepting the very gender hierarchies that Fetterley and Pryse argue can be critiqued within regional literature. If "regionalism marks that point where region becomes mobilized as a tool for critique of hierarchies based on gender as well as race, class, age, and economic resources," as they argue, that possibility does not seem to materialize in the Pollyanna novels (14). However, while the novels do not overtly challenge hierarchies of gender, we must not forget that Pollyanna is successful in changing the town of Beldingsville through the glad game, even if she fails as a regional writer. Perhaps Pollyanna's failure as a writer is one of the ways in which the novel conceals her constructive activities.

In "Spinning Sympathy: Orphan Girl Novels and the Sentimental Tradition," Joe Sutliff Sanders interprets *Pollyanna* in the tradition of sentimental American literature, arguing that the orphan girl novel "offers girls dreams of power and a roadmap to achieving that power through what would later be called 'sympathy'" (41). He argues further that "to exercise that power, girls would have to accept profound limitations" (41). According to Sanders, Pollyanna's limitation and source of sympathy is her irrepressible sadness and later in the novel her inability to walk. Through these limitations, he argues, Pollyanna is able to elicit enough sympathy to get other characters to do whatever she wants. Sanders is essentially arguing that Pollyanna and other orphan girls use a critically dismissed literary mode in a subversive way. In other words, they use their marginalized status to their advantage. We might interpret Pollyanna's failure as a writer in *Pollyanna Grows Up* in the same light. Through a convoluted series of events, her failure as a writer results in her marriage to the wealthy Jimmy Pendleton. The end results are not subversive, but the process is. Just as Pollyanna conceals her construction of the town's identity under the guise of a constructed child in the first novel, she conceals her orchestration of a proposal through the guise of a constructed woman. Thus, we could revise Fetterley and Pryse's assumption that regional writers either "accept the assumptions of the regionalizing premise" or "take exception to these assumptions" (7) by acknowledging that sometimes a regional writer does both.

Porter's Pollyanna novels demonstrate similar discursive complexity in their representation of economic class and ethnicity. For instance, the child characters in these novels—Pollyanna, Jimmy Bean (later Pendleton), Jamie Murphy (later Carew), Jerry Murphy, and Sadie Dean—all start out poor, most of them orphans. *Pollyanna Grows Up*, in particular, addresses social and class inequalities through the wealthy Mrs. Carew's efforts to remodel the tenement buildings she owns (including the one Jerry Murphy's family inhabits) and to support poor young women (such as Sadie Dean) who come to the city to find work. Because Pollyanna, Jimmy, Jamie, and Sadie Dean all flourish under the protection of wealthy adopted parents or benefactors, the novels seem to suggest that there is no natural hierarchic relationship between different social or economic classes. In fact, Mrs. Carew's establishment and patronage of a house for young respectable girls who work as secretaries and in retail shops suggest a desire to protect a very marginalized and preyed-upon population. However, the novel demonstrates a clear preference for children whose biological background is respectable. The children who find wealthy parents or patrons, for instance, all come from respectable parents: Pollyanna is a biological member of the wealthy Harrington family, Jimmy is the biological nephew of the wealthy Mrs. Carew, Jamie is the educated son of a vaguely defined character known as the "Professor," and Sadie Dean is the daughter of a minister. The one child in the novel who does not find a wealthy patron is Jerry, the newspaper boy who comes from an undeniably poor, working-class family. The novel is thus careful to separate out those characters who have questionable backgrounds from those who have an essentially genteel genealogy, a tendency that can be seen in Mrs. Carew's patronage of respectable girls over "fallen" ones and Aunt Polly's objection to Jimmy as a husband for Pollyanna until it is revealed that he is the biological nephew of the wealthy Mrs. Carew. Thus, the novel does not seem to discriminate according to economic resources, but does maintain essential class distinctions.

Lower-class characters are also singled out in Beldingsville through their use of regional dialect. Jane A. Stoneback's argument that "The use of country dialect and the rich regional flavor that marks the dialogue of such characters as Nancy and Old Tom typify the 'local color' fiction popular early in the twentieth century" (1044) implicitly recognizes this distinction. It is significant that the characters who "typify" this literature are servants. The wealthy or highly educated residents of Beldingsville—Aunt Polly, Mr. Pendleton, Dr. Chilton, Reverend Ford—do not speak with any regional dialect, which indicates a link between dialect and class. While

Pollyanna occasionally speaks with a hint of dialect, such as her exclamation that "there doesn't anybody need any pictures with that to look at" (15), for the most part she speaks Standard English. The maid Nancy and the gardener Old Tom, however, provide plenty of examples of exaggerated regional dialect in their speech, such as Old Tom's admonition to Nancy to "Go on with yer jokin' . . . Why don't ye tell me the sun is a-goin' ter set in the east ter-morror?" (7). *Pollyanna Grows Up* demonstrates the same links between dialect and class through the character of Jerry. When Pollyanna gets lost in the East End of Boston, the only person she can find who speaks English is Jerry, a young newspaper boy who speaks an urban regional dialect that Pollyanna has trouble understanding. She thinks to herself, "he does talk funny. His words *sound* English, but some of them don't seem to make any sense with the rest of what he says" (37). The fact that Jerry never learns to speak Standard English in the novels reflects his inherited working-class background.

According to Brodhead, the association of regional dialects with ethnicity is a fundamental characteristic of regional literature because it allows the consumers of regional literature—the wealthy, urban leisure class—to maintain a superior distance from the supposed subject of that literature. More specifically he argues that, for urban audiences uneasy with the increasing populations of immigrants, "Regional fiction . . . could be considered as an exclusion mechanism or social eraser, an agency for purging the world of immigrants to restore homogenous community" (136). The fact that Pollyanna meets Jerry in a neighborhood populated by Italian immigrants who do not speak English confirms this link between regional dialect and ethnically inflected English in the Pollyanna novels. Since, as Brodhead argues, "Ethnically deformed speech—what else is dialect?—is the most fundamental requirement of the regional genre" (136), the exaggerated regional dialects of Nancy and Old Tom might be seen in the context of urban anxieties over immigration. The ultimate purpose of this identification of "the foreign" in regional literature, according to Brodhead, is "to master it in imaginary terms" (137). Thus, in addition to affirming early-twentieth-century hierarchies of gender, nation, and age, *Pollyanna* and *Pollyanna Grows Up* also ultimately affirm hierarchies of class and ethnicity, as well.

It is important to note that Brodhead's identification of regional literature as a product marketed toward the urban leisure class tends to accept the assumption that the marginalized perspectives of region, class, ethnicity, and gender are intersectionally aligned in this type of literature. In other words, his definition of regional literature as a containment strategy for nonhegemonic discourses discourages the critical identification of resistance. Even though an earlier section of this chapter argued that there is no essential link between marginalized constructed categories, the *Pollyanna* novels nevertheless seem to support Brodhead's assumption. However sympathetic the female, lower-class, or ethnically marked characters may be, they are nevertheless caught up in ideological discourses that insist on their marginalization—at least by the end of the second novel. Despite the fact that Pollyanna seems to be a constructed child, there are more opportunities for region to be used as "a tool for critique of hierarchies based on gender as well as race, class, age, and economic resources" (Fetterley and Pryse 14) when she is still a child. For instance, the poor orphan Jimmy Bean speaks with a lower-class accent while he and Pollyanna are children, which makes his adoption by the wealthy Mr. Pendleton highly unlikely. By the time he and Pollyanna are adults in *Pollyanna Grows Up*, he speaks Standard English and is revealed to be the biological nephew of the wealthy Mrs. Carew. In addition, he is essentially living with Mrs. Carew in Boston by the end of the second novel. Thus, essential categories of class, economic status, dialect, and region have fallen into place because of the actions of the adult Pollyanna. In other words, when Pollyanna becomes an adult, hierarchic boundaries that were previously critiqued are affirmed and restored. Thus, we need to recognize not only that constructed ideological hierarchies exist within a matrix of intersectionality, but also that intersectional alignments can change.

Conclusion

This chapter has not attempted to give a complete account of the intersectionality of the child, the region, and the nation in Porter's Pollyanna novels. Given the complexity of these categorical umbrellas, such a task would not be possible in a chapter of this length. However, I do point out some of the necessary steps for such a study. Perhaps the most important point to remember is that hierarchical markers of identity such as age, region, and nation do not exist independently, nor are they essential or static. Genre categories such as "children's literature" and "regional literature" do not change the fact that concepts such as the child and the region are always enmeshed in a shifting and complex matrix of social hierarchies. Porter's *Pollyanna* novels may ultimately affirm the hierarchic superiority of early-twentieth-century discourses such as the nation and the city, but the total picture is more complex. Shifting and unexpected intersectional alignments allow for moments of critique of other assumed hierarchies, such as gender and class.

Works Cited

Baum, L. Frank. *The Wonderful Wizard of Oz.* 1900. Mineola, NY: Dover, 1996. Print.

Brodhead, Richard H. *Cultures of Letters: Scenes of Reading and Writing in Nineteenth-Century America.* Chicago: U of Chicago P, 1993. Print.

Cadogan, Mary, and Patricia Craig. *You're a Brick, Angela!: A New Look at Girls' Fiction from 1839 to 1975.* London: Victor Gollanez, 1976. Print.

Fetterley, Judith, and Marjorie Pryse. *Writing Out of Place: Regionalism, Women, and American Literary Culture.* Urbana: U of Illinois P, 2003. Print.

Griswold, Jerry. *Audacious Kids: Coming of Age in America's Classic Children's Books.* New York: Oxford UP, 1992. Print.

Jewett, Sarah Orne. "A White Heron." *A White Heron and Other Stories.* Boston and New York: Houghton, Mifflin, 1886. Print.

Porter, Eleanor H. *Pollyanna.* Stilwell, KS: Digireads.com, 2005. Print.

———. *Pollyanna Grows Up.* USA: Seven Treasures, 2009. Print.

Pryse, Marjorie. "Reading Regionalism: The 'Difference' It Makes." *Regionalism Reconsidered: New Approaches to the Field.* Ed., David Jordan. New York: Garland, 1994. 47–63. Print.

Rudd, David. "Theorising the Theories: How Does Children's Literature Exist?" *Understanding Children's Literature,* 2nd ed. Ed. Peter Hunt. London and New York: Routledge, 2005. Print.

Sanders, Joe Sutliff. "Spinning Sympathy: Orphan Girl Novels and the Sentimental Tradition." *Children's Literature Association Quarterly* 33.1 (Spring 2008): 41–61. Print.

Stoneback, Jane A. "Pollyanna: The Glad Game." *Beacham's Guide to Literature for Young Adults,* vol. 3. Eds. Kirk H. Beetz and Suzanne Niemeyer. Washington: Beacham, 1990. 1041–44. Print.

Taylor, Kristin N. "Home to Aunt Em: Sentimental Adoption in L. Frank Baum's *The Wonderful Wizard of Oz.*" *Children's Literature Association Quarterly* 34.4 (Winter 2009): 379–93. Print.

Turner, Frederick Jackson. *The Frontier in American History.* New York: Henry Holt, 1920. Print.

Part 3

ADAPTED *POLLYANNA*

10

The Gospel of Good Cheer: Innocence, Spiritual Healing, and Patriotism in Mary Pickford's *Pollyanna*

ANKE BROUWERS

The first movie adaptation of Eleanor Porter's successful novel (and its Broadway adaptation by Catharine Chisholm Cushing) was released in 1920. The film was a financial success and its critical reception was predominantly one of praise. A review of the picture by *Moving Picture Story* critic Frederick James Smith ended with the gushing words: "we need more of Mary Pickford, and more Pollyannas" ("Letter" 103). Smith's article, which made no discernible distinction between the film's star and the literary character she played, appears to have unambiguously advocated a particular type of picture—a nostalgic and pastoral evocation of a world of optimism and communal harmony—and a particular type of star—the optimistic and hopeful child-woman. In other words, it urged for a fictional world and heroines that were strikingly at odds with post-World War I modern society and Hollywood star culture. Yet, for all the praise it received, *Pollyanna* also courted derision, even outward hostility, by those who thought its reputation as harmless and clean entertainment would set a moral and aesthetic standard that most filmmakers in Hollywood were unwilling to adopt.

Any discussion of the 1920 adaptation of *Pollyanna* is inevitably bound up with its star, Mary Pickford, whose particular star persona and unprecedented power within the film industry cannot be separated from any picture she made. Moreover, *Pollyanna* was a special event: it was Pickford's first release for United Artists, the studio she had co-founded with Charlie Chaplin, Douglas Fairbanks, and D. W. Griffith the previous year. The company was to distribute the independently produced films of its owners, who thereby ensured themselves complete creative control as well as greater financial gains. *Pollyanna* was therefore an important film in the history of its distribution company, and also marked the beginning of a new phase in the career of its star, who had commanded top box-office results since the mid-1910s. Pickford's belief in self-reliance, a theme both within the narrative of the film and a stated goal of the new studio, proved personally and financially satisfying since, with a gross of over a million dollars, *Pollyanna* was a big hit.

The decision to adapt *Pollyanna* was a safe bet: the book, its sequel, and the play were still hugely popular, while the basic material resembled Pickford's most popular previous roles such as Rebecca in *Rebecca of Sunnybrook Farm* (Neilan 1917), Gwendolyn in *The Poor Little Rich Girl* (Tourneur 1917), Judy Abbot in *Daddy-Long-Legs* (Neilan 1919), and Sara Crewe in *The Little Princess* (Neilan 1917). Overall, *Pollyanna* complemented Pickford's screen persona as expressed through these characters that were, in the words of film historian Kevin Brownlow, "extremely attractive, warm-hearted, generous, funny—but independent and fiery-tempered when the occasion demands" (*Parade* 120). Pickford had steadily appropriated, cultivated and consolidated these properties since 1914 (starting with Edwin S. Porter's adaptation of *Tess of the Storm Country*) through filmic and extra-filmic means. The success of *Pollyanna* was confirmation that the Pickford child-woman could still pull in the crowds but also carried with it the slightly disturbing implication that perhaps this was the (only) way audiences preferred their star to be: a perennial, happy-go-lucky child-woman.

The 1920 adaptation of *Pollyanna* also reflects some key concerns of the society in which it was released: a postwar, post-sacred, and post-sentimental climate. Pickford's film version affirms *Pollyanna*'s (and Pickford's own) relationship to Christian Science and other metaphysical movements in America and demonstrates how its resonance clearly rests on its secular yet spiritually inspired motivations. Additionally, *Pollyanna* stands as both high point and saturation point of a culture of sentimentality, with its emphasis on "feeling right" closely connected to some of Christian Science's main tenets. Aesthetically, *Pollyanna* asserted a strong influence on the development of Hollywood, in which the presence of strong emotional address, empathic ability, and genteel morality served as markers of quality. *Pollyanna*'s date of release (January 1920) is also significant: the film was released into a cultural climate still largely defined by the Great War, in which war-related fads such as Spiritualism, war-imagery and art, as well as war trauma dominated. Bearing in mind Pickford's reputation as a patriotic star and the film's sustained focus on spiritual health, optimism, and physical recovery, regarding *Pollyanna* as the star's final patriotic picture is productive.

A Doctrine of Health and Happiness:
Pollyanna and Spiritual Growth

In *Audacious Kids* (1992), Jerry Griswold argues that American children's books of "the golden age" (1865–1914) shared an obsession with "positive thinking" and "the emotions of young children," and that a preoccupation with "health," or the lack thereof, figured either as an element of plot or as metaphor (xi, 17). He takes *The Secret Garden* (1910) and *Pollyanna* (1913) as clear examples of the latter, given that they are quite literally stories of convalescence that echo the self-help ethics and positive thinking central to Mary Baker Eddy's Christian Science as well as other late-Victorian quasi-religious movements. Eddy's movement tied personal health, religious devotion, and spiritual development to feeling and thinking "right" (i.e. positively, empathetically) and, like the sentimental worldview her doctrine often echoes, insisted that man is spiritual, not material. Griswold even describes Burnett's novel as a "secret" endorsement of Christian Science (18).

Indeed, the period of Eleanor Porter's and Mary Pickford's intellectual and spiritual development not only coincides with the golden age of American children's literature, it was also the golden age of the so-called "Great American Mind Cure" (Douglas 32–33). Ann Douglas has noted how many of the female doctors active in the wake of Eddy's heyday focused on "preventive medicine," in a sense advocating the Pollyanna-like idea that positive—"glad"—thoughts could keep you healthy, and that many of our perceived ailments were in fact merely doctors' inventions or figments of our own unhappy dispositions (133). Eddy wrote on the subject in *Science and Health with a Key to the Scripture* (1875): "You embrace your body in your thought, and you should delineate upon it thoughts of health, not of sickness. You should banish all thoughts of disease and sin and of other beliefs included in matter" (line 25). Eddy's recommendations made clear that through positive, healthy thoughts, every American citizen could be in control of his or her own healthy disposition. The notion of self-reliance is essential here and it blends nicely with the Victorian belief in the perfectibility of character and conduct through emotional exercise and self-discipline.

The spiritual self-help Eddy provided was accompanied by the more prosaic self-help industry of prescriptive literature (books on manners, courtesy, etiquette, domestics, and conduct) that promised success in life if practiced faithfully. The prescriptive literature market had been booming from the mid-nineteenth century onward (Newton 3). A dramatized version of this advice was in part supplied by domestic sentimental fiction, in which flawed but morally intact heroines presented models for living through idealized behavior (or life lessons) or private demonstrations (e.g. thoughts, soliloquies, or authorial asides). *Pollyanna* can be seen as the fictionalized embodiment of the kind of model behavior that prescriptive literature or improvement therapies usually promoted through dicta, anecdotes, or aphorisms. Drawing connections between domestic and advice literary traditions and early American narrative film, Paula Marantz-Cohen has argued that silent film stars quickly took over the exemplary function of their literary predecessors in presenting models to emulate via facial soliloquies (narratives of the face in close-up) and through extra-filmic appearances in fan magazines or testimonial advertising (156).

From a very early stage in her career, Mary Pickford's image was marketed and consumed as a model of the idealized American girl- and womanhood of the early twentieth century. This position was negotiated and strengthened through her contribution to the do-it-yourself industry. Between 1915 and early 1917, she published a syndicated advice column, pleasantly entitled "Daily Talks with Mary Pickford." In this column, Pickford proffered her readers the necessary tools to do "it"—find happiness, health, professional success, love, selfhood—all presented in line with traditions of self-healing and improvement therapies based on the power of our thoughts and feelings. The persona or literary voice emerging from the "Daily Talks" was a "little Mary," modeled on an amalgam of heroines of American children's and adolescent's fiction. Biographer Eileen Whitfield notes how Pickford's voice in the columns "reads like a cross between Louisa May Alcott [. . .] and a fan magazine," but the morals of the columns rely on the dicta and conduct of Pollyanna, Mary Lennox, Cedric Fauntleroy, Sara Crew, Anne Shirley, and Jo March, as well as on their sainted mothers and fathers or teachers such as Marmee, Dearest, or Miss Stacy (153).

If Porter's message embraces the evangelical promise that a child would lead the masses toward redemption, as Griswold notes, its filmic adaptation complicates this message by replacing Porter's innocent child with a commodified star image (Griswold 232). Even so, the star in question was Mary Pickford, an actress whose masquerade as a child was both established and accepted, and who could boast "sacral" or spiritual associations (see Brouwers 316).[1] The addition of *Pollyanna* to Pickford's repertoire replenished and affirmed her own existing star persona, but it also afforded the literary character an even more wide-reaching influence as

a spiritual role model. The novel's message of positive thinking, its celebration of radical innocence, rural family life, and small-town solidarity
appealed to Pickford's public persona and private personal beliefs. Partly
because of Pickford's already established repertoire (family-friendly fare)
and her reputation as "America's Sweetheart," confirmed by trade papers
and fan magazines as early as 1914 (see "Paramount Program" 343), she
needed a strong, non-ambiguous association with innocence to continue
to portray childhood, even when she was in her thirties and a divorced
(and remarried) corporate head to boot. She relied on a radical innocence, because a sentimental type of innocence, in itself Manichean, left
no room for ambiguity. Moreover, the representation and thematization
of innocence also allowed for a deeply felt response from her spectators.
Art philosophers and film historians alike have identified the appeal and
effectiveness of teary genres such as melodrama and sentimental fiction
in their reliance on the mechanics of innocence (or virtue) at first misrec-
ognized but later revealed (Midgley; Williams).

A final, important rapport between Pickford and the novel was the
endorsement of the principles of Christian Science, to which she had
become attracted after her divorce in 1919, and of which she became a
loyal devotee in the twenties (Whitfield 288; Slide 31). Pickford's attraction
to Christian Science was no anomaly in Hollywood circles. Prominent
female directors of the teens, well known for their social and politically
engaging films, like Lois Weber and Ida May Park, had a "strong regard"
for it (Slide 31). Lois Weber even twice adapted the 1903 novel *Jewel: A
Chapter in Her Life*, by Clara Louise Burnham, first in 1915 (as *Jewel*) and
again in 1923. The novel's motto, "and a little child shall lead them," as well
as its well-known endorsement of Christian Science, strongly prefigure
Pollyanna. The novel lacks an actual glad game, but features a young girl
melting the frozen emotional lives of curmudgeons and dysfunctional
families. Eddy's emphasis on the transformative power of our thoughts are
metaphorically and visually transferred to the figure of the child who does
not yet understand or accept unhappy facts (such as illnesses or failing
social fabrics), and who reverses the traditional direction of knowledge
transfer by placing wisdom in the hands of youth. Marcia Landy notes
how the 1923 remake of *A Chapter in Her Life*, "in its use of the child as an
agent of transformation . . . works (self-consciously) as a utopian fantasy,
with the young girl working as a magical guide through the conflicted
landscape of the middle-class family" (100). Pickford, who was thought of
by her fans as "just a little girl," was easily accepted as a sacral and guiding child (Studlar 355). The remake of Burnham's novel may have seemed

especially timely after the success of *Pollyanna*, but despite *A Chapter in Her Life*'s artistic qualities, it suffered from Universal's limited distribution as well as from a growing *Pollyanna* backlash, which would render all overtly sweet or unflinchingly optimistic films suspect (Stamp). For a while, at least, *Pollyanna* seems to have been the secular answer—a "social savior" for Griswold—to post-sacred concerns, offering a model on how to be and endorsing self-healing qualities such as optimism and faith in oneself as strategies to tackle life (233). The film also reflected the persistence of a sentimental worldview in popular art forms and entertainment as well as Pickford's reliance on and belief in the validity and relevance of sentimental values such as innocence, empathy, and virtue at a time when postwar society increasingly seemed to negate these values.

The Persistence of Innocence: *Pollyanna* and Sentimentalism

Ann Douglas remarks that, much like *Pollyanna* (and American children's fiction in general), many novels of the twenties were obsessively concerned with "regaining and maintaining a state of health" (132). In this shared concern, Douglas detects an urgent, historical cause, which was largely absent from the children's novels: the psychological traumas of the Great War and its aftermath. Comparing the therapeutic war memoirs of British and American authors Robert Graves (*Goodbye to All That*, 1929), Siegfried Sassoon (*Sherston's Progress*, 1939) and Ernest Hemingway (*In Our Time*, 1925; *A Farewell to Arms*, 1929) with Porter's *Pollyanna* (1913) and Eleanor Abbot's *Molly Make-Believe* (1910), *The Sick-a-Bed Lady* (1911), and *The White Linen Nurse* (1913), Douglas suggests that the continued success and appeal of these "heroines of convalescence" can be explained by how they provided some form of imaginative healing for their audience and for post–World War I society in general. I will elaborate on Douglas's compelling argument by explaining *Pollyanna*'s success as largely the result of this promise of healing and recovery.

Obsession with self-healing aside, there is apparently little common ground between *Pollyanna* and the war novels such as the ones cited by Douglas; and indeed, as Lea Jacobs has pointed out, the continued appeal of novels like *Pollyanna* did not coexist all too peacefully with changing public and critical tastes regarding aesthetic norms (stylistic and thematic) for the popular arts (literature as well as film). Qualities that had been heralded in the past, such as the careful selection of "appropriate" subject matter, decorum, and the celebration of moral values became suspect and were regarded as old-fashioned (Jacobs 9). In addition, there was a strong tendency in popular and modern (as well as modernist) novels and poems toward uninhibited "truth-telling"—an emphasis on a confrontation with the "horrors of life" (Douglas 31). *Pollyanna's* optimism and sentimental make-believe adhered to Victorian ideals but clashed with the burgeoning modernist aesthetics, which defined itself in opposition to all things sentimental, a mode and tradition associated with women writers, mass and spectacular art, and children's fiction (Clark 1990). The gradual "decline" of sentiment during the 1920s is evidenced by the stylistic and thematic innovations in Hollywood deriving from non-sentimental genres or traditions, such as literary Naturalism, symbolism or aestheticism, the advent of consumer culture and Jazz Age morality (Jacobs 39). The adaptation of Porter's novel in 1920 places *Pollyanna* at the pinnacle and saturation point of sentimental aesthetics that had characterized American culture in the previous century as well as much of mainstream cinema of the 1910s. If sentimentality is understood, as it usually is, as false, unearned, deceptive, self-congratulatory, and reality-distorting sentiment (Midgley; Jefferson; Savile), its incompatibility with "the hard facts of life" so much praised by the modern spirit, is self-evident. The essence of Pollyanna's game was of course all about the refusal to surrender to things as they are.

Yet instead of dismissing this lack of "terrible honesty" as either foolish or immoral, Griswold has described the attitude of Porter's Pollyanna as "a subversive alternative to maturity" (234). If maturity is to be equated with facing the realities of life, Porter's heroine does not, despite the title of the literary sequel, ever quite "grow up," an act that defies both biological inevitability and societal expectations. Griswold further describes Pollyanna as a "cunning trickster" and as a "master of reverse psychology," whose stubborn refusal to accept misfortunes or punishments for what they are results in her getting what she wants (232). Griswold's reading thus finds subversion and rebellion in the same qualities that have been the cause of much of the novel's critical disdain. The critical reception of the 1920 film version illustrates the mixed feelings critics and reviewers harbored regarding Pollyanna's message, in particular in light of the cultural climate in which it appeared. As one reporter in *Variety* noted: "With considerable force, it asserts that the world is a nice place to live in. A fat lie this, but it helps to believe it, and so anything able to make us believe it is as valuable as a blue river diamond mine" (qtd. in Brownlow, "Rediscovered" 169). Clearly, Pollyanna's worldview denied the truth—was "a fat lie"—but in late-Victorian appeasing style, this could be seen as a valuable quality.

Ambivalence characterizes other revelatory appraisals in leading fan magazines: in *Photoplay*, the film was described as both a nuisance and "an inspiration" (Brownlow, "Rediscovered" 169). *Moving Picture Classic* editor Frederick James Smith wrote a gushing open letter to the actress in praise of the film. Smith's praise is tempered by his confession of the inner struggle he experienced between his reverence for the truth and his desire for its denial:

> The calm, critical side of our brain tells us that it is a sugar-coated view of life as it isn't and never was, but the dream-side of us stirs—awakens. What, then, of criticism? You have given us a golden flash into something intangible, never to be attained perhaps, but sacred, far inside our hearts. You have made us forget the realities of today. If we ever reach the point where you fail to touch us, Mary Pickford, we will know that our ideals have gone. ("Letter" 103)

Pollyanna/Pickford—in Smith's letter they become interchangeable—was evidence of a lingering idealism in society. The constant oscillation between the appreciation either of truth or make-believe, youth or maturity, can be grasped also in Smith's review of Pickford's *Through the Back Door* (1921), released eighteen months after *Pollyanna*. Here he wondered, "Can it be that we are growing up too fast for our films? Is it possible that this juvenile food is too weak for us?" (Smith, "Review" 78).

Smith's later skepticism was in tune with some other disavowing appraisals of *Pollyanna*, such as the one voiced by director D. W. Griffith who, at the time, was a business partner of Pickford and known to dwell on Victorian ideals and American idylls himself. Griffith condemned the film's "fake philosophy of gilded bunkum" and labeled it a menace ("a handicap") to those who would actually try to apply it to real life (qtd. in Rosen 39). Griffith's identification of the worldview as hokum, and of the inapplicability of the glad game to real life, is telling. The *New York Times* called the possibility of a real-life Pollyanna "a provocation to a justifiable homicide" (qtd. in Basinger 38). Surely, these criticisms may have had something to do with the fact that *Pollyanna* was not only a smash hit, it inspired a devotional clamoring for more "Pollyanna pictures" ("more of Mary Pickford, and more Pollyannas"). Both Pickford and screenwriter Frances Marion had been quite happy with the result when the film came out, but then did a full one-eighty, condemning the film in retrospect (Marion 67; Brownlow, "Rediscovered" 196; Eyman 89). Their changing perspective is perhaps the clearest indication of the increasingly low status of sentiment and the rise in status of "terrible honesty."

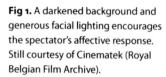

Fig 1. A darkened background and generous facial lighting encourages the spectator's affective response. Still courtesy of Cinematek (Royal Belgian Film Archive).

Fig 2. The scene of Pollyanna's arrival in Beldingsville offers Mary Pickford ample opportunity to display her physical comedy skills. Still courtesy of Cinematek (Royal Belgian Film Archive).

If the *Times* wondered why Pickford could not grow up (and instantly provided the answer by comparing her to Peter Pan), her eternal youth and innocence were also broadly perceived as a familiar and reassuring fact—evidence that not all had changed for good, that it was still possible to revisit childhood, a time *before* the unpleasant reality of mature life represented most directly by the war (Studlar 350). *Pollyanna*'s celebration of a prelapsarian and nostalgic past even came in a nostalgic *form*: it echoed Pickford's own adaptation of *The Poor Little Rich Girl* (Tourneur 1917) and *Rebecca of Sunnybrook Farm* (Neilan 1917) in performance style, small-town stereotypes (including a returning cast member from those films), locale, and the mix of pathos and sometimes very physical or cunning comedy.

The film opens at the deathbed of Pollyanna's father. It is here that we are introduced to Pollyanna's kind and caring nature as well as to her glad game. The scene's dramatic climax is mostly played out in lengthy and beautifully lit medium-close shots of Pollyanna, which provide the spectator with ample time to be affected by the little girl's tears and Pickford with the opportunity to act at once glamorous and tragic (see Fig. 1). Only moments later, the spectator is invited to enjoy the comedy of Pollyanna's stormy arrival in Beldingsville: the scene consists of Chaplinesque slapstick routines, as Pollyanna has to fight heavy wind and rain and even gets knocked over in the end (see Fig. 2). This oxymoronic mix of moods and styles was noted by some critics, most notably film academic Frances Patterson, who praised the film's double-edged and ironic inter-titles (Patterson 105). One classic scene reveals the filmmakers' awareness of the potential tiresome quality of the glad game: during dinner with an antsy Aunt Polly, Pollyanna spots a fly on the table. In all her goodness, Pollyanna promises the fly that it shall go to heaven one day, and then cheers on delightfully when Aunt Polly smashes it dead. This scene plays like the perverse reverse of a classic scene in Laurence Sterne's *Tristram Shandy*, a satire of domestic misunderstanding, in which Uncle Toby mercifully tells a fly that had been pestering him for a long time, "Go poor devil, get thee gone. Why should I hurt thee—This world is wide enough to hold both thee and me" (Sterne 148).

The film's contemporaneous mixed reception also marks the beginning of what James Elkins has described as the general loss of empathy, an "icy" detachment, in our experience of art works (126). Elkins is concerned with our responses to paintings, but his observations are relevant to our engagement with the other arts as well. If *Pollyanna* was once genuinely moving to some (represented most notably by *Moving Picture Story's* Smith—"we need more Pollyannas"), it was also met with cool, even hostile, detachment from others ("a provocation to a justifiable homicide" qtd. in Basinger 38). In discussing the teary and effusive albeit quite possibly genuine and certainly socially acceptable response people had to eighteenth-century sentimental art, Elkins notes that if a work of art was once understood as a "friendship" or "a new affection," we have now "forgotten to initiate intimacy with objects" (121). Today, works of art seldom move us to tears or elicit strong emotional responses, and it can be difficult to imagine audiences responding intensely to paintings we would classify as sentimental (unearned, false) or emotionally manipulative. Today the story of *Pollyanna*, and in fact Mary Pickford's entire repertoire, as well as the medium she appeared in (silent film), is generally greeted with unease, skepticism, even derision. The notion that the message of *Pollyanna* once succeeded in profoundly affecting viewers and critics alike now appears odd.

Pollyanna and the Great War

The explanation for the movie's contemporaneous effect may hinge on the fact that *Pollyanna* had a distinct emotional and spiritual relevance for a postwar and "post-sacred" society. Brooks explains the rise and transformation of melodrama in the context of the gradual "loss of the tragic vision" in post-revolutionary Europe looking for a new, secularized, moral value system (15). After World War I, as Thomas Slater notes, the moral vacuum became even more urgent (106), which would explain the popularity of *Pollyanna*, a secular saint, even though the film remained completely silent on the world crisis. The film's positive message of self-reliance and recovery thus becomes an alternative strategy (or therapy) for dealing with the war's aftermath. Pickford's silence had nothing to do with queasiness on the subject: she had unflinchingly and patriotically engaged with the war before (in 1917 and 1918), both on-screen and off, and would do so again the following year in *The Love Light*, a much darker antiwar film (written and directed, incidentally, by *Pollyanna*'s screen-writer, Frances Marion).

When *Pollyanna* was produced and released, the Great War and its effects were still very much felt in various aspects of American society, and would continue to be felt throughout the twenties. The war officially ended on November 11, 1918, but its aftermath continued to influence (inter)national politics and domestic and global economies. It remained at the forefront of the public mind as well as in the arts. As Leslie Midkiff Debauche asserts, "The fresh memories of the battlefield and the home-front fostered contemporary interest in the political results of the Great War. These memories also provided iconography, plot twists, themes, costumes, and characters for movie-makers in the immediate postwar period" (161). The war remained a subject of Hollywood movies both because of its continued timeliness and historical interest, but also for more pragmatic reasons: Hollywood had a large store of war-related material that created a surplus when the conflict suddenly ended, and could not change production so quickly. On the other hand, anticipating war fatigue, Hollywood would often downplay the fact that a movie was war-related in favor of other aspects of a story: its romance, its universal theme of bravery, self-sacrifice, and so on (Midkiff Debauche 161–65; Brownlow, "The War" 172). Several postwar films mixed their war-themed (sub)plots with a renewed interest in the metaphysical, most clearly in Spiritualism, which, as Tom Gunning notes, "was having a resurgence after World War I due to the desire to communicate with the war dead" (47). Its spiritual dimension certainly contributed to the 1921 success of *The Four Horsemen of the Apocalypse* (Ingram, written by June Mathis), a movie that found broad appeal thanks as much to its foreboding message of the dangers of war—envisaged by a mystical seer, its spectacular *mise-en-scène* larded with images of apocalyptic doom—as to its new star, Rudolph Valentino.

D. W. Griffith, who would heavily criticize *Pollyanna* the next year, himself dabbled with Spiritualism in *The Greatest Question* (1919), another war drama in which a mother is briefly reunited with her fallen son through supernatural means. Spiritual presence and communication with the dead would also appear in less middlebrow cultural works. In *One of Ours*, Willa Cather's Pulitzer Prize–winning novel, the presence of the novel's hero is still felt by his mother in the house after his demise on the battlefield. Unlike Griffith's exploration of the continuing mother/son connection after death, Cather does not treat the supernatural element melodramatically, nor does it structure the novel's plot. However it does provide the narrative with an affective closure for the novel's protagonist, and perhaps for the reader as well.[2]

Hollywood's Soldiers: Pickford and Patriotism

Mary Pickford had been a visible and ardent patriot during the war years. Apart from starring in patriotic (even propagandistic) war movies like *The Little American* (DeMille 1917) and *Johanna Enlists* (Taylor 1918), Pickford had helmed national fundraisers, godmothered troops, and donated large sums of money to war relief (Brownlow, "The War" 103; Beauchamp 86). It was sound business for any star to stress their patriotism off-screen, but for Canadian-born Pickford the matter had even greater urgency. *The Little American*, originally slated as "The American Girl," was a straightforward propaganda piece. The rather traditional melodrama plus love story plot was made more poignant by stirring inter-titles, a spectacular sequence in which a passenger's ship (significantly called the *Veritania*) is torpedoed by the Germans, the usual bestial behavior from German soldiers and officers (stereotypical "evil Huns" were a staple of war-related films), and several shots of Pickford saluting and clutching the American flag. As the quintessential American girl caught up in a European conflict, Pickford stands as a figure of civilization and moral superiority: hers to claim from her nationality as well as her gender.

Her second war-related feature, *Johanna Enlists*, was conceived as propaganda but in a much more veiled fashion (Brownlow, "The War" 169). The film was based on *The Mobilization of Johanna* by Rupert Hughes, an author who had published frequently about war in general and the Great War in particular despite his lack of personal experience as he was prevented from enlisting by a medical condition. In *Johanna Enlists*, patriotism is not conceived of as participation in actual battle on European soil, but instead focuses on what the home front can contribute. Pickford plays Johanna, a foolish and dreamy girl who discovers purpose and womanhood through a chance encounter with the army. When Johanna's family of farmers accommodates a passing regiment, Johanna learns that real patriotism can also be achieved through domestic excellence and by being pleasing to the eye. Only at the end of the story, when all the romantic battles are won, is the conflict in Europe alluded to in quite explicit terms: in a frontal shot addressing the camera, Johanna/Pickford turns to soldiers and spectators and instructs them to "cure" Europe. An inter-title reads: "And don't you come back until you have taken the germ out of Germany." *Pollyanna* can be placed among these patriotic productions in the way the film flatly *denies* the fact that the Great War has, in Willa Cather's later phrasing, left the world broken, and by continuing to speak of the global conflict in terms of sickness, health, and curing. During the war, patriotism (donating money or enlisting) was presented as the means to cure Europe from its germs.

In a fitting echo of the actual process and development of traumatic disorders, as theorized by Freud, *Pollyanna* can be seen to stand for Pickford and Marion's delayed grasp of the haunting experience of war, while their next film together, *The Love Light*, would bring to the fore the symptoms of psychological collapse as a result of war trauma—hysteria, empathic paralysis, and amnesia. Film historians have noted how the tone and message of war films of the mid-twenties contrast with the sentimentalized individual heroics and justifications of war in films produced during the Great War, predictably so in straightforward propaganda but also in more indirect war-related pictures. The postwar climate clearly affected the generic pattern of war films of the second half of the twenties, most notably *The Big Parade* (Vidor 1926) and *What Price Glory* (Walsh 1926). These genre films express great ambivalence about the heroics of dying for one's country and openly meditate on the futility of war. More subversively, they also question the morality of the war film as a form of "male adventure story," with the introduction of a new stock cast of characters in both literature and film adding flawed, cowardly, critical, or cynical characters to the martial hero protagonist (Jacobs 132; Hynes 214–15).

The Love Light's brutal (and largely true) narrative shows "the tidal waves of war" reaching the distant shores of a simple fishing village. One story line, focusing on the temporary mental collapse of its heroine Angela/Pickford, is particularly compelling because it actually shows war trauma in the most explicit terms. In the third and final act of the film, Angela must recover not only from the shock of a romantic betrayal by a German spy but also from the subsequent deaths of her brothers and from giving birth to a child who symbolizes her lover's duplicity and her personal loss. An inter-title explains:

> For months Angela's mind
> lay sleeping,—stunned
> by successive shocks of
> sorrow—innocent victim
> of a far off conflict.

Angela's experience results in traumatic symptoms (hysteria) after a brief period of repression (a sleeping mind) and apathy. It is not impossible that Marion was familiar with Freud, or with early writings on shell-shock (which appeared from 1915 onward), and the careful depiction of traumatic symptoms—anxiety, apathy, paralysis, hysteria—is striking. The idea that hysterical suffering comes mainly from memory, as Freud and Breuer famously proposed in *Studies in Hysteria* (first published in 1895), is clearly adopted in a scene in which Angela awakens from her catatonic state after reliving shocking memories of the recent past. The scene shows Pickford registering a series of conflicting emotional states—unresponsiveness, endearment, repulsion, panic, hope—in close-ups. Angela's hysterical condition is also aligned with a combination of the modern phenomena both clinicians (and Freud specifically) linked with trauma in general: sexual repression or forbidden desire within restrictive (bourgeois) family structures (in the film exemplified by Angela's love for a German spy) and the industrial revolution causing industrial accidents and large-scale conflicts (exemplified by the Great War). Considering the difference in tone of both pictures, *Pollyanna* and *The Love Light* symbolically represent the different consecutive symptoms of traumatic experiences and, in their story material, offer two possible cures or trajectories of recovery: through denial and optimism or through remembrance and perseverance.

Postwar *Pollyanna* continued this metaphor of convalescence. Unlike the novel and the play by Catherine Chisholm Cushing (which also served as an important source, as the opening credits acknowledge), the film fully dramatizes Pollyanna's fateful accident and her subsequent recovery. In the book, the accident is referred to in retrospect, in a single vague paragraph, and by Pollyanna herself in a short, if enthusiastic, letter closing the book that swiftly narrates her first steps in a medical rehabilitation center. In order to meet public expectations and star requirements—a star like Pickford needed scenes in which she could be both active (performing the action instead of narrating it) and emotionally moving—these events required explicit staging. The visualization of these spectacular and cathartic scenes additionally endowed the Pollyanna character with a somewhat heroic status. In the film, the central accident is the result of Pollyanna jumping in front of a car in order to save a toddler. The scene is particularly convincing as it was filmed in reverse, giving the impression that Pickford performed a dangerous stunt (Eyman 134). The script also features Pollyanna and Jimmie Bean fighting in a scene that ends with Jimmie telling Pollyanna to "just go on and die." This ominous curse makes the actual accident (which came as no surprise to the audience familiar with the story) even more sympathetic and paves the way for an emotional scene of forgiveness and consolation between the two children.

After the accident Pollyanna discovers some perks to being sick: Aunt Polly suddenly calls her "dear," and even places a kiss on her brow. Pollyanna reasons in an inter-title:

"It's so good to have
you love me, Aunt
Polly, I—I'm really
glad I was hurt."

This optimism comes before she receives the news that she will never walk again, and she nearly quits playing her game since the prospect of living without the use of her legs is emotionally paralyzing as well. And thus, as an inter-title explains, Pollyanna's "songs of gladness are temporarily hushed," but the "rainbows" of happiness and hope, a visual theme in the movie's illustrated inter-titles, soon return when Dr. Chilton is finally allowed into the household. Dr. Chilton realizes that his ability to cure Pollyanna is entirely up to his patient's state of mind. He promises:

I *am* going to make
you well, Pollyanna,
because . . . you have
faith in me.

Indeed, it would appear that "faith" is essentially all that is needed to make Pollyanna well again, and that the specialists called in at Aunt Polly's urging, as an inter-title emphasizes, have been unable to help her because she has no faith in them. Ultimately, it is the combination of faith in the healing capacities of Dr. Chilton (whom we never see perform a medical treatment) and an optimistic belief in herself that bring about Pollyanna's complete recovery. Her miraculous triumph is presented as a religious as well as a personal victory, and the scene takes full advantage of the sympathetic power of the moment: Pollyanna is in the downstairs parlor, surrounded by her aunt, Mr. Pendleton, Dr. Chilton, Jimmie Bean, Nancy, and Tom. The tension of the moment is too much for Jimmie, and he dashes outside to cry over what he believes will be a failed attempt. Before Pollyanna actually tries to walk, we are given an undisturbed gaze on Pickford's face in a ravishing and glamorously diffused close-up. With a devout and determined look on her face, she looks up to the heavens and then looks blissfully into the camera while mouthing, "I believe . . . I can walk again." A smile, and then finally, in fashion both pathetic and slightly comic, she manages to stumble across the room, collapsing in her aunt's arms. Kevin Brownlow's observation that the scene resembles the adaptation of George Cohan's Broadway hit *The Miracle Man* (1919), in which a healing Patriarch miraculously succeeds in enabling a crippled boy to walk again, strengthens the scene's spiritual implications ("Rediscovered" 169). Additionally, the sight of the crippled star walking again might have spoken to the well-known image of wounded, paralyzed, and scarred soldiers who had returned from the war. On an allegorical level of another kind, the scene also implies that, as an independent producer, Pickford could stand on her own two feet.

Pollyanna's Hollywood

War trauma aside, *Pollyanna* apparently also struck a chord with more general audience psychology, eulogizing the rupture from childhood and decrying the vicissitudes of modern life (including Hollywood films and Hollywood mores in general). Frederick James Smith championed the film for its depiction and resuscitation of "youthful innocence and childhood dreams" (Smith, "Letter" 103). Smith's language comes across as dreamy, perplexed, almost spiritually affected, and those in the business of picture making certainly did not appreciate his call for "more Pollyannas." The film was praised by the National Board of Review, just as the founding of the Motion Pictures Producers and Distributors Association (MPPDA) in 1922 ushered in a new period of censure on a moral basis (Aronson 39). As the list of banned subjects grew, a vigilant form of censorship became a force to be reckoned with, even if actual censorship was hardly ever exercised, since most film content was censored before it went into production. Despite the general tone of moral vigilance, however, the call for more Pollyanna pictures never materialized as the Jazz Age and more naturalist and war-weary film productions of the mid-twenties set new aesthetic and moral standards. On the other hand, an actual decline of sentiment never truly materialized—Hollywood has never banned sentiment or sentimentality, or the idea of a "Pollyanna picture." Even if *Pollyanna* was outwardly condemned ("the Pollyanna period has passed," wrote Frances Marion in 1937), a Pollyanna-like ideology and characters remained at the heart of influential, "classical" Hollywood production. Powerful players like Marion and Pickford, and other pioneers and industry titans like Charlie Chaplin, Frank Borzage, Cecil B. DeMille, John Ford, King Vidor, along with producers and studio heads like Samuel Goldwyn, Louis B. Mayer, and Darryl Zanuck, tapped into the fictional world offered by *Pollyanna*. These were all deeply sentimental filmmakers, but most of them were capable of adapting their inherent sentimentality to the changing tastes and cultural shifts introduced by the Jazz Age (a favorite narrative strategy of these filmmakers was to contrast the old types and the new, with the old mostly winning out).

As a film overtly addressing and confirming the power and possibility of faith, spiritual healing, trauma, recovery, self-reliance, and optimism, Pickford's adaptation of *Pollyanna* was infected by the spirit of its time and by the career, persona, and private concerns of its star. Oddly, although it captured current tendencies and concerns, the film also became almost instantly regarded as hopelessly naïve and outdated, even if these ideas, in a more muted form, would remain at the core of Hollywood fare and aesthetics for years to come.

As *Pollyanna* became obsolete, so too did its star; Pickford's career slowly went into decline during the twenties and she retired from filmmaking in the early thirties. However, she remained active behind the scenes (at United Artists), and even cashed in on the Pollyanna philosophy once again in 1934, when she published a semi-spiritual booklet, *Why Not Try God?*, a short tract championing the power of positive and happy thoughts. In 1920 her film adaptation of *Pollyanna* brought her a smashing financial success, and it seems that in 1934 her interpretation of Christian Science with a Pollyanna-esque twist brought her spiritual calm as well. As the book providentially became a bestseller, it was also proof that, ultimately, optimism pays.

Notes

1. Pickford was typically described as "divine" (Lindsay "Congo" 104), "heavenly," or even "Madonna-like" (qtd. in Wagenknecht 10), like a "fairy" and "not from this world" (qtd. in Basinger 59). Poet Vachel Lindsay praised the "sustained Botticelli grace of 'Our Mary'" ("Art" 4).

2. The novel also addressed the "psychological wounds" of war, anticipating medical and societal acceptance that came much later. Cather solemnly notes the soldiers' inability to reconnect with life after they return from battle, a clear reference to the traumatic symptoms of the then as-yet-unnamed phenomenon of shell-shock.

Works Cited

Abbot, Eleanor. *Molly Make-Believe*. New York: Century, 1910. Print.

———. *The Sick-a-Bed Lady*. New York: Century, 1911. Print.

———. *The White Linen Nurse*. New York: Century. 1913. Print.

Aronson, Michael. "Movies, Margarine and Main Street." *American Cinema in the 1920s: Themes and Variations*. Ed. Lucy Fischer. New Brunswick: Rutgers UP, 2009. 23–45. Print.

Basinger, Jeanine. *Silent Stars*. London, CT: Wesleyan UP, 2000. Print.

Beachamp, Cari. *Without Lying Down: Frances Marion and the Powerful Women of Early Hollywood*. Berkeley: U of California P, 1997. Print.

The Big Parade. 1925. Dir. King Vidor. Copy from the International Museum of Photography and Film, George Eastman House. Film.

Brouwers, Anke. "There Was Something about Mary: Mary's Perfect 'Little American.'" *Stories and Portraits of the Self*. Eds. Helena Carvalhão Buescu and João Ferraira Duarte. Amsterdam: Rodopi, 2007. 307–20. Print.

Brownlow, Kevin. *The Parade's Gone By . . .* Berkeley: U of California P, 1968. Print.

———. *The War, the West, and the Wilderness*. New York: Random House, 1979. Print.

———. *Mary Pickford Rediscovered: Rare Pictures from a Hollywood Legend*. Los Angeles: Henry N. Abrams and AMPAS, 1999. Print.

Burnham, Clara Louise. *Jewel: A Chapter in Her Life*. New York: Grosset & Dunlap, 1903. Print.

Cather, Willa. *One of Ours*. New York: Albert A. Knopf, 1922. Print.

Clark, Suzanne. *Sentimental Modernism: Women Writers and the Revolution of the Word*. Bloomington: Indiana UP, 1991. Print.

Cohen, Paula Marantz. *Silent Film and the Triumph of the American Myth*. London: Oxford UP, 2001. Print.

Cushing, Catharine Chisholm. *Pollyanna, the Glad Girl, a Four Act Comedy*. New York: Klaw & Erlanger, 1915. Print.

Debauche, Leslie Midkiff. *Reel Patriotism: The Movies and World War I*. Madison: U of Wisconsin P, 1997. Print.

Douglas, Ann. *Terrible Honesty: Mongrel Manhattan in the Twenties.* New York: Noonday, 1995. Print.

Eddy, Mary Baker. *Science and Health with Key to the Scriptures.* Boston: Christian Scientist Publishing, 1875. *Project Gutenberg.* October 2002. Web. 28 July 2013.

Elkins, James. *Pictures and Tears.* London: Routledge, 2001. Print.

Eyman, Scott. *Mary Pickford: From Here to Hollywood.* Toronto: Harper Collins, 1990. Print.

The Four Horsemen of the Apocalypse. 1921. Dir. Rex Ingram. Archive.org. Web. 18 September 2013. Film.

Graves, Robert. *Goodbye to All That.* London: Anchor, 1929. Print.

The Greatest Question. 1919. Dir. D. W. Griffith. Museum of Modern Art, New York. Film.

Griswold, Jerry. *Audacious Kids: Coming of Age in America's Classic Children's Books.* New York: Oxford UP, 1992. Print.

Gunning, Tom. "True Heart Susie." *The Griffith Project. Vol. 10 (1919–46).* Ed. Paolo Cherchi-Usai. London: BFI, 2006. 18–27. Print.

Hemingway, Ernest. *In Our Time.* New York: Boni & Liveright, 1925. Print.

———. *A Farewell to Arms.* New York: Charles Scribner's Sons, 1929. Print.

Hughes, Rupert. "The Mobilization of Johanna." *Hearst's* September–October 1917. Print.

Hynes, Steven. *A War Imagined: The First World War and English Culture.* New York: Pimlico, 1991. Print.

Jacobs, Lea. *The Decline of Sentiment: Hollywood Cinema in the 1920s.* New York: Columbia UP, 2008. Print.

Jefferson, Mark. "What is Wrong with Sentimentality?" *Mind: New Series* 92 (October 1983): 519–29. Print.

Johanna Enlists. 1918. Dir. William Desmond Taylor. Mary Pickford Film Institute. Film.

Landy, Marcia. "Movies and the Changing Body of Cinema." *American Cinema in the 1920s: Themes and Variations.* Ed. Lucy Fischer. New Brunswick: Rutgers UP, 2009. 95–119. Print.

Lindsay, Vachel. *The Congo and Other Poems.* New York: Macmillan, 1915. Print.

———. 1915. *The Art of the Moving Picture.* New York: Modern Library, 2000. Print.

The Little American. 1917. Dir. Cecil B. DeMille. Mary Pickford Film Institute. Film.

The Love Light. 1921. Dir. Frances Marion. Milestone, 2001. Film.

Marion, Frances. *Off with Their Heads!* New York: Macmillan, 1972. Print.

Midgley, Mary. "Sentimentality and Brutality." *Philosophy* 54 (1979): 385–89. Print.

The Miracle Man. 1917. Dir. George Cohan. Print presumed lost. Film.

Newton, E. Sarah. *Learning to Behave: A Guide to American Conduct Books Before 1900.* Westport, CT: Greenwood, 1994. Print.

"Paramount Program." *The Moving Picture World.* New York: Chalmers (October–December 1914): 343. Print.

Patterson, Frances Taylor. *Cinema Craftsmanship: A Book for Cinematographers.* New York: Harcourt, Brace and Howe, 1920. Print.

Pickford, Mary. "The Portrayal of Child Roles." *Vanity Fair* (1917), n.p. Rpt. in Kevin Brownlow, *Mary Pickford Rediscovered: Rare Pictures from a Hollywood Legend.* Los Angeles: Henry N. Abrams and AMPAS, 1999. 30, 32. Print.

——. *My Rendez-Vous with Life*. New York: H.C. Kinsey, 1935. Print.

——. *Sunshine and Shadow*. New York: Doubleday, 1955. Print.

——. *Why Not Try God?* New York: H.C. Kinsey, 1935. Print.

Pollyanna. 1920. Dir. Paul Powell. Cinematek. Film.

The Poor Little Rich Girl. 1917. Dir. Maurice Tourneur. Mary Pickford Film Institute. Film.

Rebecca of Sunnybrook Farm. 1917. Dir. Marshall A. Neilan. Mary Pickford Film Institute. Film.

Rosen, Marjorie. *Popcorn Venus: Women, Movies and the American Dream*. New York: Avon, 1973. Print.

Sassoon, Siegfried. *Sherston's Progress*. London: Faber & Faber, 1939. Print.

Savile, Anthony. "Sentimentality." *Arguing about Art*. Eds. Alex Neill and Aaron Ridley. London: Routledge, 2004. 315–19. Print.

Slater, Thomas J. "June Mathis: A Woman Who Spoke Through Silents." *American Silent Film: Discovering Marginalized Voices*. Eds. Thomas J. Slater and Gregg Bachman. Carbondale: Southern Illinois UP, 2002. 201–16. Print.

Slater, Thomas. "June Mathis' Valentino Scripts: Images of 'Male Becoming' After the Great War." *Cinema Journal* 50.1 (Fall 2010): 99–120. Print.

Slide, Anthony. *Silent Topics: Essays on Undocumented Areas of Silent Film*. Toronto: Scarecrow, 2004. Print.

Smith, Frederick James. "Mary Had a Little Tear." *Motion Picture Classic* (September 1917): n.p. Print.

——. "Letter to Mary Pickford." *Motion Picture Classic* (March 1920): 103. Print.

——. "Review of Through the Back Door." *Motion Picture Classic* (August 1921): 78. Print.

Stamp, Shelley. "Exit Flapper, Enter Woman: Or Lois Weber in the Hollywood Jazz Age." *Framework: The Journal of Cinema and Media* 51.2 (Fall 2010): 358–87. Print.

Sterne, Laurence. *The Life and Opinions of Tristram Shandy*. London: Cochrane, 1832. Print.

Studlar, Gaylyn. "Oh, 'Doll Divine': Mary Pickford, Masquerade, and the Pedophilic Gaze." *A Feminist Reader in Early Cinema*. Eds. Jennifer M. Bean and Diane Negra. Durham: Duke UP, 2002. 349–73. Print.

Tess of the Storm Country. 1914. Dir. Edwin S. Porter. Mary Pickford Film Institute. Film.

Vasey, Ruth. *The World According to Hollywood, 1918–1939*. Exeter: U of Exeter P, 1997. Print.

Wagenknecht, Edward. "Introduction." In Raymond Lee, *The Films of Mary Pickford*. New York: Castle, 1970. 9–11. Print.

What Price Glory. 1926. Dir. Raoul Walsh. International Museum of Photography and Film, George Eastman House. Film.

Whitfield, Eileen. *Mary Pickford: The Woman Who Made Hollywood*. Kentucky: UP of Kentucky, 2007. Print.

Williams, Linda. "Melodrama Revised." *Refiguring American Film Genres: Theory and History*. Ed. Nick Browne. Berkeley: U of California P, 1998. 42–88. Print.

11

"Almost a golden glow around it":
The Filmic Nostalgia of Walt Disney's *Pollyanna*

K. BRENNA WARDELL

The 1960 film adaptation of Eleanor H. Porter's *Pollyanna* by Walt Disney Productions can be regarded as a work of recovery. The late 1950s was a period infused with nostalgia for turn-of-the-century American life and a desire to reconnect with a sense of innocent fun and community coherence in a period in which social, economic, and cultural shifts had created anxiety about families and the state of the nation itself. The film's creators reveal their nostalgia through a focus on play in the film's form and narrative, which, in conjunction with period details such as costumes and songs, creates a sunny, nostalgic picture of small-town American life in the early 1900s.

"*Pollyanna* has almost a golden glow around it when you look back and think of it as the adventures of children and the way they affect the adults they come in contact with," notes film historian Stacia Martin in the feature "*Pollyanna:* Making of a Masterpiece" in the Vault Disney DVD Collection of the film (2002). Rather than focusing on twenty-first-century reactions to the film, this chapter analyzes *Pollyanna*'s 1959 production and 1960 release; however, I begin with Martin's words because they capture not only the nostalgia for a past, seemingly more simple era in American life that pervades the Disney adaptation, but they also set up the figurative and literal glow, conveyed through form and narrative, that is one of its central features. A brief examination of the film sets up its similarities to, and differences from, Porter's novel, as well as from an earlier film adaptation released in 1920. Historical background on the nation and the film industry, including Walt Disney Studios, in the 1950s is then provided for cultural and industrial context. Finally, a close reading of the aural, visual, and narrational emphasis on play within the film demonstrates how play is employed by the film's creators to recover a sense of a cohesive American identity while building a utopian vision of the nation's past.

While the film and Porter's novel differ in a number of ways, the novel's essence—the transformation of an early-century town by the 12-year-old orphan Pollyanna—remains the same. After traveling to her wealthy aunt's home in Harrington (the novel's Beldingsville, Vermont), Pollyanna uses her glad game to win over the household staff and the townspeople, including the grumpy, invalid Mrs. Snow and the town's fire-and-brimstone minister, Reverend Ford. Through her play with Jimmy Bean, a boy who lives in the town orphanage, Pollyanna also encounters the reclusive Mr. Pendergast (the novel's Mr. Pendleton), and Edmond Chilton, a doctor recently returned to town.

In a plotline that marks a significant departure from the novel's narrative, a fracture between the townspeople and Polly develops over what to do about the town orphanage, endowed by Polly's father. The mayor advocates a new building, while Polly supports repairs to the existing structure. While the townspeople are initially reluctant to defy the autocratic Polly, they plan a charity bazaar to raise funds for a new orphanage. Almost everyone in town takes part in the bazaar, with the notable exception of Polly. Pollyanna is forbidden to go, but she manages to escape her attic room and attend the celebration.

Pollyanna's evening ends in tragedy, however, when she is paralyzed after she falls from a tree while climbing back to her room. Aunt Polly reluctantly consults Dr. Chilton, who arranges for surgery in the city; however, he worries that Pollyanna seems to have lost hope because she no longer plays the glad game. Word of Pollyanna's injury reaches the townspeople, who flock *en masse* to Aunt Polly's house. Dr. Chilton carries Pollyanna downstairs to greet them, and their joyful thanks for everything she has done for them quickly restores her spirits. While Porter ends her novel with Pollyanna's first tentative steps and then details Pollyanna's full recovery in the sequel *Pollyanna Grows Up* (1915), the film ends with Pollyanna still impaired, although on her way to surgery and a hopeful outcome. The final shots of the film show Pollyanna and a reconciled Polly and Dr. Chilton off to the city by train, with the entire town on hand to bid them farewell. As the train leaves the station, an updated version of the town's name is shown on a sign—it reads "Harrington: 'The Glad Town.'" As this summary reveals, the 1960 film adaptation adheres relatively closely, on the whole, to the spirit of the novel despite its plot differences. At the same time, it also engages with elements of the 1920 film adaptation, which stars Mary Pickford.

On the surface, the two films appear very different on both the level of narrative and form; however, a closer examination reveals some interesting parallels. The 1920 film has a much shorter running time than the 1960 film—58 minutes in comparison to 134 minutes—thereby limiting its room for narrative and character development. Technical differences between film production in the eras in which the films were produced, such as the contrast of silence to sound and black and white to color, along with shifting audience expectations of the visual, aural, and narrational capacity of cinema, influence each film's final shape. At the same time, the films are linked on the level of content and form in a shared focus on play and, with that play, a sense of an emotional buoyancy conveyed via a light-filled *mise-en-scène*.

This focus on playfulness and luminosity in each film can be seen as a response to the demands of adapting *Pollyanna* for film. To communicate the novel's theme of "gladness" through the film medium, the cast and crew of each film version emphasize this theme visually through the appearance of the film's world and its characters. The creators of the 1960 film also add aural elements of dialogue, sound effects, and music to parallel and augment this visual cheerfulness.

To create the look and tone of the 1960 film, director and screenwriter David Swift and his crew provide an emotional sunniness through their use of formal details, especially *mise-en-scène* choices such as high-key lighting and colorful costumes, augmented by cheerful period and original music; together, these produce "a golden glow" that is both figurative and literal (Martin). A narrational highlight on play on the part of both children and adults further advances the novel's focus on gladness. At the same time as these components of form and narrative are used to recreate the novel's atmosphere and message of cheer, they also produce a sense of nostalgia for a seemingly more easygoing, sociable period in American history. This can be seen especially strongly in the focus on community coherence in the two sequences that bring the townspeople together before and after Pollyanna's accident: the charity bazaar and the gathering at Polly's house. Together, these aspects of Disney's *Pollyanna* create a film text that evokes a sense of nostalgia for a supposedly more innocent, hopeful time in viewers' lives—their childhood—while also engaging with the nation's past: a past set before World Wars I and II and the subsequent social, economic, and political changes wrought by wartime and war recovery. As this engagement with history is crucial to this argument, a brief sketch of the history of the period and the production is provided before a move to an exploration of the film and the aspects of form and narrative within *Pollyanna* that undergird the argument.

1950s America and Hollywood: Success and Struggle

Between the century's early years and the late 1950s, the United States went through rapid economic, sociopolitical, and technological changes that transformed the nation internally, while simultaneously resulting in increased global prominence. The post–World War II years of the 1950s saw many U.S. citizens enjoying unprecedented economic success, although the situation for the nation's film industry, particularly the major Hollywood studios, was much less settled. A combination of factors challenged the dominance of the film studios and altered the nature of film production, distribution, and exhibition. In *Movie-Made America: A History of American Movies*, film theorist Robert Sklar details these challenges, beginning with the ruling in *United States v. Paramount Pictures* in 1948 that led to the dismantling of vertical integration (272–73). Utilizing vertical integration—the ownership of not only film production, but also of distribution and exhibition branches—studios had been able to make films, distribute those films through their own distribution arms, and then exhibit the films in studio-owned theaters. As a result of the ruling, studios had to shed their distribution networks and sell their theatres, retaining only their production facilities, many of which were significantly scaled down during the period.

Added to these economic problems were the repercussions of the House Un-American Activities Committee (HUAC) hearings from the late 40s and into the 50s. As Sklar notes, the hearings associated many Hollywood workers with the threat of Communism (249–68), and had a significant impact on cinema attendance and on perceptions of the movie industry as a whole.[1] Other developments that led to significant changes in American culture and society, including shifts in the film industry, were the growth of freeways and suburbs and the resulting decline of the inner cities; the mixture of attention to and anxiety over young people and youth culture; and the beginnings of the civil rights movement. Together, these changes created concern on the part of many Americans about the cohesion of the nation's families and worries about the nation's social fabric as a whole.

For the film industry, however, perhaps the most daunting challenge was the competition from the new medium of television, which threatened the industry's command of viewer dollars. To counter dwindling audience numbers, many film producers utilized contemporary technology and highlighted the unique visual and aural qualities of the film medium that set it apart from television. For example, some producers created epic spectacles in brilliant Technicolor that utilized widescreen formats such as Cinemascope, including *The Robe* (Koster 1953) and *Ben-Hur* (Wyler 1959), while others turned to decidedly adult adaptations of contemporary plays, articles, and books, such as the sexually fraught *A Streetcar Named Desire* (Kazan 1951), the gritty *On the Waterfront* (Kazan 1954), and *Blackboard Jungle* (Brooks 1955).

Another tactic that studio heads used to draw in audiences was to focus on the genres that seemed to resonate mostly strongly with the public; of these, as Sklar notes, westerns, costume melodramas, and comedies proved particularly popular (283). The popularity of comedy could explain why Swift, like Frances Marion and Paul Powell (the screenwriter and director, respectively, of the 1920 film), emphasizes the comic aspects of Porter's story, drawing from the novel or, in some cases, creating new incidents.[2] Attention to contemporary audiences interests and sensibilities, and an understanding of their distance from early-century mores, was certainly important for Swift. On his commentary for the Vault Disney Collection DVD, Swift notes that he deliberately sought to leaven the book's more overt sentimentality with touches of humor in consideration of contemporary tastes, and he points to star Hayley Mills's facility with comedy as a central reason for the success of her performance and for the longevity of the 1960 adaptation.

The popularity of genres such as comedy and costumed spectacle may have kindled the interest of Walt Disney and his studio in adapting *Pollyanna*, a text whose period setting could create the opportunity for lavish scenes, while the innocent, family-friendly nature of the story aligned with Disney's own reputation as a producer of works, whether media texts or the newly-built Disneyland theme park, that could appeal to both adults and children. At the same time, the Disney studio was transforming in response to the socioeconomic demands of the period. As Neal Gabler notes in *Walt Disney: The Triumph of the American Imagination*: "If the studio and the staff were different from the ones over which Walt had presided before Disneyland, so now were the films they produced. For one thing, animation had practically disappeared; in the five years after *Sleeping Beauty* the studio produced only two animated features, *101 Dalmatians* and *The Sword in the Stone*. . . . The emphasis had shifted to live action films" (585).

Walt Disney's interest in engaging with bygone eras through these live-action films is revealed by an examination of their titles and their content for, like *Pollyanna*, a number were set in previous centuries, some specifically in the nation's past. For example, *Johnny Tremain* (Stevenson 1957) is located in Boston during the Revolutionary War, the popular *Davey*

Crockett television series (directed by Norman Foster and compiled as the 1955 movie *Davey Crocket: King of the Wild Frontier*) is set in the early half of the nineteenth century in Tennessee and Texas, and *Old Yeller* (Stevenson 1957) takes place in nineteenth-century Texas. Preceding *Pollyanna* as a work of early-twentieth-century small-town nostalgia is *So Dear to My Heart* (Schuster 1948), set in 1903 in a fictional town in Indiana. This list argues for the studio's interest in wedding family-friendly stories with tales situated in the American past.

This background on 1950s America and the state of the Hollywood studios, including Disney, explains why both *Pollyanna*'s audience and the film's creators might be interested in a work from earlier in the century—one that recreates an idyllic past, at least momentarily, via the film medium. A close reading of the film's formal and narrational aspects will detail how these work to produce for viewers a glowing, nostalgic glimpse into that past.

Formal Choices: Creating a "golden glow" through Sight and Sound

Formal choices, particularly in the selection of *mise-en-scène* elements such as lighting and costume, are essential in creating the sense of gladness and play delineated in the narrative. For example, the choice of the lighting of interior and exterior scenes, and of specific characters, is one of the primary ways in which Swift and his crew created a "golden glow" on both an emotional and perceptual level. Watching the film, one is struck by the brightness of the images, with all of the exterior location scenes apparently filmed in brilliant sunshine and the interior scenes brightly lit, even in the few sequences in which characters express emotional gloom.[3] These lights illuminate exterior settings that display a pastoral abundance full of blooming flowers and green fields. There is, in fact, an interesting temporal aspect to both lighting and setting. Given the abundance of flora and the bright golden quality of the light, Pollyanna appears to arrive in the summer; however, although time passes as she transforms the townspeople's lives, neither the exteriors nor the interiors visibly shift to mark seasonal changes. The town of Harrington may, as the film opens, be a pleasant space, yet Pollyanna seems to bring with her something extra: an eternal summer whose visible glow augments the internal transformation that she creates in the townspeople's hearts and souls.

That the film literally glows is important in understanding the ways in which it conveys its blithe tone, maintains a focus on the transformation of the townspeople, and nods to the genres of comedy and musicals. For example, the brightness of the *mise-en-scène* creates a distinct emotional affect in viewers, insisting on a sense of lightheartedness even in more dramatic, even frightening, moments—such as Pollyanna's refusal to play the glad game following her accident. While Pollyanna's rejection of the glad game does create a momentary sense of emotional depression, especially given Pollyanna's predicament, the high-key lighting of the scene, reinforced by the light-colored costumes of the actors and the overall decor, assures the viewer that this gloom is temporary and fleeting.

If the film in general has a literally lighthearted look, this is particularly true of the appearance of Pollyanna herself. Film theorist Richard Dyer notes in his book *White* that *mise-en-scène* elements, particularly lighting, can not only be used to differentiate certain individuals from others on-screen—a necessary act in developing character and plot—but can also associate these individuals with a sense of spirituality, almost otherworldliness, and purity. As Dyer notes, there is a tendency on the part of many artists and thinkers to associate paleness with positive moral/spiritual values: "In Western tradition, white is beautiful because it is the colour of virtue. This remarkable equation relates to a particular definition of goodness. All lists of the moral connotations of white as symbol in Western culture are the same: purity, spirituality, transcendence, cleanliness, virtue, simplicity, chastity" (72). This association of whiteness or light with spirituality is, Dyer argues, particularly the case in regard to white women or girls and the ways in which they are lit and photographed: "Idealized white women are bathed in and permeated by light. It streams through them and falls on them from above. In short, they glow" (122). In Disney's *Pollyanna*, the lightness of Mills's blond hair, combined with the brightness of the sunshine (whether artificial or real) and the pale colors of many of her costumes, creates a sense that Mills as Pollyanna is literally, as well as figuratively, associated with light and with the emotional/spiritual implications of such light. In this particular use of lighting the film echoes the 1920 adaptation, in which bright lighting consistently picks up the pale face and blond ringlets of Pickford's Pollyanna, particularly in close-up shots, and makes her appear to glow.[4]

Pollyanna's is not the only palely glowing face in the 1960 adaptation, although she receives special attention; in fact, it is noteworthy that Harrington's population is entirely white. (In contrast, *Polly* [1989] and its sequel *Polly: Comin' Home!* [1990], two later adaptations of *Pollyanna* produced by Walt Disney Television, feature a cast that is largely African American in productions set in a small Alabama town in the 1950s.) Given the film's production in the late 1950s, when issues of racial equality became a theme, overtly or covertly, of so many contemporary media texts, this is important, as it makes the film's nostalgic bent potentially problematic. The argument may be made that a viewer might not expect a small New England town in the early years of the century to have much racial or ethnic diversity, yet the uniformity of whiteness on-screen creates a sense of omission. This lack contrasts with the 1920 film, in which an African-American woman and child appear, albeit in a manner that is curious—the woman chides Pollyanna for chatting with the child as he washes himself in a water trough—and cursory, in that these characters are afforded only a few minutes of screen time and then disappear.

The result is that one might read the distinct whiteness of Disney's Harrington as a conservative move, a nostalgia on the part of its producers for a time before the sociopolitical turmoil of the civil rights movement, a yearning for a time when communities, whether towns or groups of people, may have seemed, at least on the surface, more cohesive. In the creation of this literally light community in the adaptation, brought together through the ministrations of the pale, blond Pollyanna, there is also an echo of Porter's novel, which largely eschews a discussion of racial or ethnic difference despite the period's waves of immigration and domestic migration, which were widely discussed in the contemporary popular press. One of the few exceptions to this in the novel is the character of Nancy, who is Irish. In the 1960 film adaptation, however, Nancy is no longer Irish, and she speaks with a distinctly American accent.

Just as lighting is essential to convey a sense of gladness on-screen, so too a gradual shift in costume styles and colors throughout the film helps the viewer appreciate the manner in which the characters are gradually transformed by Pollyanna and her game: moving from gloom and isolation to gladness and community involvement. For instance, Polly initially appears in dark colors and heavy fabrics, such as the deep blue dress accented with abundant jet beading she wears when Pollyanna first meets her. However, her costumes gradually lighten as she becomes closer to Pollyanna and more integrated into the community. As the film progresses, she begins to dress in costumes such as a light gray dress accented with white, a dress in light blue, and, in the film's finale, a pale pink and white dress that mirrors Pollyanna's own flowered pink and white dress with pink bows. Pollyanna's costumes are consistently light-colored, although on the whole she too moves to brighter, lighter colors as the story progresses and the sense of gladness within Harrington grows.

The use of such a bright *mise-en-scène*, particularly the high-key lighting, generically ties the film to film genres such as the comedy and the musical, which normally feature this lighting style. In fact, with its brilliant lights, colorful turn-of-the-century costumes, and period songs, the film recalls a famous musical of Hollywood's Golden Age: *Meet Me in St. Louis* (1944), directed by Vincente Minnelli.[5] Music is, in fact, a vital aspect of the film's playful, nostalgic mode, and while *Pollyanna* is not a musical per se, attention to its soundtrack reveals the manner in which specific aural choices amplify the visual choices I have discussed.

Notably, the film's aural elements support and emphasize the film's nostalgic mode and lighthearted touch. For example, the music in the title sequence, with its lush, lilting orchestration, quickly sets the aural tone and augments the pastoral, almost timeless appearance of the setting. At the same time, certain unusual musical punctuations highlight specific moments, reinforcing the sense of play that is so central to the film's narrative. For example, as a little boy swings into the water in the film's opening, the camera focuses on a large steam locomotive crossing over the stream, moving toward the viewer; at the same time, the soundtrack contains not simply the sound effects of the locomotive, but also the addition of a musical "choo-choo" from the orchestra. This addition both reinforces the presence of the train and playfully comments on it. So too, a little later in the title sequence a boy, later revealed to be Jimmy Bean, is seen running by a family sitting in a broken-down motorcar with the father underneath the car, attempting to fix it. As Jimmy runs by the motorcar in one direction, a horse-drawn cart moves by it in the opposite direction. The camera fixes on the departing cart, and the musicians draw the viewer's attention to the moment by playing the "clip clop" of the horses' hooves.

This deliberate use of sound, as Claudia Gorbman notes in "Classical Hollywood Practice" from *Critical Visions in Film Theory*, is known as "mickey-mousing" (181), and it aurally hints to the viewer that in beginning to watch *Pollyanna* he/she is entering a lighthearted, playful world.[6] At the same time, this mickey-mousing of the train and the cart serves to comment on these particular aspects of early-twentieth-century life that would, by 1960, seem delightfully strange to young viewers and quaint relics of a bygone time to older viewers. In the instance of the contrast of the broken-down motorcar versus the jaunty movement of the horse cart, with the sound emphasis given to the latter, there is an additional element of meaning at work, for in the focus on the cart there seems to be an argument for the pleasures of a simpler kind of technology and, with it, a slower pace of life. Together, these elements of the title sequence help to emphasize the playfulness and innocence, and the nostalgia for both, that will fill the rest of the film.

The film's aural elements also create a nostalgic hail to viewers in the use of era-appropriate music in concert with composer Paul J. Smith's original work. Period tunes such as "When You and I Were Young, Maggie" and "I'll Take You Home Again, Kathleen" help not only situate the film authentically in the early twentieth century, but also evoke the past for listeners who may have grown up hearing these songs. Music also provides a way to demonstrate the increasing playfulness and cohesion of Harrington's inhabitants thanks to Pollyanna. For example, when Pollyanna and Nancy, Polly's maid, have begun to bond, Pollyanna leads Nancy in an impromptu singing of the traditional round "Early One Morning": the twining of their voices together and the cheerfulness of the song emphasizing their new camaraderie and breaking down any sense of barriers—whether socio-economic or emotional—between them.

So, too, music plays an essential role in the bazaar scene, indicating how the fractured community has come together in joyful play. Medium shots and close-ups of the musicians playing for the dancers, such as an older lady beaming as she enthusiastically pounds away on some drums, stress the participatory nature of the music-making and the manner in which Pollyanna has united the townspeople despite their differences.

This association of music and community is emphasized toward the conclusion of the bazaar, when Pollyanna and some other little girls, dressed to create a living American flag, sing "America the Beautiful." The choice to have Pollyanna sing a solo highlights her central role in the narrative and in the town's transformation, while numerous close-ups of the townspeople responding to her song stress the emotional affect of the moment. That the choice of song references the history and beauty of the nation makes the moment nostalgic on both an individual and communal basis, and the decision to have Pollyanna deliver the song makes the character a conduit for this sense of shared history and patriotism.

The Power of Play

In addition to the formal choices—visual and aural—I have noted, the focus on play conveyed by the narrative's arc is an essential way in which the adaptation creates a sense of overt sunniness. Play as actual play and as a goal, a way of life, is central in the film, with Pollyanna the chief proponent/instructor of this through her glad game. Images of children at play, individually and together, are central tropes of the film, as they are of the 1920 version, and set a tone of lighthearted fun and innocence within the pastoral, small-town setting.

The initial moments of the film's title sequence, for instance, quickly introduce this trope of play and its importance in the film. The screen goes from dark to pale to reveal the naked backside of a little boy who swings on a rope, jumps into a stream, and then joins his friends, who are already splashing in the water. The camera then follows another boy, Jimmy Bean, as he races with a giant toy hoop around town, finally approaching the train station where Pollyanna will shortly alight. Once there, he places a piece of chain on the tracks in order to see how the train will flatten it. While Jimmy's actions in the title sequence may seem mundane, even superfluous, to the main narrative action of Pollyanna's arrival in Harrington, they support the trope of play within the film. So does a later segment, added by Disney himself, which shows Jimmy, on a visit to the creek with Pollyanna, ducking his head underwater and blowing bubbles at a fish.[7] Moments of this kind, woven throughout the film, let the viewer know that play is an essential, and desired, aspect of the world of *Pollyanna*.

After Jimmy and Pollyanna meet, the two are often shown at play: taking turns being leader and instructing each other in new ways to play. For instance, Jimmy encourages Pollyanna to climb trees and shows her how to leave her attic bedroom via the giant tree outside her window. Similarly, Pollyanna teaches Jimmy the potential for play even within the dark, gloomy space of Mr. Pendergast's home. As in the novel, she notices the beautiful rainbows that Mr. Pendergast's prisms, hanging from his lamps, cast on the walls, and in the film she soon gets both Jimmy and Mr. Pendergast interested in creating such "rainbow-makers." Here, a child's play spreads not only to other children, but also to adults. Mr. Pendergast's subsequent interest in such play and in the children themselves not only foreshadows his later adoption of Jimmy, it also indicates his re-entry into the Harrington community.

While one might expect to see Pollyanna and her fellow children at play, the film also demonstrates the manner in which Pollyanna's playfulness, particularly her glad game, spreads to encompass the adult townspeople, regardless of differences such as gender or class. The culmination of this community play is, as noted, the added plotline of the bazaar, a sequence that shows the entire town, with the exception of Polly, in celebration:

dancing, eating, and playing games under bright lights as upbeat music plays. One of the booths features a dunking tank, in which members of the town pay to attempt to hit a target and send a clown (a costumed townsperson) into the water. The transformation of Reverend Ford from an isolated, oppressive preacher earlier in the film to a good-natured father to his flock is revealed in his interaction at this booth as, at the urging of some onlookers, he takes a turn. Patiently responding to the jeers of the clown when he misses his first few throws, he notes, lightheartedly, that he always wanted to see this particular townsperson baptized. Then, to cheers from the onlookers, he succeeds in hitting the target and dunking the clown. The joyfulness of this extended sequence, in which Reverend Ford and the film's other characters come together for a good cause, is then counterbalanced by Pollyanna's accident and the contrast between play/no play when Pollyanna tries and fails to play the glad game.[8]

Pollyanna's dismay when she realizes the result of her accident and her angry statements—"It was a silly game, I hate it. I never want to play it again. Leave me alone"—demonstrate her separation from the game and from the sense of celebration she has helped to create. However, the appearance of the townspeople at Polly's house, carrying flowers, puppies, food, toys, and other delights, quickly counterbalances her gloom. As she is carried among the townspeople, Pollyanna's interaction with them emphasizes the importance of the girl—and her game—in their lives, and augments the sense of a town-wide celebration begun in the exuberant bazaar sequence. For example, Mr. Pendergast reveals that he has adopted Jimmy and that the two will continue to make rainbow-makers; as Mr. Pendergast says, they plan to spend their lives in an act of play—"just hanging prisms"—a work that not only can please the two of them, but that also has the potential to spread a sense of gladness to others.

Finally, the film's finale marks the culmination of the adaptation's focus on play, particularly the playing of the glad game. The entire town assembles to bid Pollyanna farewell and the camera lingers on the word "Harrington" on the town's sign, which is now nicknamed "The Glad Town." Not just a few individuals, but the entire town has been changed due to the power of Pollyanna and her play.

Myth-making

This focus on play works to create a land in a state of perpetual innocence and joy: a vision of an ideal, and idealized, America of pleasure and equality. That *Pollyanna* takes place in a world before World War I, a war that heralded the horrors of modern warfare and touched the lives of millions of people around the globe, can explain why the pre-war setting of *Pollyanna* may have indeed seemed for viewers in 1960 and beyond a much more innocent and idyllic time. Certainly, contemporary reactions to the film focused on *Pollyanna* as a nostalgic project, in a manner that was both positive and negative. For instance, in his chapter on *Pollyanna* in *The Disney Films*, film critic Leonard Maltin reproduces a review from Arthur Knight, a writer for the *Saturday Review*, who views the film's wistfulness about the past and its subject matter in a very positive manner:

> *Pollyanna* has the feeling for Americana, the nostalgic glow of a simpler, gentler way of life that has characterized most of the Disney live-action features.... There is warmth here.... More fundamental, there seems to be a genuine belief that the art of positive thinking, as practiced by Eleanor H. Porter's little heroine, is every bit as applicable today as when the "glad game" was first invented. (172)

Yet Maltin also includes a review from *Time* that, as he notes, contains very tempered praise, writing, "*Time* magazine, in a curiously backhanded yet favorable review, called the film 'the best live-actor movie Disney has ever made,' qualifying that remark by calling it a 'Niagara of drivel and a masterpiece of smarm'" (172). The *Time* review indicates the manner in which a mid- to late-century viewer might view Pollyanna and her early-century world, at least Disney's version of it, as flawed, even suspect, given, as I have noted, factors such as the simplistic nature of its vision of an America that elides differences such as class and race.

Perhaps for reasons of this kind, and despite Swift's efforts, as noted earlier, to adapt the film's tone for a contemporary audience, the film was not a box-office success. While acknowledging the appeal of the film's lavish look and experienced cast of veteran actors such as Jane Wyman and Adolphe Menjou, Maltin notes that "*Pollyanna*'s gross of $3,750,000 fell short of the $6 million goal, and Walt Disney thought he knew why. 'I think the picture would have done better with a different title,' he explained. 'Girls and women went to it, but men tended to stay away because it sounded sweet and sticky'" (172).

The 1960 film production of *Pollyanna* was a work of recovery, an attempt to reconnect with a particular vision of American childhood and America, from a studio that specialized in such visions. Taken individually and together, the film's visual and aural elements and narrative arc contain the potential not only to connect viewers with their own childhoods, but also to hail those viewers in a more general sense, replaying a vision of a perfect childhood and of an idyllic location for that childhood: small-town America. Of course, the film, like the book, is a fantasy, but, as Martin notes, there is no denying that it has "almost a golden glow" around it.

Notes

1. In a chapter titled "Adapting Children's Literature" from *The Cambridge Companion to Literature on Screen*, Deborah Cartmell discusses the increasing conservatism of Disney, as displayed in his sociopolitical actions and reflected in his films: "In addition to visual anchorage, was an ideological agenda that Disney brought to the stories, reflected in his founding role in the Motion Picture Alliance for the Preservation of American Ideals (the foundation of the Hollywood blacklist). It's no accident that the rise of Disney coincided with debates about the morality of the cinema and American values, and a very conservative view of the family is common to all of these films" (170).

2. However, the nature of this comedy and how it is conveyed is an area of difference between the films. For example, the creators of the 1920 film focus on physical comedy, with a few ironic asides to viewers via the title cards, while much of the humor of the 1960 film is created via dialogue, coupled with reaction shots that emphasize character moments.

3. This use of brightly lit exteriors mirrors that of the 1920 film, in which many scenes take place outside in what appears to be bright sunshine. Both films appear to have been shot in California—with the exteriors of the 1920 production resembling locations in Southern California and the 1960 film shot in Northern California around Santa Rosa—which creates a visual link between the two.

4. At certain emotional junctures, Pickford's character is shown with her eyes heavenward, as if communicating with the divine, which enhances the suggestion of her special, expressly spiritual nature.

5. The connections between the two films go beyond the early-century setting and a central use of music. Both films seem to construct their settings, the St. Louis of *Meet Me in St. Louis*, and the Harrington of *Pollyanna*, as utopian spaces. In *Meet Me in St. Louis* the pleasant, pastoral environs of St. Louis are contrasted with the city to which the family may have to move: New York. In *Pollyanna* Harrington is imagined as a lovely place with unhappy people. The addition of the bazaar sequence, in which the town's people display their transformation under Pollyanna's influence as they celebrate together, is also similar to the fair that is so central to the plot and music of *Meet Me in St. Louis*. For example, in his 1994 essay "Meet Me in St. Louis: Smith, or The Ambiguities," Andrew Britton notes:

> If "St. Louis" suggests a myth of the organic community in a lost Golden Age, then the idea of "the fair" is the furthest reach of the myth—"It must look like a fairy land." The last moments of the film—the camera tracking in to a huge close-up of Esther's face on her rapt, repeated murmur of "Right here where we live"—convey an achieved

union of the "normal"/everyday and the miraculous. They put forward, implicitly, for the spectator's consent, the proposition that "your home town too is miraculous if only you stop to look at it." (164)

6. Gorbman notes that "Music making action on the screen explicit—'imitating' their direction or rhythm—is called mickey-mousing (after musical practices used in the early Disney sound cartoons)" (181). The use of such "mickey-mousing" in *Pollyanna* not only aligns the film with the Disney output as a whole, but particularly connects it to the overt playfulness and visual and aural experimentation of the early Disney films. For example, in Disney's *Steamboat Willie* (1928), one of the first synchronized-sound cartoon films released in Hollywood, Mickey Mouse creatively manipulates the bodies of a variety of animals, from a duck to a cow, in order to produce a variety of sounds for his own enjoyment and to entertain Minnie Mouse.

7. In this sequence the children go down to a stream and Jimmy sticks his head underneath the water. The camera shares his point of view to reveal the magical nature of this underwater environment. As Jimmy looks around underwater, he/the viewer sees an effects-created fish, who also notices him. This leads to a switch in perspective as the fish/viewer views Jimmy imitating the open, bubbling mouth of the fish. Disney conceived of the moment and had it shot by a second unit without Swift's knowledge; in fact, Swift relates that he did not learn of it until he saw the dailies.

8. Swift notes that Disney showed great interest in the project, investing in it not only creatively and financially, but also emotionally. As Swift and several other interviewees on the DVD extra note, Disney carefully watched the film's dailies, which often brought him to tears. Disney also insisted that the lengthy bazaar scene, which Swift desired to trim, remain intact.

Works Cited

Braudy, Leo. "Stage vs. Screen." *Theater and Film: A Comparative Anthology*. Ed. Robert Knopf. New Haven: Yale UP, 2005. 352–60. Print.

Britton, Andrew. "Meet Me in St. Louis: Smith, or The Ambiguities." *Britton on Film: The Complete Film Criticism of Andrew Britton*. Ed. Barry Keith Grant. Detroit: Wayne State UP, 2009. 157–74. Print.

Cartmell, Deborah. "Adapting Children's Literature." *The Cambridge Companion to Literature on Screen*. Eds. Deborah Cartmell and Imelda Whelehan. Cambridge: Cambridge UP, 2007. 161–80. Print.

Dyer, Richard. *White*. London: Routledge, 1997. Print.

Gabler, Neal. *Walt Disney: The Triumph of the American Imagination*. New York: Alfred A. Knopf, 2006. Print.

Gorbman, Claudia. "Classical Hollywood Practice." *Critical Visions in Film Theory*. Eds. Timothy Corrigan, Patricia White, and Meta Mezaj. Boston: Bedford/St. Martin's, 2011. 165–85. Print.

Maltin, Leonard. *The Disney Films*. New York: Crown, 1973. Print.

Pollyanna (Vault Disney Collection). 1960. Dir. David Swift. Perf. Hayley Mills, Jane Wyman, Adolphe Menjou. Walt Disney Video, 2002. DVD.

Porter, Eleanor H. *Pollyanna*. Boston: Colonial, 1913. Print.

Sklar, Robert. *Movie-Made America: A Cultural History of American Movies*. New York: Vintage, 1994. Print.

Watts, Steven. *The Magic Kingdom: Walt Disney and the American Way of Life*. Boston: Houghton Mifflin, 1997. Print.

12

Pollyanna: Transformation in the Japanese Context

MIO BRYCE

Eleanor Hodgman Porter's *Pollyanna* was introduced in 1916 to Japanese readers through Tsuchiko Hironaka's translation, entitled *Pareana* [Pollyanna]. Published by a Christian publisher soon after its original publication in 1913, it was a complete translation, but the circulation and initial popularity of the story were limited.[1] Published during the short Taishō period (1912–26), which was characterized by wide-ranging political and socio-cultural democratic movements, this translation appealed especially to well-educated, urban young people of the upper- and middle-classes who were beginning to enjoy Western philosophy and cultural material in their daily lives. After freedom of religion had been promulgated in 1873 with the Meiji Restoration, Christianity was re-established, not only through churches but also through Christian schools. As one of the seed-beds of translated Western children's literature, Christian organizations provided eminent translators (Takita; Copeland 99–158), including both Tsuchiko Hironaka and Hanako Muraoka, the translators of *Pollyanna*. *Pollyanna* was one of several well-known western children's stories published in magazines and/or as books during this period of social change.

Pollyanna, followed by *Pollyanna Grows Up* (1915), has been translated and adapted to a range of media in Japan, including picture books, manga, and anime. Visual media offered diverse images of Pollyanna, from the slender and ladylike figure illustrated by Jun'ichi Nakahara in *Junior Soreiyu* (a girls' magazine) in 1956, to the tomboyish young girl with a stubby body in red overalls in the anime *Ai Shōjo Porianna Story* [The Story of Pollyanna: Girl of Love] (1986), directed by Kōzō Kusuba. The anime represents the most radical Japanese adaptation of Pollyanna, as it was adapted for a much younger audience.

This chapter examines adaptations of Eleanor Hodgman Porter's *Pollyanna* (1913) and *Pollyanna Grows Up* (1915) in Japanese sociocultural and psychological contexts, with specific reference to the anime, and to the sources for the anime: the popular Japanese translations by Hanako Muraoka, *Shōjo Pareana* [Girl Pollyanna][2] and *Pareana no seishun* [Pollyanna's Adolescence], as well as the first translation, *Pareana* [Pollyanna], by Tsuchiko Hironaka. These translations and anime adaptation reflect the history of translated western children's literature in the early modern era in Japan, and provide insights into how the story and titular character have been adapted for different audiences.

Translated Western Children's Stories in Early Modern Japan

Japan's modern era began with the Meiji Restoration in 1868, which led to an influx of a wide range of Western ideas and artifacts—policies, legal, military, and social systems, science and technologies, philosophies, and education. Literary works, most of which were in English, including children's literature, were introduced through translations and adaptations—initially poems, followed by novels, drama, and critiques (Yanagida 167). Japan's cultural borrowing was aggressive, complex, and ambiguous; in fiction, alterations were often made to plots, characters, settings, and tone "to tame and modify the foreign to fit domestic sensibilities" (Miller 13). Canonic Western literature played a significant role as an educational apparatus in Japan's modernization.

Translated children's stories have special historical and sociocultural significance and formed an essential part of Japanese childhood experience. Few literary works had been written exclusively for children before the early modern period, partly because childhood was not recognized as a distinct period of life. The limited availability of Japanese stories meant that translated Western stories were the main source of children's literature in the early modern period, and consequently Japanese children's literature was developed largely under Western influence and inspiration.

Many children's stories were introduced as adaptations or abbreviated versions, some of which altered the setting and names of characters. For example, Lewis Carroll's *Alice's Adventures in Wonderland* was published as *Ai-chan no yume-monogatari* [Ai/Love's Dream Story] in 1910, and Johanna Spyri's *Heidi* as *Kaede monogatari* [The Story of Kaede/Maple] in 1925. In the case of *Pollyanna*, an adaptation with illustrations by Machiko Tanimura appeared in 1955, in which 14-year-old Pollyanna was named Michiko and Aunt Polly, Chikako.

Western children's stories, both translations and adaptations, have played an important role in the history of Japanese children's literature, coexisting with indigenous Japanese children's literature. The conceptual importance of translated Western stories lies in cultivating positive ideas of independence, personal strength, and love, both in collectivistic Japanese society and in the minds of individuals. Texts such as Louisa May Alcott's *Little Women* (first translated in 1891), Frances Hodgson Burnett's *A Little Princess* (1893), and, of course, Porter's *Pollyanna* series were particularly momentous for girls in Japan.[3] They not only provided entertainment and information about western cultures to their young readers, but also helped shape the concept of girlhood as a positive and enriching experience through adventurous and earnest female characters. Japanese girls were able to gain confidence in their individuality by sharing childhood experiences with girls in Western countries. The differences between the real situations of the Japanese readers and those of the characters in British or American middle-class families, though, suggest that these stories were probably read as exotic fantasies. This situation continued between the 1950s and the 1970s, when many collections of Western stories for girl readers were compiled with clear editorial intentions of providing strong, active, and positive role models for Japanese girls (Satō).

Japanese Appropriation of *Pollyanna* in Translations

A translated story is, in a sense, independent from its original text, as the translation involves multi-faceted retelling and cultural appropriation. As John Stephens and Robyn McCallum state, "because retellings do not, and cannot, also reproduce the discoursal mode of the source, they cannot replicate its significances, and always impose their own cultural presuppositions in the process of retelling" (4). Japanese translations often deviate from the original texts significantly because of the nature of the target language—Japanese is highly contextual, hierarchical, and gendered. Each character's utterance hence needs to be differentiated through the complex use of speech styles and the level of (in)formality based on the age, gender, and class status of the speaker in the specific situation.

Readers are assumed to share common cultural schemata, knowledge, and emotional alignment with the creators, and in this respect Japanese literature tends to favor suggestiveness over articulation. As Donald Keene puts it, "the unexpressed is as carefully considered as the expressed, as in a Japanese painting the empty spaces are made to have as strong an evocative power as the carefully delineated mountains and pines" (9). Readers and audiences are therefore expected to involve themselves imaginatively and empathetically to decode the material from the viewpoint of the creator. The space left for the reader to fill may be larger than that envisaged in Wolfgang Iser's concept of gaps, yet more controlled due to the tacit consent and the cultural and emotional relationship between the author and the reader.[4]

Translators are not only the transmitter of the text; they are also the first readers. Their personal readings determine the characterization of protagonists, which is evident in, for instance, the speech styles and vocabulary they select. To make verbal communications come across as natural speech, translators often need to make radical changes based on their gauging of the interplay between the original text and the reader's assumptions. Until recently, however, translators have been reluctant to omit anything in the original and used a distinct translation style that was verbose, formal, and often disjointed. Both Hironaka's and Muraoka's translations exhibit such tendencies, and these techniques occasionally cloud the integrity of the characters.

Speech styles reveal not only the character's personality, status, education, and cultural backgrounds; in Japanese, subtle shifts in address can also reveal specific interpersonal relationships. Class consciousness is expressed less explicitly in modern Japanese from the postwar period, when egalitarianism had been promoted strongly. By the time the anime version of *Pollyanna* was produced, most Japanese perceived themselves as middle class. Combined, these elements result in significant discrepancies between the original and the Japanese translations.

In the original, Polly's and Nancy's utterances are distinguished by class dialect: Polly is (overly) formal—"I wish you to stop your work and listen" (9)—and her sentences are carefully structured. In contrast, Nancy's speech is uneducated (as indicated by malformed words such as, "you . . . told me this mornin' ter hurry" [9]). Nancy's syntax is also disorganized and ungrammatical. The status difference between the two is marked linguistically, and also by Nancy's repeated use of the formal title "ma'am": "'Yes, ma'am; I will, ma'am,' she stammered" (9). Their differences in language are consistent throughout the story.

In Hironaka's translation,[5] Polly's enunciation is precise and well structured. She uses *omae* (an informal form of "you," often expressing the speaker's higher status) to refer to Nancy, and ends the sentence with *okiki nasai* [please listen], confirming her superiority and firmness, reflecting her status and education. This expression is often used by parents and teachers when they are reproaching their children or students. The wording suggests that Polly's voice is somewhat deep and masculine. Nancy, on the other hand, stammers (although only at the beginning), and correctly uses humble language for herself (*kashikomarimashita* for "certainly" and *orimashita* for "was doing"), and a respectful, honorific form (*osshaimashita* [said]) for Polly (2).[6] Nothing about her language suggests a lack of education.

Polly becomes rougher and more hostile in Muraoka's translation (1962). She shouts at Nancy, uses plain and casual forms, lacks elegance and formality, with the result that she comes across as a hostile, dictatorial old woman.[7] For instance, Polly's use of words such as *odamari* [be quiet] and *iiwake* [excuse][9] add a rougher and more uncaring tone than that attributed to her in Hironaka's text. Nancy, on the other hand, offers polite responses which resemble those in the Hironaka translation.[8] She seems slightly stronger because words such as *ōisogi* [quickly], but the emphasis is on Nancy's vulnerability. The replacement of the speech reporting tag "miserably" with "*kawaisō ni*" [poor thing] (7), encourages readers to emotionally align with Nancy and then with Pollyanna, who is also subjected to Polly's vicious tongue.[10]

There is, however, a further complication—style shifting. In Japanese, the speech styles of participants are frequently and fluidly altered to reflect dialogical dynamics (Jones and Ono). When a speaker uses casual linguistic forms, it signifies their higher, or at least equal, standing to others who speak more politely. In Hironaka's translation, after the above dialogue Polly also uses plain and casual forms frequently, often ending sentences with -*sa* or *dane* [to confirm or stress]—both of which have a roughness that is associated with male speech. Polly's change of speech mode suggests that her initial formality is not her typical language style, but is employed specifically for the purpose of scolding Nancy. Nancy is also capable of style shifting. In both translations, she speaks properly in a polite and humble form to Polly and uses casual dialect in private and in conversation with characters such as Old Tom. Polly's dominance over Pollyanna is emphasized in Muraoka's translation, as exemplified in their first meeting, where Polly speaks bluntly using short sentences in plain, casual form, ending them with or without particles (-[*da*]*yo*, -*kai*, -[*da/ga*] *ne*, -[*no*]*sa*—all of which are typically used by men). Her hostile, domineering language contrasts with the soft, formal, polite language of Pollyanna, who ends her sentences with particles (–*no*, -*noyo*, –*wa*), which are exclusively used by women.

Furthermore, the portrayal of Pollyanna as a frail, lonely child is underlined in Muraoka's translation. For example, at the station, Pollyanna is simply described as "standing quite by herself" in the original (Porter 21).

However, in the Japanese version, the words *kawaisō ni* [poor thing] and *shombori to* [with a sad and lonely air] (20) were added to stress her sense of loneliness and dejection, which is then contrasted with her excitement and profound relief when she sees Nancy.

Pollyanna is then illustrated as a "cute, adorable, endearing" [*kawairashii*] little girl. In the dialogue between Timothy and Nancy, just after their return with Pollyanna to Polly's mansion, the word *kawairashii* is inserted before "kid" in Timothy's assertion "It'll be more fun here now, with that *kid* 'round . . ." and again before the word "blessed" in Nancy's phrase "it'll be somethin' more than fun for that *blessed* child" (26; emphasis added). The adjectives *kawaii* and *kawairashii* [cute] are often used with the aforementioned *kawaisō* [pity, poor thing]. Consequently, their use firmly establishes Pollyanna's cuteness, innocence, and vulnerability as her essential attributes within the story, as well as within Japanese cultural and psychological contexts.

The emphasis on cuteness—*kawaii* and *kawairashii*—is another appropriation, as Japanese have been fascinated, even obsessed with childlike innocence as a core quality of cuteness since the ancient period, as depicted in Murasaki Shikibu's *The Tale of Genji* and Sei Shōnagon's essay *Pillow Book* in the Heian period (794–1185). *Kawaii* is an evaluative yet ambiguous term, which reflects the user's affectionate gaze and desire to protect the object of gaze—an object that is small, soft, and fragile, as exemplified by angelic images of infants. According to Kinsella, *kawaii* or "cute" essentially means "childlike" (220): it celebrates innocent, simple, and vulnerable social behavior and physical appearance. It is an overarching term, and comic value has become an essential element of the concept. It is important to note that the object's spiritual and sexual innocence are vital qualities of cuteness. In the case of the anime *Pollyanna*, cuteness is constructed through her small, round body, expressive eyes and face, outgoing personality, and friendly mannerisms, and ensures her essential virtue.

Although Muraoka's translation is popular and was used as the basis for the anime, it is nevertheless old-fashioned and often inconsistent in its representation of speech styles. The anime makes significant alterations in order to suit a younger, 1980s Japanese audience, making Polly's speech more polite and feminine, whereas Pollyanna's speech is childlike and more appropriate to her behavior. As a visual mode, the anime also expresses power relationships by the body size and shape of each character. Polly is thus tall, solid, and has a long, angular and pale face; Nancy is smaller, slender, and has an egg-shaped head and a smooth, feminine face; Pollyanna is stubby and short; she barely reaches Polly's waist.

An Orphan Girl in Overalls:
Japanese Appropriation of *Pollyanna* in Anime

The anime is entitled *Ai shōjo Pollyanna Story*. The combination of the two nouns, *ai* [love] and *shōjo* [girl], is unusual and employed to characterize Pollyanna as a center of mutual love. Her ability to love and her desire to be loved, as suggested by the title of the concluding song—"*ai ni naritai*" [I want to become your love], are highlighted. Although the term *ai* [love] and the kanji (Chinese character) were introduced through Buddhist texts in the ancient period, the use of the term changed in the early modern period under Christian influence. It generally refers to what the Greeks classified as *storge*—a trusted, selfless love, like that shared between family members—and is distinguished from romantic or erotic passion. Depicting mutual affection and friendship between different age groups is not easy in Japan, where hierarchy dictates codes for interaction. Therefore, framing the title in this way is an effective means of defining the focus of the series. The anime portrays people's love for Pollyanna in her hometown, especially Mr. and Mrs. White, who intend to foster her and buy her a red-checked gingham dress before her departure. In this context, her love cannot imply romantic or sexual elements, and so a young, childish identity is established by her atypically youthful characterization.

The anime was directed by Kōzō Kusuba and produced by Nippon Animation as part of *Sekai Meisaku Gekijō* [World Masterpiece Theatre]. It comprised 51 episodes (approximately 24 minutes each) divided into two parts. Part One (episodes 1-27) roughly corresponds to Porter's *Pollyanna*, and Part Two (episodes 28-51) roughly corresponds to *Pollyanna Grows Up*. The correspondence is only rough because, as I shall expand below, the narrative departs markedly from Porter's originals. The series was broadcast by Fuji Television Network in prime time (7:30–8:00pm) on Sundays. It won an Agency for Cultural Affairs Award for Excellence in Film for Children's Television in 1986 and the Atom Award (the award for TV anime) in the Japan Anime Festival in 1987. The character designs were by Yoshiharu Satō, who was later responsible for character design and directed animation for Studio Ghibli's *Tonari no Totoro* [My Neighbor Totoro] in 1988. The target audiences of the World Masterpiece Theatre were young children and their mothers, hence the stories were adapted accordingly. The alterations include the removal of explicitly Christian motifs and the darker aspects of human nature (e.g., malice, jealousy) and addition of cute animals and episodes of cheerful human interactions, especially with friends (S. Araki).

In the anime *Pollyanna*, many memorable scenes and episodes from the novel are adapted to make it a touching story of adults and children working together to create loving homes. An audience familiar with both the original and the translations can also enjoy the comparison. As is common in children's stories in Japan, pathos and a sense of realism are enhanced in the anime. The timeframe of the anime is significantly shortened to only two years, and the addition of tears and laughter make it more emotionally extreme. The anime is explicit in its portrayal of death and sorrow, as exemplified in the addition of a scene depicting Dr. Chilton's heroic death after falling from a cliff on the way home from a house visit on a stormy night. The tragedy is particularly dramatic as it takes place on a joyous occasion—on the night of an intimate party to celebrate Pollyanna's recovery. In the anime version, Polly's marriage to Dr. Chilton lasts less than two months.

Many episodes were added to portray Pollyanna's cheerful and often comical interactions with others, particularly with Jimmy, to balance the sadness of the story with humor. Songs in the series also focus on such emotions, using word-sets related to tears and memories. As a result, Pollyanna's sorrow and joy are effectively contrasted, demonstrating her ability to face difficulties, do her best to stay positive, and live life to the full.

The opening scene of the first episode of the anime establishes *Yokatta sagashi* [searching for things that made me feel glad] as a theme for the series. Running in her overalls with her pet Chipmunk on a mountain slope, Pollyanna stumbles and falls to the ground, where she pretends to be unconscious until Chipmunk anxiously touches her face. As she leaps up with a smile, she finds bright yellow flowers and happily exclaims "*Yokatta!*" [I'm glad!]. She picks them and runs to her mother's grave to offer them there. This short opening captures and condenses essential details of the narrative and its central character. Pollyanna's young and boyish identity is emphasized by her overalls, infant-like body, and behavior: energetic yet vulnerable, sensitive yet mischievous, and possibly self-centered. The trick played on Chipmunk could be read as her ability to influence others' feelings. Her friendship with Chipmunk represents her love of all living creatures as well as her loneliness. She demonstrates *Yokatta sagashi* by changing her negative experience—falling down a hill, getting dirty and scratched—to a source of joy in finding the flowers.

However, this scene is quickly connected with her love of her deceased mother, whom she cannot remember, and her daily visits to the grave. The sequences are constructed to emotionally engage the audience. According to Mitsuko Horie, who voiced the character, she made her

voice consciously happy and lively to allow the audience to contrast her
cheerfulness with her situation as a motherless child, and consider her
unspoken sorrow. The mother–child bond is highlighted in the anime
even more strongly than in the original. From the outset, Pollyanna's story
is shadowed by death and lost love, highlighting her determination to live
positively, which encourages the audience to admire and pity her.

The glad game in the original text is also reconceptualized in the anime
series. It is renamed *Yokatta sagashi*, employing a colloquial and childish phrase. This phraseology conveys the lightness in the original, unlike
Muraoka's literary and overly formal translation, *yorokobi no asobi* [game
of joy]. Furthermore, it uses past tense, *yokatta* [it/I was good], indicating
that Pollyanna's game focuses on what one can find here and now. She then
shifts her attention to the potential solution—something that can relieve
an individual's distress. Such quick emotional shifts are more commonly
seen in children than in adults. Pollyanna exclaims "*yokatta!*" while clasp-
ing her hands theatrically, signaling her completion of a game. The acts of
"*yokatta!*" generally occur several times in each episode throughout the
series to establish consistency, although sometimes they seem repetitive,
even forced.

The anime does not include the famous episode with the crutches,
but instead directly connects the glad game to Pollyanna's loneliness as a
motherless child. Her father initiates the game in clear relation to "rejoicing texts" in the Bible in order to console her. Moreover, he firmly and
patiently teaches her to be positive using *Yokatta sagashi* when Pollyanna
complains that she cannot eat ham and eggs—a delicacy she looks forward to eating once a week—asserting that without them, she does not
want to eat her bread and milk. Her disappointment is expressed as anger.
Here, the crutches are replaced with a familiar dish for Japanese children,
ham and eggs, and its deprivation shows their humble life. Similarly, when
Pollyanna complains about Mrs. White's scolding, he again tells her to be
grateful she has someone who genuinely cares for her. He then asks her
to bring her mother's handheld mirror and shows her the ugly reflection
until she regains her usual cheerful and positive outlook. These short
sketches reveal how young and immature Pollyanna is, and how carefully
her father nurtures *Yokatta sagashi* in order for it to become her mainstay
after his death. His last words for her are a request that she continue to
play the game.

As an embodiment of *Yokatta sagashi*, Pollyanna is metaphorically a
prism to refract people's perspectives and feelings and to break barriers
within and between individuals. Although the game is an important tool,

or "a set of crutches rather than a cure" (Mills 92), it functions effectively when explored alongside Pollyanna's childlike pathos and curious, non-stop conversation. Particularly in the Japanese context, without her child-ishness, the glad game could be understood as unsolicited meddlesome imprudence, as Polly worries in the original. She is able to heal others in this way because she is a young, innocent child who simply enjoys chat-ting with people.

In contrast with the original, Pollyanna's behavior is perceived in the Japanese context as intrinsically that of a young child rather than a girl on the brink of puberty. She is cheerful and lively, yet can be assertive and self-centered. She is talkative, a quality that is rarely praised in Japan. It is unsurprising, then, that the anime lowers her age from eleven to eight and depicts her as though she were even younger, more active, tomboyish, and athletic. Pollyanna's childishness is embodied in her infantile physique; a short, stubby, large-headed figure, her height is only half the size of an adult, which allows her to jump to hug someone but also to be cuddled. As Gunther Kress and Theo Van Leeuwen argue, the "grammar of visual design" (1) plays a vital role in the production of meaning. Pollyanna exhibits her capacity to create intimate love, but also illustrates her vul-nerability and desire to be cared for, through such movements. Her hair is light brown and shoulder-length with two small braids and rather messy. She wears a simple light pink shirt, rolled up reddish (or dark pink) over-alls, and simple shoes without socks. Her appearance in the anime series contrasts starkly with her description in the original text as "slender . . . with two fat braids of flaxen hair hanging down her back" (Porter 21).

Pollyanna's tomboyish behavior complements her appearance. She walks briskly and often runs like a small child. Her physique resembles that of Heidi in the anime *Arupusu no Shōjo Haiji* [Heidi: Girl of the Alps] (1974), who comes to live in the Alps with her grandfather when she is five, but Heidi wears dresses and skirts despite her life in the mountains.[11] In addition, in the anime Heidi is portrayed as being less talkative and more perceptive. Pollyanna's peculiar childlikeness also contrasts with another popular character, An in *Akage no An* [red-haired An/Anne of Green Gables] (1979) in World Masterpiece Theater. In this anime version of the Canadian children's classic, An is depicted as a thin, dreamy girl of average size. She is not particularly pretty, but the text presages future beauty and her development is the focus of the story.

Pollyanna's overalls, which she wears most of the time throughout the anime series, ground her identity in otherness and asexual childlike innocence. They suit her tomboyish behavior, making it easier for her to climb trees, walk on the parapet, and turn somersaults and tumble in a state of uncontrollable joy (for example, when her father makes a recovery, when she arrives at Beldingsville station, and in the dress shop). In Japan, overalls are generally worn by infants and young children, and red overalls were commonly worn by very young girls in the 1980s, when the anime was made. Other popular, overall-wearing girls include Peko-chan (from 1950), the original mascot character of a confectionary and restaurant company; Fujiya, who is a cheerful and energetic 6–year-old (100 cm tall and weighing 15 kilograms); Hello Kitty (from 1974), Sanrio's best-known original character; and a girl robot Arare-chan (in Akira Toriyama's humorous manga and anime, *Dr. Slump*, from 1980). Nevertheless, it is unusual for a girl over the age of eight to wear overalls. Polly definitely disapproves of her niece's attire: she notes that dirty clothes that obscure whether the wearer is a boy or a girl are wholly inappropriate for a member of the respected Harrington family. In fact, Pollyanna is mistaken for a boy by Micky (Jerry) when she gets lost in Boston in Part II. Polly does provide Pollyanna with stereotypical girls' clothes, which Pollyanna only wears occasionally. Other girls in the anime wear dresses (for example, her friends Karen and Sadie), and thus the overalls are used to mark out Pollyanna's special qualities. Moreover, the overalls have a special significance for Pollyanna as her father used to say that they suited her best. Nancy intends to throw them away, but after seeing Pollyanna's attachment to them, she allows the little girl to continue wearing them when she plays outside—her time to "live" (Porter 43; Kusuba Anime episodes 6 and 7). The overalls become her uniform, subtly indicating Polly's acceptance of her niece.

Pollyanna's infantilization reflects the Japanese perception of childhood innocence—known as *dōshin* [child's heart]—which is considered a central human quality. The concept has been promoted by Miekichi Suzuki's magazine for children, *Akai tori* [Red Bird], especially through the stories of Mimei Ogawa. Ogawa's symbolic stories depict children's innocence as a longing for an ideal society (Kawahara). Although these stories are criticized for failing to portray real children—instead illustrating an idealized, nostalgic image of the child—*dōshin* is widespread and is particularly evident in manga and anime.

By depicting Pollyanna's short outburst about the lack of ham and eggs, the anime also indicates that her cheerfulness is not innate: it demands effort—*kenagesa*—another idealized quality in a child. There is no exact English equivalent of the term *kenagesa*, which depicts a child's brave and spiritual effort to try their best despite their powerlessness, and which evokes sympathy from others who are older and stronger. Pollyanna's first night in the attic room demonstrates this quality. She agrees to sleep in the dark attic and holds her candle and goes up to her room, although she is scared. She is shocked by the waving shadows of the cloth bags in the attic, runs into her room, and then her candle goes out. She falls on the bed and cries herself to sleep, still wearing her overalls. She also demonstrates *kenagesa* later when she chooses to undergo a risky, five-hour operation and endure a painful rehabilitation.

Pollyanna's vulnerability as a young and immature child is further dramatized with additional episodes. For example, she and her friend Karen are chased by an angry bear in the forest where they go to find strawberries for her dying father. In Beldingsville, when she meets Jimmy for the first time, she is walking on a parapet of a wooden bridge and nearly falls, but is rescued by Jimmy. A similar, more serious, incident occurs near the close of the anime (Part II), when she nearly falls from a log lying across a river, and is again saved by Jimmy. In Boston, Pollyanna is attacked by three boys in the dirty, narrow street, and falls on the ground. She is pathetic; brandishing her wooden walking stick helplessly, she starts to cry. Eventually she escapes and sits down to cry again, and this is when she meets Micky. Although he is a total stranger, she hugs him when he offers her help, and falls asleep as he carries her home. Such behavior does not accord with her age of eight or nine, let alone the young teen character in *Pollyanna Grows Up*. These snapshots reveal the energy with which she embarks on adventures but also her immaturity, vulnerability, and need to be cared for.

Pollyanna must be depicted as a young child not only because of her childish behavior, but also because of her lack of social conformity. She expresses her emotions spontaneously with little regard for others' feelings. She not only runs through the house and bangs doors but also turns somersaults and tumbles to express joy, even in front of Polly in a dress shop, even though she is aware that such behavior is unacceptable. Pollyanna shifts her attention, perspectives, and moods quickly, even abruptly. She is unusually frank in expressing herself, as exemplified by her question as to whether Aunt Polly is rich. Once she is determined to help, she is persistent, as seen in her continuous approaches to Pendleton. Pollyanna's childlikeness is enhanced in the anime, where she laughs and cries far more frequently and explicitly than the Pollyanna of the original and the translations. Her tears may also be used (strategically) to persuade adults to comply with her wishes, for example, when Mrs. Carew prohibits Pollyanna from searching for the missing Chipmunk in Boston.

Assertiveness is not regarded positively in Japan, and so her childishness must be emphasized if she is to avoid criticism.

Pollyanna's love of living things is also an essential part of her child-likeness. The bond between child protagonists and their animal friends are typical in the World Masterpiece Theatre, and are used to illustrate children's innocence. Pollyanna asks Polly not to kill flies and is excited to read about flies. This may also remind some Japanese of an ancient story, *Mushi mezuru himegimi* [The Princess who loved insects], in a collection of short stories from the late Heian Period, *Tsutsumi chūnagon monogatari* [Tales of Tsutsumi chūnagon],[12] which inspired Hayao Miyazaki to create manga (1982–94) and anime (1984), *Kaze no tani no Nausicaä* [Nausicaä of the Valley of Wind].[13] Pollyanna's bond with Chipmunk is also comparable to Nausicaä's bond with her fox-squirrel Teto. Their scientific interest and love of living things are positively depicted, yet could be regarded as socially inappropriate.

These attributes indicate Pollyanna's otherness, in that she is neither able nor does she wish to read the context nor to conform to "friendly authoritarianism," as Yoshio Sugimoto terms it (271), which is a serious fault in collectivistic Japanese society. Horie, the voice actor for Pollyanna, points out that Pollyanna follows her own path without trying to guess what others are thinking or feeling [*sasshinai*]. Polly's habitual gesture of touching her throat represents Japanese confusion and discomfort when confronted with her niece's incompliance to friendly authoritarianism.

Pollyanna's otherness can be interpreted in terms of Masuko Honda's concept of the otherness of children, or of her genealogy of *mojamoja* [shock-headed, bushy-haired child characters] like Peter in Heinrich Hoffmann's *Struwwel-Peter* (1845), who is initially ostracized because of his uncivilized appearance and mannerisms but who becomes the savior of the society. Pollyanna's otherness may also be considered in relation to Japanese ethnological concepts of the *marebito* [guest] or *ijin* [person of a different kind], who visits a community periodically to revitalize it with his or *Pollyanna* her spiritual power. In a study of Japanese folk-tales, Tōji Kamata notes the frequency with which gods take the form of a child. Although Kamata does not discuss *Pollyanna*, the qualities Kamata observes are evident in Porter's character, and this may explain why the novel has been so well received in Japan. Pollyanna's particular form of otherness is familiar to an audience familiar with indigenous folktales.

Pollyanna's otherness is further emphasized by her status as the orphan daughter of a poor missionary. This rich narrative strategy fits well in Japanese empathy-focused culture with its strong sensitivity and receptivity toward loneliness, regarding sympathy as the most essential human trait. The first episode of the anime is titled *Kyōkai no chiisana musume* [a little girl of the church], establishing her Christian identity. This aspect of Pollyanna's identity is somewhat unusual, as religious references are usually removed in anime (for instance, in the anime *Heidi, Girl of the Alps*). The episode is followed by "*Tōsan shinanai de*" [please don't die, Father!], and "*Oka no ue no sambika*" [hymns on the hill] before her departure for Beldingsville in "*Mishiranu machi e*" [toward an unknown town]. The anime also presents Pollyanna's move to Aunt Polly's home as being Pollyanna's father's desire and her own choice. These added scenes frame Pollyanna's story as a mission to continue her father's work by helping unhappy people with *Yokatta sagashi* and her mother's desire to be reconciled with Polly. Pollyanna brings back her mother's handheld mirror, which prompts Polly to recall her happy girlhood with Jenny.

That Pollyanna is the orphan of a dedicated missionary secures her innocence and empathy, as well as otherness in the Japanese context. In Japan the Christian community has always been small (less than 1 percent of those who profess religious belief) and missionaries rare. Missionaries tend to be depicted as self-sacrificing, benevolent helpers rather than as religious leaders. The setting therefore has a strategic advantage in portraying the orphan girl as a perfect recipient of the reader's sympathy—as an innocent and unfortunate victim of a tragic consequence of her father's noble, selfless commitment to help others. Furthermore, as missionaries, they are placed outside the social hierarchy. It is hence not uncommon for them to have wealthy family or relatives, enabling the orphan girl to cross the borders of the social classes. These conditions are important in the Japanese context to imbue the story with realism, maintaining Pollyanna's integrity and self-esteem in the face of her inevitable dependence on others.

Pollyanna is introduced as an innocent stranger to the new host community, where her quest for her own place is enacted through her interactions with people around her. This is another element to which Japanese girls could be wholeheartedly drawn. Japan has an established patriarchy in which girls can be treated as outsiders within their family of origin, as they are expected to marry and become a member of another family. Yukari Fujimoto's ontological questions—"who am I" and "where is my place"—are the most recurring and fundamental questions in *shōjo* manga, and these questions apply to writing for girls across genres. Unlike the original, the anime confines Pollyanna within her childhood and family of origin. Many episodes in the original were removed or reinterpreted.

This is particularly evident in the portrayals of her interactions with Jimmy Bean. There is a hint that their close friendship may evolve into romantic love, but within the narrative it is suppressed mainly by Pollyanna's asexual childishness. Much like in the original, she enjoys her friendship with Jimmy, yet often seems inconsiderate about his feelings. For example, she leaves him abruptly to join Dr. Chilton and does not understand his mixed feelings of jealousy and sympathy for Jamie. Throughout the anime, Jimmy steadily grows and shows maturity, confidence, and empathy. His masculine qualities surface through his determination; he shows *kenagesa* when he accepts that he will not find a home of his own and so builds a home of his own in Pendleton woods. He also develops friendships with Old Tom, Timothy, and Nancy. After he is adopted by Mr. Pendleton, Jimmy also develops a genuine father–son relationship with him, but without neglecting his other friends. Jimmy and Tom occasionally help each other overcome their respective crises when they bitterly question God's actions—Pollyanna's injury and Dr. Chilton's death.

Pollyanna and Jimmy's friendship is based on an equal standing, although curiously gendered in the later episodes. Although they are still children, Jimmy becomes taller and more masculine, whereas Pollyanna looks even younger and more dependent than at the beginning of the story. This is particularly evident in the episode where, attempting to cross a river on a fallen tree to pick flowers on the other side, she slips and is left hanging from the log. This is based on the episode where Jamie loses self-control due to his inability to rescue Pollyanna from an angry bull, and his failure is contrasted to Jimmy's successful rescue. Nonetheless, in the anime, Pollyanna's failed adventure is self-inflicted, caused by her over-confidence, and once she fails she is frightened and calls for help pitifully until Jimmy rescues her.

Pollyanna's independence and strength decrease throughout the series. Her self-development is somehow halted, confined as she is to a limited view of childhood. Polly, on the other hand, develops into a motherly figure, wholly unlike the bitter, solipsistic, old Polly in the original. With the emphasis on Pollyanna's youthfulness and vulnerability, the pair embody an interdependent mother–child bond (*amae*) that Takeo Doi sees as the fundamental and possibly ideal human relationship (1971). This is a significant deviation from the original, not only from the characterization of each protagonist but also within the framework of the story. The final scene of the anime also conveys familial warmth in childhood through the sibling bond of Pollyanna and Jimmy. They play with snowboards and Pollyanna falls on Jimmy in the snow. Pollyanna's behavior is particularly immature for her age, and this scene confirms their genuine intimacy—her childish nature and her dependence on Jimmy. Such childishness entails a certain nostalgic quality, which may be the crystalized embodiment of the ideal *dōshin* [child mind].

Conclusion

The anime adaptation of Eleanor Hodgman Porter's *Pollyanna* and *Pollyanna Grows Up* to a Japanese context created the most radical Japanese transformation of the original by infantilizing Pollyanna. Her physique, appearance, utterances, and behavior remain intact and successfully impressed the anime's audience with her cheerful, childlike innocence and *kenagesa* [child's brave and best effort]. The strategic infantilization was justified to engage the young target audience in the 1980s, as indicated by the high viewer rate at that time. The anime successfully rejuvenated the popularity of the original and engaged many young audiences. Since then, it has been rerun many times through different channels, including NHK satellite television BS2 in 2000 as part of *BS Meisaku Anime gekijō* (BS Masterpiece Anime Theater) and ANIMAX (a satellite television for anime). It was also released on VHS in 1987 and again in 1997 and on DVD in 2000 by Bandai Visual, but only in Japanese. Part I was also reorganized from Polly's perspective and released as a 90-minute complete version in 2002. Although the popularity has gradually faded, the anime remains a considerable favorite in the mind of the Japanese.

Pollyanna's peculiar infantilization was a necessary appropriation of the protagonist and her glad game, *yokatta sagashi*, for the Japanese context. Nonetheless, the anime considerably simplified her portrayal, limiting her maturation as well as the development of the narrative. This is in contrast to the anime *Akage no An* [*Anne of Green Gables*], in which An's overly poetic and sophisticated utterances make an intriguing incongruence with her behavior (Somer), allowing the development of a richer narrative.

Nonetheless, almost all works in the *World Masterpiece Theater* are from western literature and like *Pollyanna* have gone through a number of thematic reconceptualizations and appropriations. For example, in *Shōkōjo Sara* [Princess Sara/*Sara Crewe*] (1985), Sara's strength, self-esteem, and intelligence are reduced to highlight her *kenagesa* and endurance of the bullying she suffers at the hands of the jealous Minchin and other characters (Hatakeyama). Budge Marjorie Wilson's *Before Green Gables* (2008), which is not young children's literature, was transformed into the anime *Kon'nichiwa An: Before Green Gables* [Hello Anne: Before Green Gables] (2009) for a very young audience. The focus is shifted from the harsh lives of adults (including Anne's parents) to Anne and her *kenagesa*. Realistic depictions of social issues are replaced by Anne's interactions with school friends, and some romances, thereby bringing cheerfulness to the narrative (Y. Araki). As represented by these examples, the script commonly employed in the *World Masterpiece Theater* is that of a young, innocent, and earnest protagonist bravely challenging the harsh realities with tears and laughter. In the process, they involve and enlighten adults and children around them.

Pollyanna's childlike innocence is the core attribute of her characterization that appeals to Japanese audiences. An analysis of how and why the anime transformed the original shows how astutely the Japanese appropriation has been implemented in the story, employing Pollyanna's excessive childlike innocence as a core human quality as well as a catalyst for an expansion of empathetic human circles.

Notes

1. Nihon Kirisutokyō kōbun kyōkai or Kyōbunkan [Christian Literature Society of Japan]. Although Hironaka's book is a good and amazingly modern translation, it is very difficult to obtain today. Hironaka's book was republished in 1956, titled *Shōjo Pareana* by the same publisher. Her surname has changed from Hironaka to Yamamoto.

2. Muraoka's translation was initially published as *Yorokobi no hon* [Book of Joy] in 1939, then *Kurige no Pareana* [Pollyanna with chestnut colored hair] in 1956 and *Shōjo Pareana* [Girl Pollyanna] in 1959.

3. Montgomery's *Anne of Green Gables* (1908) has been loved and has had a strong influence on Japanese readers, although it was not published in translation until 1952.

4. For example, Matsuo Bashō's most popular haiku, *Furuike ya, kawazu tobikomu, mizu no oto* [An old pond. A sound of water created as a frog jumped in]. *Kawazu* (frog) can be singular or plural, but readers are expected to imagine the faint sound created by a small frog jumping into an old pond: that is, the poet/reader is alone in silence and may be thinking of the significance of one's fleeting presence against the eternity of nature. If one imagines many frogs, although grammatically correct the picture becomes a comical sketch rather than an insightful poem.

5. Polly says "*Watashi ga omae ni hanashi wo suru toki wa, shigoto o yamete, watashi no iu koto o chanto okikinasai*" [when I talk to you, please stop your work and listen properly to what I say].

6. Nancy stammers, "*ha, hai, kashikomarimashita*" [y-yes, certainly] then "*Ano, kesa hodo atokatazuke a hayaku shite shimau yōni to osshaimashita node, tsui hataraite*

orimashita. . . ." [As you told me this morning to finish work quickly, without thinking I kept on working. I am sorry].

7. Polly then says in plain and casual form, "*Watashi ga yonda ra, shigoto o yamete watashi no iu koto o kiite moraitai ne*" [when I talk to you, I expect you to stop work and listen to what I say].

8. Nancy's response, "*kesa wa ōisogi de atokatazuke o suru yōni to osshaimashita node, tsui shigoto ni ki o toraremashite*" [as you told me to clear up very quickly, I was only thinking of the work].

9. Polly's response is "*Odamari. Nancy. Iiwake wa kikitaku nai yo. Chūi shite moraitai no sa.*" [Be quiet, Nancy. I don't want to hear your excuse. I just want you to be attentive].

10. Polly's hostility and roughness is intensified in Jibu Ōsaki's adapted and illustrated book, *Pareana monogatari* [The Story of Pollyanna], published in 1929 by a Christian publisher, Nichiyō sekaisha.

11. This anime was also produced by the World Masterpiece Theater (which involved the renowned animator Hayao Miyazaki and producer Isao Takahata). The design of Heidi's hair is changed from long to short, based on advice given by the Johanna Spyri Museum that her grandfather does not have time to take care of her long hair (Kanō 52).

12. The anime was directed by Isao Takahata, and Hayao Miyazaki was involved in the first part.

13. Eiichi Mitani asserts that it is unusual that the story suggests that the princess's peculiarity is not fated but self-determined (19–20).

Works Cited

Araki, Shōji. "Nihon hon'yaku bungakushi ni okeru *Haiji* [Heidi] hon'yaku." *Gunma daigaku shakai jōhō gakubu kenkyū ronshū* 15 (2008): 171–94. Web. 11 June 2013.

Araki, Yōko. "Budge Marjorie Wilson cho, *Before Green Gables: Animation Kon'nichiwa An Before Green Gables* tono sōiten to sono kōka." *Keiwa gakuen daigaku Jimbun shakai kagaku kenkyūjo nempō* 9 (2011): 135–48. Web. 11 June 2013.

Copeland, Rebecca L. *Lost Leaves: Women Writers of Meiji Japan.* Honolulu: University of Hawaii Press, 2000. Print.

Doi, Takeo. *Amae no kōzō.* Tokyo: Kōbundō, 1971. *The Anatomy of Dependence,* trans. John Bester. Tokyo: Kodansha International, 1981. Print.

Fujimoto, Yukari. *Watashi no ibasho wa doko ni aru no?: Shōjo manga ga utsusu kokoro no katachi.* Tokyo: Gakuyō shobō, 1998. Print.

Hatakeyama, Chōko. "Saiwa no hōsō keitai kenkyū: House shokuhin Sekai Meisaku Gekijō daiissaku *Shōkōjo Seira* [Sarah] (1985) no baai." *Baika joshi daigaku bunka hyōgen gakubu kiyō* 4 (2007): 65–75. Web. 11 June 2013.

Hironaka, Tsuchiko. *Pareana.* Tokyo: Nihon Kirisutokyō kōbun kyōkai, 1916. Print.

Honda, Masuko. *Ibunka to shite no kodomo.* Tokyo: Kinokuniya shoten, 1982. Print.

Horie, Mitsuko. "Cast Interview 2." Supplement of *Ai shōjo Pollyanna story* (DVD). Tokyo: Nippon Animation, 2000. Print.

Iser, Wolfgang. *The Act of Reading: A Theory of Aesthetic Response*. Baltimore: Johns Hopkins UP, 1978. Print.

———. "The Reading Process: A Phenomenological Approach." *Modern Criticism and Thought: A Reader*. Ed. David Lodge. London: Longman, 1988. 188–205. Web. 11 June 2013.

Jones, Kimberly, and Tsuyoshi Ono. "The Messy Reality of Style Shifting." *Style Shifting in Japanese*. Amsterdam and Philadelphia: John Benjamins, 2008. 1–7. Print.

Kamata, Tōji. *Oi to shi no folklore*. Tokyo: Shinyōsha, 1990. Print.

Kanō, Seiji. *Nihon no animation o kizuita hitobito*. Tokyo: Wakakusa shobō, 2004. Print.

Kawahara, Kazue. *Kodomo-kan no kindai: "Akai tori" to "dōshin" no risō*. Tokyo: Chuokoronsha, 1998. Print.

Keene, Donald. *Japanese Literature: An Introduction for Western Readers*. Charles E. Tuttle, 1977. Print.

Kinsella, Sharon. "Cuties in Japan." *Women, Media, and Consumption in Japan*. Ed. Lise Skove and Brian Moeran. Honolulu: University of Hawai'i Press, 1995. 220–54. Print.

Kress, Gunther, and Theo Van Leeuwen. *Reading Images: The Grammar of Visual Design*. London and New York: Routledge, 1996. Print.

Kusuba, Kōzō. *Ai Shōjo Porianna Story*. 13 vols. 1986. Tokyo: Nippon Animation (Bandai Visual, distributor), 2012. DVD.

Miller, Scott J. *Adaptations of Western Literature in Meiji Japan*. New York: Palgrave, 2001. Print.

Mills, Alice. "Pollyanna and the Not So Glad Game." *Children's Literature* 27 (1999): 87–104. Web. 11 June 2013.

Mitani, Eiichi, and Gen'e Imai, eds. *Tsutsumi Chūnagon monogatari and Torikaebaya monogatari*. Tokyo: Kadokawa shoten, 1976. Print.

Muraoka, Hanako. *Shōjo Pareana*. Tokyo: Kadokawa shoten, 1962. Print.

———. *Pareana no seishun*. Tokyo: Kadokawa shoten, 1962. Print.

Porter, Eleanor H. *Pollyanna and Pollyanna Grows Up*. 1913, 1915. Ware: Wordsworth, 2011. Print.

Satō, Motoko. "Gender to jidō bungaku: hon'yaku, saiwa no shiten kara." *Zusetsu Jidō bungaku hon'yaku daijiten*. Vol. 4. Tokyo: Ōzorasha, 2007. 30–34. Print.

Stephens, John, and Robyn McCallum. *Retelling Stories, Framing Culture: Traditional Story and Metanarratives in Children's Literature*. New York: Garland, 1998. Print.

Sugimoto, Yoshio. *An Introduction to Japanese Society*. 2nd ed. Cambridge: Cambridge UP, 2003. Print.

Takita, Yoshiko. "Wakamatsu Shizuko and *Little Lord Fauntleroy*." *Comparative Literature Studies* 22.1 (1985): 1–8. Web. 11 June 2013.

Tanimura, Machiko. *Nanairo no niji* [seven colors of rainbows]. Tokyo: Popurasha, 1955. Print.

Yamamoto, Tsuchiko. *Shōjo Pareana*. Tokyo: Kyōbunkwan, 1956. Print.

Yanagida, Izumi. *Meiji shoki hon'yaku bungaku no kenkyū*. Tokyo: Shunjūsha, 1961. Print.

13

Pollyanna in Turkey:
Translating a Transnational Icon

TANFER EMIN TUNÇ

Over the past eighty-five years, Eleanor Hodgman Porter's *Pollyanna* (1913) has become one of the most popular, yet debated, American children's novels in Turkey. In the English-speaking world, the protagonist has been embraced as an advocate for female children who mimics the admirable qualities of the traditional boy-hero—honesty, trustworthiness, bravery, resourcefulness, rationality, and resilience (Goulden and Stanfield 193–94). In Turkey, Pollyanna has similarly gained social currency as an empowering icon who, over a number of generations, has conveyed a message of acceptance, optimism, and forgiveness that has provided young Turkish readers with personal motivation and inspiration.

Like the title character herself, the novel *Pollyanna* has also experienced its own Turkish trajectory. From the moment it was introduced to the country in 1927, it has undergone numerous print translations and reincarnations, even inspiring theatric and cinematic adaptations, including the Turkish Pollyanna-like character "Ayşe." However, as this chapter will illustrate, each subsequent generation (the 1920s, 1950s, 1970s, and today) has created new translations and adaptations, all of which reflect their respective time periods socially and politically. Consequently, over the years, the novel has been used in Turkey as a vehicle for the spreading of various ideologies—ranging from pro-Western sentiments in the mid-twentieth century to Islamism in the early twenty-first century. This has inevitably complicated the politics of translating and adapting this American text (with Western, Christian values) in a predominantly Muslim country grappling with larger issues of modernity and identity.

Pollyanna's Arrival and Adaptation in Turkey

As Shirley Marchalonis explains,

> the popularity of *Pollyanna* went far beyond that of the best-selling novel.
> Something about the chief character caught the public imagination. After
> Porter's death other writers were commissioned to carry on the series. . . .
> There was a play version of *Pollyanna* in 1915; the book was translated into
> various languages, including Turkish . . . *Pollyanna* Clubs appeared through-
> out the country, and in 1960 a film version was released. The heroine's name
> has entered the language; *Webster's Third International Dictionary* defines a
> Pollyanna as "one having a disposition or nature characterized by irrepress-
> ible optimism and a tendency to find good in everything; an overly and often
> blindly optimistic person; an irritatingly cheerful person." (Marchalonis)

Clearly, the publication of Porter's *Pollyanna* in 1913 ushered in a global
phenomenon "with forty-seven printings by 1920, a successful film and
a series of twelve sequels, [some] by other hands" (Hunt 205). Pollyanna,
with her glad game and the "Christian positivism" it implied, became "a
byword for cheerfulness," which was what a world on the verge of war
needed in 1913 (Hunt 205).

Similarly, the translation of *Pollyanna* into Turkish coincided with a
major period of social and cultural upheaval in the country—the transition from the Ottoman Empire to the Republic of Turkey—with the first
translation of *Pollyanna*, or *Poli Anna* (spelled as it would be pronounced
in Turkish), appearing in 1927. Translated by Vedide Baha and published
in Ankara by *Hakimiyyet-i Milliye Matbaası*, it was book number six in
the *Türkiye Himaye-i Etfal Cemiyeti (Türkiye Çocuk Esirgeme Kurumu)
Çocuk Külliyatı*, or the Turkish Department of Children's Services Corpus
of Children's Literature (the first book in the series was Johanna Spyri's
Heidi). The original translation by Baha was given as a gift to the first
president and founder of the Turkish Republic, Mustafa Kemal Atatürk
("Atatürk'ün Özel Kitapları"). This edition was produced in Ottoman
Turkish script, which resembles Arabic, because it was printed before
the language reform of 1928 when the Latin alphabet was adopted and
the Turkish language was purged of Arabic and Persian words as part of
a nationalistic project to "purify" it of foreign influences. The Ottoman
Turkish translation was transcribed into Latin script, which also included
some "new" Turkish word substitutions, in 1931, and was published by

Matbaacilik ve Neşriyat in Istanbul. Other translations followed in 1948, 1958, and 1973, and it is estimated that over twenty different versions of the book exist on the market today (Kansu-Yetkiner, "Anthroponym Translation" 82).

Like Americans, Turks have also been fascinated by Pollyanna, a girl whose positivism has been translated and adapted through different media to fit the Turkish context, often promoting a distinct ideology in the process. In addition to numerous editions of the novel (the translational politics of which will be discussed later in this essay), *Pollyanna* has entered other areas of Turkish culture, including theater and film. It was first adapted to the stage under the title *Pollyanna* by *Devlet Tiyatrosu* [Turkish State Theater] as a children's musical during the 1956–57 season. It played in the Turkish capital, Ankara, and was directed by Haldun Haluk Marlalı with a musical score by İlhan Usmanbaş ("Devlet Tiyatroları"). It was subsequently revived by two female directors (a rarity in Turkish theater), Melek Ökte Saltukalp Gün and Asuman Bora Kutal, during the 1959–60 (Ankara) and 1989–90 (Diyarbakır) seasons, respectively. Recently, it was staged by the *Masal Gerçek Tiyatrosu* [True Fairy-Tale Theater] during the 2008–09 Istanbul season, with a new script written by Reha Bilgen, who was also the director, and Burcu Tekin ("*Pollyanna*").

Although *Pollyanna* is quite popular with today's Turkish children, both as a play and a novel, previous generations are probably more familiar with the tale as a work of literature and a Turkish film adaptation, *Hayat Sevince Güzel* (1971), which translates as *Life is Beautiful When You Love*.[1] Directed by Temel Gürsu, the film is based on Porter's novel (which is uncredited) but incorporates Turkish cultural elements, including names: Pollyanna becomes Ayşe, played by Zeynep Değirmencioğlu, who also starred in a film adaptation of *Snow White*; her aunt is named Handan and not a variation of Ayşe's name (Pollyanna/Aunt Polly); and Dr. Chilton becomes Doktor Ferit.[2] The locations are all Turkish as well: turn-of-the-twentieth-century Beldingsville, Vermont, becomes 1970s Ayvalik, a coastal town on the Aegean Sea. The costumes also reflect 1970s Turkey: Ayşe, who is around sixteen and not eleven, wears gypsy skirts, mini-skirts, and exposes her midriff in the second half of the film ("Hayat Sevince Güzel").

Most of the film is spent along the town's boardwalk, where Ayşe meets and charms numerous odd characters, persuading them to change their outlook through her song and dance routines. Other major characters include Deli Amca (or "crazy uncle," an adaptation of Mr. Pendleton), who is depicted as an angry, stingy eccentric who allegedly tortures children for stealing fruit from his garden, and Ömer (Jimmy Bean), a street urchin who spends his time playing tricks on the old man. Some elements remain true to Porter's original. For example, the origin of the glad game, which is called *memnun olmak oyunu* in Turkish, remains the same—the crutches found in the missionary barrel instead of the desired doll, and the notion that Pollyanna should be glad that she does not need them. However, the film has been overwhelmingly Turkified, and begins when Ayşe is sent away from her village after the death of both parents: we learn her father was a *muallim*, or teacher, who led an impoverished life with his family in a remote part of Turkey. Initially, Ayşe is dressed as a peasant girl—complete with local accent—and is shown crying at her parents' grave while explaining to them she must leave to live with her wealthy aunt. On the train ride to her aunt's home, she is harassed and mocked by the passengers, who joke about her provincial ways and ask her to sing a song to entertain them. She is also travelling with her dog Boncuk [Bead], who is expunged from the train since dogs are prohibited. This is also the first time the audience witnesses Ayşe playing the glad game: she tells Boncuk he must be glad (*memnun*, which translates more accurately as "pleased") they are stopping the train just for him instead of tossing him out the window while the train is in motion. Doktor Ferit, who is described as an unfortunate man who lost his love and has been away from the town for years, is also on the train, and arrives along with Ayşe. Their paths divide, but only temporarily.

As in the original novel, Ayşe is also met at the station by the family servant, Peyker (Nancy), and confronts her unsympathetic Aunt Handan at her waterfront home, where she forbids Ayşe to talk about her parents because her mother ruined the family (her marriage caused their father's death) by running off and marrying a peasant (in this Turkish, secular adaptation, religion is deemphasized and class difference, modernity, and the country/city divide are emphasized far more than in the original novel). Handan also informs Ayşe that her parents paid the price for their "cursed love" by dying young, and that she has made a great sacrifice by agreeing to adopt Ayşe, a dirty little "mountain goat." Handan, who sports a mini-dress, orders Peyker to get Ayşe out of her soiled peasant clothes, take her to the Turkish bath, and to be careful when she combs Ayşe's hair—if any insects fall out they will have to delouse her.

Ayşe is relegated to a shabby backroom without a mirror, which makes her glad, for, as she expresses to Peyker, it is far better than the room in her village house and now she will not have to look at her freckled face. As soon as Peyker leaves, like Pollyanna, Ayşe climbs out the window and down the tree, and in this case, does not run up a hill but down to the beach. Peyker finds her there, and that is when Ayşe tells her about the glad game. When they return home, Handan tells Ayşe that from now on she will eat meals with the servants as a punishment for being late and not following her rules. Ayşe willingly goes to the kitchen, where she shares the traditional herbal cures she learned from her father with the household staff. Peyker then brings Ayşe to town on a shopping trip, where they talk about some of the locals, including Deli Amca, Ömer, and her aunt's former fiancé, Doktor Ferit. Ayşe becomes determined to reunite the couple, who are angry with each other for an unspecified reason.

Along the way, Ayşe befriends the crabby invalid Zehra (Mrs. Snow), to whom she brings not calf's foot jelly but meat and chickpea stew (a traditional Turkish dish). She also becomes an avenger of injustice: she compels the local blacksmith to take responsibility for his illegitimate daughter, whom the local children call "a bastard," by marrying her mother. In one important scene, Ayşe is invited to a party by the local spoiled rich kids, where they mock her provincial ways and peasant-girl mannerisms, in particular her speech, clothing, and the fact she was a shepherdess (she even gives them a sample of the dance she performed in the fields while rounding up the animals). While the hostess suggests that she can earn money by entertaining guests at weddings and celebrations (she will obviously need to earn a living as her aunt has positioned her as a servant), a young man, Ali, comes to her rescue and takes her home. Handan becomes infuriated when she sees Ayşe in a stranger's car and explains to her niece that she is no longer in the village and that such behavior will not be tolerated. To save herself and Ayşe from further embarrassment, Handan, who is constantly shown reading European magazines, gives her a makeover that includes modern "city" clothing (mini-skirts, cropped tops, and long gowns), a new hairdo (her braids are traded in for a bouffant), jewelry, heels, and cosmetics. Her formerly bushy eyebrows, which signified the fact that she was a peasant girl, are also plucked and shaped, and she is suddenly transformed into an attractive young lady. She takes speech, etiquette, posture, sewing, and piano lessons—all designed to erase her peasant class markers—thus completing her Eliza Doolittle–like change.

The "new and improved" Ayşe is even more effective than the peasant girl: not only does she win the affection of Ali and reunite feuding friends, but she is also able to persuade grouchy Zehra to eat and gain a positive outlook on life. She begins to melt the cold heart of her aunt, who allows her to keep a stray cat and Boncuk, Ayşe's dog, who somehow finds his way to their home. Ayşe finds Ömer a home with, predictably,

Deli Amca, who lost his six-year-old son, Doğan, on Father's Day after he fell from one of his fruit trees (this explains why the old man guards his garden with a gun—to scare aware children and prevent another life from being lost). She is also able to convince the townspeople to hold a fundraiser for the rest of the local orphans, which her aunt, in a fit of stubbornness, prevents her from attending (this is at the center of the Disney film adaptation, so the change here is not a Turkification of the novel per se, but rather a response to other cultural manifestations of *Pollyanna*). Once again, she escapes through the window and joins the fundraiser, where the townspeople show their gratitude by giving her the doll she has always wanted. On her way back into her room, however, Ayşe falls from the tree and is paralyzed. After Boncuk pushes the door open and Ayşe overhears a conversation about her paralysis between Handan and Doktor Ahmet, Doktor Ferit is called in to treat the distraught girl, and amidst the preparations for surgery in Istanbul, the love between Handan and the physician is rekindled. Ayşe's spirits are lifted by a group visit from the locals, which includes the spoiled rich kids who once mocked her, and they persuade her to have the operation.

The film thus has a happy ending, promoting not only an ideology of forgiveness—that life is more beautiful when one loves—but also one of modernity, suggesting that personal transformations—whether they involve sentiments, or even class standing and comportment—are possible and even desirable. This message was a particularly powerful one in Turkey in the early 1970s because, at that time, the country was in political turmoil, caught in a clash between those who embraced western influences and those traditionalists who did not, as well as those who favored autocratic military rule in the name of order, and those who believed in the tenets of democracy, whether personal or political. *Hayat Sevince Güzel*, which presents numerous compromises between divergent sides, invariably conveys the notion that everyone, including former (political) enemies, could live in peace and harmony, even if they did not always agree—a potent and possibly subversive message in 1971, especially for a children's movie.

Pollyanna and the Politics of Translation

The translation, adaptation, and interpretation of *Pollyanna* in the Turkish context is an ideological battle that has spanned eight decades, delving far deeper than the messages of peace and modernity espoused by the

1971 film. As Neslihan Kansu-Yetkiner explains, translations of *Pollyanna* have often reflected the social and political climate of the country at the time of translation, a phenomenon she illustrates through her analysis of the character names (anthroponyms) found in four versions of the novel: *Poli Anna* (1931, the first translation to be written in Latinized Turkish script), *Pollyanna* (1948 and 1958), and *Gülenay* (or "Smiling Moon") (1973), a cultural adaptation by Kemal Bilbaşar, also known as E. Bilbaşar ("Anthroponym Translation" 80). As Kansu-Yetkiner notes, a major shift occurred between the 1930s–1950s and the 1970s that involved a transition from "foreignization imposed through late Ottoman westernization attempts . . . [and] by the Translation Bureau as a . . . tool of [the] westernization process" (1930s–1950s) to a "domestication" of *Pollyanna* that sought to deemphasize foreign influences and promote a nationalist agenda that would placate both the republican elite and the Islamic front (1970s) ("Anthroponym Translation" 79). As the Turkish context elucidates, the translation of proper names is a difficult task to begin with, and is further complicated by the intertwining of translational practices and socio-political factors including "geographical belonging, history, specific meaning, playfulness of language and cultural connotations" (Kansu-Yetkiner, "Anthroponym Translation" 80).

The Turkish Translation Bureau, which supervised the 1948 and 1958 translations of the novel, was established in 1940 and functioned until 1967 as a tool of the state-regulated modernizing forces in Turkey that sought to westernize the country, especially through language reform and by exposing the population to both foreign and domestic literature (Kansu-Yetkiner, "Anthroponym Translation" 83). During the early years of the Bureau, "works were translated in full without any omissions, additions, [or] changes . . . in order to fully convey the spirit of the works. . . . [They] were recreated in Turkish as faithfully as possible, using a readable, easily understandable, simple, and unelaborated Turkish" (Aksoy). However, as time progressed, political ideology began to infiltrate literary translations, ranging from the pro-U.S. and pro-West sentiments of the 1950s to the nationalistic and militaristic sentiments of the 1970s, which was in essence a backlash against "foreign influences" by members at both ends of the political spectrum.

The political shifts that occurred in Turkey between the 1930s–1950s and the 1970s affected translations of *Pollyanna*. Kansu-Yetkiner provides numerous examples of this phenomenon through her analysis of character, institutional, and place names. For instance, Pollyanna Whittier was translated as Poli Anna Waytır or Woyter in 1931, was retained in its original form in the 1948 and 1958 versions translated by the state-run bureau, and became Gülenay Haksever, which means "Smiling Moon Justice-Lover," underscoring Pollyanna's optimism and fairness, in the 1973 translation. Tom the Gardener is Mister Tom in 1931, Bay (Sir) Tom in 1948, Mösyö or Monsieur Tom in 1958, and finally the provincial (or even proletarian) Bahçıvan Duran Ağa [Duran the Head Gardener] in 1973. The 1958 translation of *Pollyanna* includes a number of other French influences (the use of French accents and titles in Turkish also denotes foreignness) including Timothée (Timothy) and Madam Snow (Mrs. Snow). Fluffy's and Buffy's names were phonetically transcribed for Turkish pronunciation in the 1931 translation (Filâfi and Pilâfi), remained in original form (Fluffy and Buffy) in 1948 and 1958, and became Çomar and Tekir in 1973. When it comes to institutions, the Christian Endeavor Society is not mentioned in the 1931, 1958, or 1973 editions, and is translated as Hristiyan Faaliyet Birliği [Christian Activity Society] in 1948. Locations such as Beldingsville, Vermont, and New York are phonetically transcribed in 1931 (Bildingroyl, Vermunt, and Nevyork) and remain in original form in 1948 and 1958; in 1973, Beldingsville becomes the Turkish city İzmit and New York becomes Istanbul. Interestingly, Little Eagle Ledge is translated as Kartal Tepesi [Eagle Peak] in 1931, Küçük Kartal Kayası [Little Eagle Rock] in 1948, Petit Aigle Kayası (a hybrid French/Turkish combination) in 1958, and returns to Kartal Kayası [Eagle Rock] in 1973. The 1973 *Gülenay* translation is also particularly noteworthy because, as Kansu-Yetkiner observes, it represents the beginning of the literary "Turkification and Islamization process, where manipulative attempts . . . [turn] *Pollyanna* into a glocalized product, introducing a glad game in which Christian positivism is substituted by Islamic tolerance" ("Anthroponym Translation" 85–87).

A controversy surrounding the Turkification and Islamization of literary classics, one of which was *Pollyanna*, emerged in July 2005, when the Turkish Ministry of Education released a suggested reading list of 100 books for elementary school children in order to standardize curricula across the country (similar lists were also released for middle and high school students). The Minister of Education simultaneously noted that the government would not be distributing these books to schoolchildren and encouraged the private sector, charities, and even newspapers to distribute the books free of charge ("İlkokulların da 100 Temel Eseri Var"). Hoping to profit from this standardized list, which included over thirty international classics such as *Pinocchio*, *Heidi*, *The Little Prince*, and *Pollyanna*, publishers all over the country hired translators to prepare the

Turkish texts and began printing budget, and often severely abridged, versions of the classics they believed would appeal to parents and children alike. The books were sold separately, as well as in 100-volume sets, with a number of newspapers joining the effort—and promoting their own sales in the process—by printing coupons that could be collected over a period of time and exchanged for the books. By August of the following year, parents, teachers, translators, the media, and even the Turkish Ministry of Education began questioning the quality of these newly retranslated classics, taking a closer look at the budget books that were being sold and distributed without much regulation. Two troubling issues emerged: First, who was translating these classics and deciding what would be abridged; and second, why was the original text being altered, and in some cases being Islamified by translators and publishers?

A number of national (*Hürriyet* and *Radikal*) and international (Britain's the *Telegraph*) newspapers began to investigate and report their findings, discovering that these classics were being brutally slashed in length because in Turkey, publications under ninety-six pages are not required to pay a publication tax (*bandrol*), thus maximizing profits ("100 Temel Esere 'İslami' Makyaj"). They also found that one Istanbul-based publisher in particular, Damla Yayınevi—whose first publication was, interestingly, Peyami Safa's *Amerika'da Bir Türk Çocuğu* [A Turkish Child in America]—was committing perhaps the most egregious abuse of these classics by "Islamifying" the texts through their "creative translations." As the *Telegraph* noted, "Pinocchio, Tom Sawyer and other characters have been converted to Islam in new versions of 100 classic stories in the Turkish school curriculum." For example, in *Pinocchio*, the title character says to Geppetto, his maker, to "Give me some bread, for *Allah*'s sake" ("*Bana ne olursunuz biraz ekmek verin . . . Allah rızası için*"). In the Damla version of *The Three Musketeers*, D'Artagnan is told that he cannot visit Aramis. As Malcolm Moore observes, "the reason would [surely] surprise the author, Alexandre Dumas" (Moore). An old woman explains: "*Onu şu anda göremezsiniz. Yanında din adamları var. Hastalığından sonra hidayete erdi*" [You can't see him right now. He is surrounded by men of religion. After his illness, he saw the light (my translation)]. In these translations, when a Creator is evoked, the Arabic word for God (*Allah*), which is specific to Islam, is used, rather than the more generic term *Tanrı* (Lord), and phrases of anticipation (such as "I hope") are replaced by *inşallah* (God-willing) (Kansu-Yetkiner, "Manipulation of Gendered Discourse" 426). Moreover, Christian religious symbols (such as churches, nuns, and priests) have been replaced by bell towers, mosques, and imams.

As the Turkish newspaper *Radikal* revealed, after the recommended reading list was released, publishing houses translated the non-Turkish texts according to their own ideological missions, mainly because the Ministry of Education promoted the publication of such budget classics without monitoring the translations and investigating the translators—the latter of which would prove difficult, since in many cases the translators' names were not mentioned (Sertkan 20–21). Not only were texts Islamified, but in some cases, characters' names were changed: Heidi's grandfather, for example, was given a Turkish name, Alp Dede, in the Nehir Yayınları version, as was Geppetto, who became Galip Dede (*dede* means grandfather in Turkish) (Salman). Even though Pollyanna is "seen by some as the embodiment of Christian forgiveness" and charity (Moore), and by others as deeply religious to the point of functioning, like her father, as a missionary of Evangelical Christian values (Turan 2010), *Pollyanna* was also not spared such alterations. Numerous examples exist in the eighty-page version of the novel published by Damla, which was translated by Ekrem Aytar ("Kitapyurdu"). For example, in the original text, Mr. Pendleton and Pollyanna's conversation about his broken leg includes clear biblical references:

> "Yes, yes; well, there's one thing I know all right, and that is that I'm flat on my back right here this minute, and that I'm liable to stay here—till doomsday, I guess."
> Pollyanna looked shocked.
> "Oh, no! It couldn't be till doomsday, you know, when the angel Gabriel blows his trumpet, unless it should come quicker than we think it will—oh, of course, I know the Bible says it may come quicker than we think, but I don't think it will—that is, of course I believe the Bible; but I mean I don't think it will come as much quicker as it would if it should come now."
> (Porter 76)

While, according to Islam, the blowing of the angel Gabriel's trumpet is a sign of the end of the world, in the Damla version of the conversation, Pollyanna substitutes the Koran for the Holy Bible and uses the word *kıyamet*—a term that specifically represents the Koran's doomsday scenario, which differs from the Christian apocalypse on a number of points, in particular the Second Coming of Christ ("100 Temel Esere 'İslami' Makyaj"). As Mr. Pendleton expresses: "*Bildiğim tek şey kıyamete kadar yatacağım*" [All I know is that I am going to stay in bed until Doomsday]. Pollyanna's response: "*Yo kıyamete kadar yatamazsınız. Yani Kutsal*

Kitap'ta yazdığına göre kıyamet *hiç beklemediğimiz bir anda kopabilir. Ama ben inanmiyorum. Yanliş anlamayın kıyametin kopacağına inaniyorum. Sadece hemen kopacağına inanmiyorum"* [No, you can't stay in bed until Doomsday. According to the Holy Book, the end of the world can strike when you least expect it. But I don't believe it. Don't get me wrong, I believe the end of the world will come. I just don't believe it will happen soon (Aytar 41, my translation)].

In another example, Aunt Polly and Pollyanna converse as follows in the original text: "'Poll*yanna!* . . . I'm surprised at you—making a speech like that to me! . . . I hope I could not so far forget myself as to be sinfully proud of any gift the Lord has seen fit to bestow upon me'" (21–22). The Damla translation collapses the dialogue, which is actually seven lines in the original text, into two sentences which removes all sentiments of the Christian sin of gluttony: "*Benimle böyle konuşman hayret verici. Soruna gelince,* Allah'*ın bana bahşettiklerinin değerini bilirim*'" [It's amazing that you're talking like this to me. When it comes to your question, I know the value of what God has given me (Aytar 15, my translation; also see Salman 21)].

Although the *Telegraph* was correct in noting that "the clumsy insertions by Islamic publishing houses have caused controversy in Turkey, which has been a strongly secular state since the 1920s" (Moore), many critics began to wonder whether these "insertions" were merely "clumsy" oversights or intentional expressions of political Islam through something as seemingly innocuous as children's books. After all in Turkey, it was common knowledge that "in the 1990s . . . there was a paradigm shift [among religious] . . . conservatives. They decided to stop [ignoring] the translation of western classics, and began to get involved in the translation business. Their involvement . . . helped them discover the [Christian] religious elements inherent in the classics, which had [been] disregarded in the course of the modernization process," which they more than willingly reclaimed and manipulated for their own ideological purposes (Sertkan 17). Turkey's prime minister, "Recep Tayyip Erdoğan . . . called for swift action to be taken against the publishers," and the minister of education at the time, Hüseyin Çelik, promised an investigation into the matter and "threatened to take legal action against any publisher which continue[d] to issue such books" (Moore). Moreover, Professor Necat Birinci, who was part of the committee that determined the 100 essential works, warned parents only to purchase books carrying the Council of Education and Morality (*Talim ve Terbiye Kurulu*) seal of approval ("Sorumsuz Yayıncılık"). However, while Minister Çelik is on record as stating that "If there are slang and swear words, we will sue them for using the ministry logo" (Moore), the ministry never mentioned anything about suing publishers such as Damla, Nehir, and Timaş for Islamifying texts.

As a follow-up to its initial statements, the Turkish Ministry of Education also stated that given the number of publishers in Turkey, it would be impossible to monitor all translations and that its function was simply to recommend books, and not create unfair competition by only supporting certain publishers. Ultimately, parents were responsible for finding "the best and most accurate" translations of foreign classics by examining their content, evaluating translators, and if necessary, asking teachers for help ("Pişkin Bakanlık!"). Shifting the responsibility to parents (many of whom are not equipped to make such decisions) and teachers allowed Damla, which illegally published books "stamped with the crest of the ministry of education," to elide accusations that it had misled the public by selling books whose content had not actually been vetted and approved by the government. Damla defended itself by maintaining that it took literary license with its translations in order to make them more relevant and familiar to children, who probably would not be able to understand direct translations of books from other cultures anyway. It denied inserting anything that was not implied in the original text and even praised itself for "livening up" its editions by avoiding "monotone" translations that would not appeal to children. It also refuted the accusation that substituting *Allah* for God (*Tanrı*) was part of a "psychological campaign" ("Sorumsuz Yayıncılık"; Sertkan 27–28). Instead, the publishing house framed this and other substitutions as attempts to adapt the works and render them more accurate and applicable to the Turkish context.

Translators in Turkey immediately voiced their opinions about the corruption of these classics, maintaining that such license not only altered the meaning and intention of great works of literature, but also tarnished their profession. As Tuncay Birkan, an executive board member of the Literary Translators Society (*Kitap Çevirmenleri Meslek Birliği*) explained, the alteration of texts according to the personal agendas of translators or publishing houses flies in the face of Turkish translational ethics. Birkan was also troubled by the fact that

> anyone could publish these books. Moreover, most of the books are not even full-text works. Whenever abridged versions are printed anywhere else in the world, it is usually noted somewhere on the book. But that's not being done here. Readers are being duped. Parents need to be careful. Many publishers are printing these 100 essential works for profit. These are not true

translations. The books should also mention the names of the translators.
(qtd. in Salman, my translation)

Nilay Yılmaz, an instructor at Istanbul Bilgi University's Turkish Language
Unit (*Türk Dili Birimi*), characterized such books as "vehicles," stating that
"if every translator or publishing house reflected its own ideology, children who read these books in elementary school may not want to reread
them in the future. When you purchase books, you also purchase their
ideology. These books are being used as vehicles" (qtd. in Salman, my
translation; Sertkan 22–23).

The president of the Association of Translation (*Ceviri Derneği*), Professor Hasan Anamur, went one step further by noting that all translations should remain true to the original text, even if that means including
"off color" language. Translations should not be sanitized or stolen from
other sources without crediting the translator and inserted with specific
ideology. Anamur also mentioned that such behavior is not only unethi-
cal but "outright brainwashing" ("Sorumsuz Yayıncılık," my translation).
Anamur's accusation that these translations constitute "brainwashing" is
particularly notable because such a politically loaded term not only suggests the manipulative dimension of translation but also, in semi-encoded
terms, conveys the danger of encroaching religious conservatism in Turkey that secularists believe is spilling over into the public sector. Turkish secularists maintain that such acts are not merely harmless oversights
but rather part of an orchestrated fundamentalist campaign to alienate
the nation from Europe and the West and to Islamicize today's youth and
tomorrow's leaders. Literature, they believe, is increasingly being cor-
rupted and used as part of this stealth campaign.

Ideology, whether religious, nationalistic, or otherwise, is always, either
implicitly or explicitly, part of children's literature. Once it has been established, it is very difficult to alter. While the books themselves may be
destroyed, they leave a lasting impact on those who have read them, especially subliminally. The Islamified versions of *Pollyanna* remain on school
bookshelves and are still sold over the Internet, imposing their worldview
through "ideological manipulations," which are "expressed, enacted, sustained and, at times, inculcated through [the] manipulative distortion of
discourse and norms of interaction" (Kansu-Yetkiner, "Manipulation of
Gendered Discourse" 422). This has even crossed into the realm of gender,
since many of the Islamic translations explicitly enforce patriarchal values
and traditional gender roles for women to the point where "what may
look like a 'mistranslation' or 'translational loss' at first glance ... [actually]

highlights the socio-political or ideological structures, processes, norms, and constraints in which [the translations] were produced" (Kansu-Yetkiner, "Manipulation of Gendered Discourse" 423). These conservative ideologies serve as interpretive frameworks for attitudes concerning not only thought but also behavior.

While feminist critiques of children's literature traditionally have centered on evaluations of male and female characters and the ability, especially of the latter, to function as appropriate role models for girls, feminist theoreticians increasingly look at the language used in this literature, and its translations, as vehicles for the construction of gendered identities and discourses. Kansu-Yetkiner describes Islamic translations of *Pollyanna* as being particularly insidious with respect to gender roles because they represent both conscious and unconscious "manipulative attempts" to legitimize "social institutions, family roles, and [the] . . . desecularization of women" ("Manipulation of Gendered Discourse" 424). These manipulative attempts include overt indoctrination or didacticism, as well as the passive communication of ideology through "the texture or the narrative of the work or conveyed through the words of the characters," including the systematic use of specific terminology, religious values, and gender roles (Kansu-Yetkiner, "Manipulation of Gendered Discourse" 424). In addition to the use of words such as *Allah* and *inşallah*, and Arabic or Persian words instead of Turkish ones (religious conservatives in Turkey often consciously select non-Turkish words as a way of resisting secularism), gender roles are also altered in Islamic translations (Kansu-Yetkiner, "Manipulation of Gendered Discourse" 427). In the original text, Porter writes:

> A father one day said to his son, Tom, who, he knew, had refused to fill his mother's woodbox that morning: "Tom, I'm sure you'll be glad to go and bring in some wood for your mother." And without a word Tom went. Why? Just because his father showed so plainly that he expected him to do the right thing. Suppose he had said: "Tom, I overheard what you said to your mother this morning, and I'm ashamed of you. Go at once and fill that woodbox!" I'll warrant that woodbox, would be empty yet, so far as Tom was concerned! (110)

However, as Kansu-Yetkiner conveys ("Manipulation of Gendered Discourse" 431), the tone of the conversation is radically different in the Timaş translation, and one that exemplifies the intimidating power of the patriarchy over women and children:

Babası oğlu Tom'a: Sana söylüyorum! Diye bağırdı, bu odun yığınını bir saat içinde kömürlüğe taşımadığını görürsem, artık başına gelecekleri sen düşün! … Evin dış kapısının önünde dikilmekte olan anne, kocasının söylediklerini duymuştu. İçini çekerek oğluna doğru yürüdü … Bak güzel oğlum, dedi. Biz bir aileyiz. Biliyorsun ki, bu ailenin en büyük yükü babanın omuzlarında. Eğer, onun yükünü paylaşmak için, elimizden gelen yardımı yapmayacak olursak, zavallı adamcağız çalışmaktan yatağa düşecek. Çok şükür, büyüdün ve güçlü bir delikanlı oldun. Babanın sana ihtiyacı var. (Gülbahçe 105)

The father to his son Tom: "I'm telling you!" he screamed. "If I don't see you taking this pile of wood to the coal cellar within an hour, just think what will happen to you." … Tom's mother had been listening to her husband's threat from outside the door. Taking a deep breath, she started walking toward her son … "Look, my handsome son," she said. "We're a family. You know that the burden of this family rests on your father's shoulders. If we don't do what we can to share his burden, the poor man is going to get sick from working so hard. Thank goodness you've grown into a strong young man. Your father needs you." (Gülbahçe 105, my translation)

Similar expressions of traditional masculine and feminine behavior exist throughout the text, all of which have the common element of devaluing women and enforcing conservative religious values. While Mrs. Benton wears a blue scarf, which she ties into a bow around her neck in the original text, in the Timaş translation she wears a white headscarf and a blue dress. Moreover, while the women of the Ladies' Aid society "sew and give suppers and raise money and— and talk" (Porter 62), the women in the Timaş translation meet to "sew, cook, collect donations, and gossip a little" (Gülbahçe 65–66, my translation) ("dikiş dikmek, yemek pişirmek, yardım toplamak ve biraz da dedikodu yapmak için bir araya gelmiş") ("Manipulation of Gendered Discourse" 430–32).

As the Pollyanna case has illustrated, translating children's classics in other parts of the world with different social and cultural values can be problematic, often trespassing beyond the acceptable limits of adaptation to "the distortion of the source text" and the manipulation and "re-writing" of works of literature for ideological purposes (Sertkan xi). While the controversy concerning the essential reading list for Turkish schoolchildren underscores this phenomenon, fortunately it has not dampened enthusiasm for western classics, and in some circles has even reignited a movement toward rediscovering the original texts in their original languages. Pollyanna continues to be a favorite among Turkish parents and children, and its worthiness as a classic has not been tarnished by attempts to manipulate its content. If anything, the controversy has made parents and readers more aware of the agendas of certain publishers, and has actually rendered consumers more active participants in what they choose to read, and not simply passive recipients of information. It has also emphasized the notion that translations and adaptations of the novel—whether literary, theatrical, or cinematic—have paralleled and reflected change in Turkey as a whole, and have served as a barometer of the nation's sociopolitical situation. Clearly, as the story of *Pollyanna* in Turkey illustrates, the ability of a novel to bridge social and political divides is always dependent on translators, publishing houses, and cultural outlets, which adapt literary originals for local consumption, more often than not with specific agendas in mind.

Notes

1. A full version of the film can be viewed at www.youtube.com/watch?v=osRC7UEPDVE.

2. Some of the name choices in the film are, like those in Porter's novel, symbolic in meaning. Some names worth noting are Ayşe, which is a popular name among the peasant class that also means "to live comfortably"; Ferit, which means a stubborn bird of prey; Deli Amca, or crazy uncle; Peyker (face); Ömer (justice); and Ali (superior).

Works Cited

"100 Temel Esere 'İslami' Makyaj." *Hürriyet*. 2006. Web. 2 June 2013.

Aksoy, Berrin. "Translation as Rewriting: The Concept and its Implications on the Emergence of a National Literature." *Translation Journal* 5.3 (2001). Web. 28 August 2013.

"Atatürk'ün Özel Kitapları." *Türk Silahli Kuvvetleri*. Entry 1562. Web. 4 June 2013.

Goulden, Nancy Rost, and Susan Stanfield. "Leaving Elsie Dinsmore Behind: Plucky Girls as an Alternative Role Model in Classic Girls Literature." *Women's Studies* 32.2 (2003): 183–208. Print.

"Hayat Sevince Güzel, 1971." *Sinema Türk 2.0*. Web. 3 June 2013.

Hunt, Peter. *Children's Literature*. Oxford: Wiley-Blackwell, 2001. Print.

"İlkokulların da 100 Temel Eseri Var." *Radikal*. 2005. Web. 2 June 2013.

Kansu-Yetkiner, Neslihan. "Anthroponym Translation in Children's Literature: Chasing E. H. Porter's *Pollyanna* through Decades in Turkish." *Interactions* 20.1/2 (2011): 79–90. Print.

———. "Manipulation of Gendered Discourse in Translation: The Case of *Pollyanna* in Turkish." *The Sustainability of the Translation Field*. Hasuria Che Omar, Haslina Haroon, and Aniswal Abd. Ghani, eds. 421–34. Kuala Lumpur: ITNM, 2009. Print.

Marchalonis, Shirley. "Eleanor H(odgman) Porter." *American Novelists, 1910–1945.* James J. Martine, ed. Detroit: Gale Research, 1981. *Dictionary of Literary Biography* Vol. 9, *Gale.* Web. 6 April 2013.

Moore, Malcolm. "Pinocchio and Friends Converted to Islam." *Telegraph.* 2006. Web. 5 June 2013.

"Oyun Arşivi—*Pollyanna.*" *Devlet Tiyatroları.* Web. 2 June 2013.

"Pişkin Bakanlık! İyi Kitabı Veli Bulsun." *Radikal.* 2006. Web. 2 June 2013.

"*Pollyanna.*" *Kitapyurdu.* Web. 5 June 2013.

"*Pollyanna.*" *Ne Var ne Yok Tiyatro Sanat.* Web. 4 June 2013.

Porter, Eleanor H. *Pollyanna.* Rockville: Arc Manor, 2008. Print.

———. *Pollyanna.* Trans. Ekrem Aytar. Istanbul: Damla Yayınları, 2005. Print.

———. *Pollyanna.* Trans. Şengül Gülbahçe. Istanbul: Timaş Yayınları, 2003. Print.

Salman, Umay Aktaş. "Hayırlı Sabahlar Hans!" *Radikal.* 2006. Web. 5 June 2013.

Sertkan, Kamer. "The Ideology of Lexical Choices in the Turkish Translations of *Oliver Twist.*" MA thesis, Dokuz Eylul University, 2007.

"Sorumsuz Yayıncılık." *Radikal.* 2006. Web. 3 June 2012.

Turan, İbrahim. "Bazi Bati ve Türk Çocuk Klasiklerinde Dini ve Ahlaki Değerler" [Religious and Ethical Values in Some Western and Turkish Classical Child Books]. *Dinbilimleri Akademik Araştırma Dergisi* 10.1 (2010): 171–94. Print.

Lessons from *Pollyanna*

MARINA ENDICOTT

I first read *Pollyanna* when I was nine, while my family was spending the summer in a borrowed Victorian rectory high on a hill in Yarmouth, Nova Scotia. A verandah wrapped around the house, a comfortable apple tree hugged up against it, and inside, in a warren of dark corners and unused bedrooms, there were a thousand places to lie and read. Crammed book-shelves lined the children's rooms where my siblings lay suffering with measles, one after another; healthy and ignored, I read my way through the days and nights all summer. After our own utilitarian city rectory, this was paradise. And I was not alone: I had the company of all those orphans.

Pollyanna too was a minister's daughter, subject to privations and exigencies I knew well, and to both the unreliable generosity of parishioners, and the polite obligation charity imposes on the poor. At Christmas and Easter and other mysterious occasions of conscience, baskets of food would appear on our porch. We too received barrels of discarded clothes. The winter before that peaceful summer, I went to school happy in a new blue smocked dress, and was met by a girl who told the class, "That's my old dress she's wearing."

So I read *Pollyanna* with fellow feeling, and recognized the practical application of the glad game as the pragmatism Janet Wesselius links with William James's philosophy in her essay: an actively employed tool to level melancholy vagaries. I appreciated, too, the critique of religious hypocrisy implied in the game, predicated (as Roxanne Harde says) "on optimism and hope, a game that suggests benevolence should be an act of love, not of social obligation."

I had come close to orphanhood a few years before, when my parents were forced to farm us out to various relatives and friends for six months while my mother underwent long treatment for breast cancer. During that lonely time, while it seemed unlikely my mother would recover, I began preparing for life as an orphan. Pollyanna's model looked like a good one to adopt: brave, sad but not undone, acknowledging the loss but continuing to live with energy in the earthly world—that "whole-hearted engagement with life that enables her to work through her mourning and come to terms with her orphanhood" (Harde).

In the summer rectory I read the book as Monika Elbert does here, comparing Pollyanna with the other orphan girls of my recent reading: Anne, Rebecca, Katy, Mary Lennox, Jane Eyre, and of course Heidi, those healing sprites and loners and eccentrics. No wonder that, in the intervals of trying on charity clothes, day and night we children played our favorite game, Orphans on a Raft: One of the orphans always fell into the sea and drowned, and was a ghost for the rest of the game, giving advice or merely appearing beyond the prow in saintly visions, shrouded in a sheer curtain.

Anthony Pavlik digs an ecocritical reading out of *Pollyanna*'s fertile ground, looking at the idealized representation of the countryside as a "natural" space for the child, and the idyll of the cultivated, civilized garden: a refuge against the filth of the wider world. Pollyanna herself functions as dirt in the book: a kind of "matter out of place." Like Anne of Green Gables, the child's physical enjoyment of the world's chaos gradually infects the antiseptic aunt. Pollyanna offered that unselfconscious absence of restraint to me as a child reader—wildness wearing a garland of loving and unencumbered charity.

That wildness and openness extends to issues of gender. Pollyanna is resolutely non-girly. Her displeasure with cooking lessons was a delightful contrast to the tiresomely perfect and claustrophobic toy kitchen created for Meg's daughter Daisy in Louisa May Alcott's *Little Men*. ("How nice it is to do it all my ownty donty self!" says Daisy, unlike Pollyanna.) In her essay, Samantha Christensen examines the complicated linkages between food and class, food and charity—even food and character—and how Pollyanna's optimism and genuine gladness makes her "virtually unpunishable." Eventually she gives even dried-up Aunt Polly a taste for the ice-cream of human kindness.

As a child, I felt the rightness of Porter's censure of Aunt Polly, who as Ashley Reese says, "generally does what is morally right, but always out of a sense of duty, begrudgingly. . . ." Reese points to another tenet the book reinforced in me: Pollyanna's "Christ-like acceptance of all people regardless of their reputations or social status."

Rereading the book now, I am a little shocked to find how strongly *Pollyanna* formed my own moral understanding, and to trace strands of its influence through my own writing. For one thing, the book is coded with distinctions of class. An understood hierarchy of natural order ensures that superior souls (non-immigrant, well-spoken white children) will rise anyhow from obscurity and that the lesser blessed, like Nancy, will find their appropriate level. Those class precepts run deep in our children's literature. I am still unpacking them, and still find myself batting aside genteel precepts that Porter and Aunt Polly and all her ilk managed to insinuate into my earliest mind about the natural nobility of good breeding, that secret that will eventually tell.

Patricia Oman cites Mary Cadogan and Patricia Craig's complaint that "Pollyanna makes no demands on the reader's ability to think. . . . Out of this sentimental rag-bag has come every cliché in the business." But Oman suggests that Pollyanna "is actually the discursive site for complex ideological struggles." One of those struggles is the definition and redefinition of family that runs through both of Porter's *Pollyanna* books: adoption of orphans, assignment and acceptance of responsibility, and the gift of a ready-made child to childless, hopeless adults. Laura M. Robinson addresses the definition-defying queerness of *Pollyanna*'s critique of heteronormative family, and points out the rarity of "common" families in Beldingsville, full of heartbroken bachelors, widows, and spinsters; the traditional married families in Porter's world succumb to troubles or die off, exposing "the extent to which the family rests on capricious and ineffectual patriarchal authority." As a child, sympathetic to Pollyanna's vision of family, the constructed kind appeared to be the best. I've been writing about constructed or deconstructed families ever since.

Pollyanna's glad remembering of her lost father has also been useful to me in later life, when in true mourning. She brings "the bugle-call" of her father's philosophy to her new life, as Harde puts it, by allowing "her father to speak again and be heard by another congregation in a way that allows her the fullness of memory and mourning."

For me it is Pollyanna's consciousness of her own deep sadness and her need for gladness that saves the book from sentimentality. She is not inanely or falsely glad, but deliberately, thoughtfully glad; and she understands how hard she will have to work not to despair. The essays in this book illuminate Pollyanna's work for me again, childhood's golden light slanting lower and more broken by shadows than on first reading, more complexly revealing our own world.

CONTRIBUTORS

Anke Brouwers is an assistant professor at the University of Antwerp and at KASK in Ghent. She has written a PhD dissertation on sentimentalism in the films of Mary Pickford and Frances Marion. Her current research interests include, film narration, film and emotion, children's cinema, American silent cinema, and intermediality.

Mio Bryce is head of Japanese studies at Macquarie University, teaching Japanese language, literature, and manga/anime. She obtained her PhD in Japanese classical literature (*The Tale of Genji*) from the University of Sydney. She is involved in interdisciplinary research into youth cultures with the English Department at Macquarie University, Australia.

Samantha Christensen is a graduate student at the University of Alberta. She is currently writing her master's thesis on food in nineteenth-century children's literature, with a particular focus on women's coming-of-age texts. She has published in *Bookbird*, IRSCL, and has a chapter in *Walking the Line: Country Music Lyricists in American Culture*.

Monika Elbert is professor of English and Distinguished University Scholar at Montclair State University. She also serves as editor of the *Nathaniel Hawthorne Review*. She coedited *Transnational Gothic: Literary and Social Exchanges in the Long Nineteenth Century* (Ashgate, 2013). She has published widely on nineteenth-century American writers. Her *Enterprising Youth: Social Values and Acculturation in Nineteenth-Century American Children's Literature* (Routledge) appeared in 2008. She also edited a special issue on Hawthorne's children's literature (*Nathaniel Hawthorne Review*, spring 2010).

Marina Endicott's *Good to a Fault* was a finalist for the 2008 Giller Prize and won the Commonwealth Writers Prize, Canada/Caribbean. Her *The Little Shadows* was shortlisted for the Governor General's award in 2011. Her new novel, *Falling for Hugh*, will be out in 2014.

Roxanne Harde is professor of English, associate dean–research, and a McCalla University Professor at the University of Alberta, Augustana Faculty. She studies and teaches American literature and culture. She has published *Reading the Boss: Interdisciplinary Approaches to the Works of Bruce Springsteen*, and her essays have appeared in several journals, including *International Research in Children's Literature*, *Women's Writing*, *The Lion and the Unicorn*, *Christianity and Literature*, *Legacy*, *Jeunesse*, and *Critique*, and several edited collections including *Enterprising Youth* and *To See the Wizard*. She is editor of *Bookbird: A Journal of International Children's Literature*.

Dorothy Karlin completed the dual degree program in children's literature and library sciences at Simmons College in 2012. She is now working in Worcester, Massachusetts, as a children's librarian.

Lydia Kokkola is professor of English and education at Luleå University of Technology in northern Sweden. Her research interests include bilingual literacy education, Holocaust fiction, adolescent sexuality, and she has begun a new project on advanced reading skills. Her latest book, *Fictions of Adolescent Carnality*, has just been released from Benjamins.

Patricia Oman is assistant professor of English at Hastings College in Hastings, Nebraska. Her research centers on issues of place and region in twentieth-century American literature and film, especially popular genres such as children's literature and Hollywood musicals. She is currently writing a monograph, based on her doctoral dissertation, titled *There's No Place for Home: The Myths of Middle America*.

Anthony Pavlik teaches English and education in the Department of Arts, Communication, and Education at Luleå University of Technology in Sweden. He is a member of the editorial board of *Children's Literature in Education*, and his publications on children's and young adult literature include articles on ecocriticism, spatial theory, literary maps, and fantasy fiction.

Ashley N. Reese is a PhD student at the University of Cambridge. Her doctoral research is on protagonists' gendered, place-based, and Christian identities in four early-twentieth-century North American texts, including *Pollyanna*. She received an M.Phil. in children's literature at Cambridge, exploring various aspects of Baum's Oz series.

Laura M. Robinson is an associate professor and head of English literature at the Royal Military College of Canada. She has published articles on Canadian children's literature, Margaret Atwood, Ann-Marie MacDonald, and *The L-Word* in addition to many articles on L. M. Montgomery's work. Her current project examines Montgomery's depiction of friendship and sexuality. Her creative writing has appeared in *Women's Studies, Wascana Review, torquere, Frontiers, EnterText*, and *Her Circle.*

Tanfer Emin Tunç is associate professor in the Department of American Culture and Literature at Hacettepe University, located in Ankara, Turkey. She specializes in women's studies and has published extensively on women's writing, including essays on Charlotte Perkins Gilman, Willa Cather, L. M. Montgomery, Caroline Gordon, Margaret Mitchell, Lillian Hellman, Lucille Clifton, Ruthanne Lum McCunn, and Wendy Wasserstein, and the book *Feminism's Unfinished Legacy: Critiques of Gender and Racial Inequality in Contemporary American Women's Literature* (VDM, 2011).

K. Brenna Wardell is an instructor of film, television, and literature, currently employed by the University of Alabama. Her research interests include gender and sexuality, media aesthetics, ecocriticism, and adaptation studies. She has presented conference papers at the Society for Cinema and Media Studies, Console-ing Passions, and What Is Television?

Janet Wesselius is associate professor of philosophy at the Augustana Campus of the University of Alberta. Her interest in pragmatism and *Pollyanna* grew out of her work on the influence of place and identity on the forms philosophy can take. She has published in feminist epistemology and philosophy of science and is currently working on a project examining the ontological implications of the metaphors we use to think about the nano-scale.

INDEX

CPSIA information can be obtained at www.ICGtesting.com
Printed in the USA
BVOW04*2221131014

369920BV00002B/3/P